BLACK MEN IN COLLEGE

Black Men in College provides vital information about how to effectively support, retain, and graduate Black male undergraduates. This edited collection centers on the notion that Black male collegians are not a homogenous group; rather, they are representative of rarely acknowledged differences that exist among them. This valuable text suggests that understanding these differences is critical to making true in-roads in serving Black men. Chapter contributors describe the diverse challenges Black men in HBCUs face, and discuss how to support and retain high-achieving men, gay men, academically unprepared men, low-income men, men in STEM, American immigrants, millennials, collegiate fathers, those affiliated with Greek letter organizations, and athletes. Recommendations for policy and practice to encourage retention and persistence to degree completion are grounded in extant theory and research. This text is a must-read for all higher education faculty, researchers, and student affairs practitioners interested in addressing the contemporary college experiences of Black men in post-secondary institutions.

Robert T. Palmer is Assistant Professor of Student Affairs Administration at The State University of New York—Binghamton.

J. Luke Wood is Assistant Professor of Administration, Rehabilitation, and Post-Secondary Education at San Diego State University.

BLACK MEN IN COLLEGE

Implications for HBCUs and Beyond

Edited by Robert T. Palmer and J. Luke Wood

Routledge
Taylor & Francis Group

NEW YORK AND LONDON

First published 2012
by Routledge
711 Third Avenue, New York, NY 10017

Simultaneously published in the UK
by Routledge
2 Park Square, Milton Park, Abingdon, Oxon OX14 4RN

Routledge is an imprint of the Taylor & Francis Group, an informa business

© 2012 Taylor & Francis

The right of the editors to be identified as the authors of the editorial material, and of the authors for their individual chapters, has been asserted in accordance with sections 77 and 78 of the Copyright, Designs and Patents Act 1988.

Library of Congress Cataloging in Publication Data
Palmer, Robert T.
    Black men in college : implications for HBCUS and beyond / by Robert T. Palmer and J. Luke Wood.
    p. cm.
    Includes bibliographical references and index.
    1. African American men—Education (Higher) 2. African American male college students. 3. African American universities and colleges. I. Wood, J. Luke, 1982– II. Title.
    LC2781.P35 2012
    378.1'982996073—dc23
    2011026466

ISBN: 978-0-415-89383-1 (hbk)
ISBN: 978-0-415-89384-8 (pbk)
ISBN: 978-0-203-15644-5 (ebk)

Typeset in Bembo and Stone Sans
by EvS Communication Networx, Inc.

Printed and bound in the United States of America on acid-free paper
by Edwards Brothers, Inc.

CONTENTS

FOREWORD

Access to college by Black students has lagged behind that of White students since the inception of higher education in this country. The upturn in admission of Black students to predominantly White institutions (PWIs) that began in the late 1960s and early 1970s was matched by increased study of the issues related to this deficiency. However, much of the earlier discussion articulated only the problems and failed to focus adequately on their solutions. Fortunately, more recent research and writing on Black student college attendance has included discussion on how to resolve many of these issues confronting students and how to help those students achieve tangible results in college completion.

One other issue that, thankfully, has shown some evolution over the past 20 years of writing on Black student college attendance is the recognition of subpopulations in the community of Black college students. In the mid-1990s, I started asking for the disaggregation of data on Black college students and its interpretation to show how Black men and Black women college students differ in perceptions, performance, and interests. Other scholars have also voiced that concern and have also called for an extension of the disaggregation of student information and research based on those data to include other characteristics besides gender. That message continues to go forth to the higher education community as an important part of the effort to aid Black students' matriculation.

Carrying this idea a step further, researchers have begun to further disaggregate the study of Black male college students in particular. As Strayhorn and Scott state in chapter 3 of this book, "much of what has been written about Black men in higher education treats them as a monolithic group whose experiences are much more similar than different. Yet a growing body of research indicates that 'they are not all the same'." Happily, the study of Black men is being expanded to focus on a number of specific subgroups among that population.

Perhaps the last of the areas where attention needs to be focused, but heretofore had not been adequately addressed, is the differences demonstrated by students at different kinds of institutions. For example, the proportion of research on students at community colleges lags behind the percentage of students who actually attend such institutions, particularly research on students of color. Likewise, there is a corresponding absence of research on students at historically Black colleges and universities (HBCUs) probably because, despite their significant contribution to the creation of an educated Black population for a century and a half, they represent today only 3% of the institutions of higher education in this country. However, as Robert T. Palmer and J. Luke Wood explain in chapter 1 of this volume, those 3% of the nation's schools produce 20% of Black undergraduate degrees, 11% of all master's degrees, 11% of all doctorates, and 20% of all first professional degrees earned by Black students.

So, it is for these reasons that I enthusiastically welcome the work that Robert T. Palmer and J. Luke Wood present in this volume. They shine a bright light on the importance that HBCUs continue to have in educating a disproportionately high number of this nation's Black male college students. More importantly, they give proper emphasis to the wonderful diversity within that Black male population on those campuses that is too often overlooked by academicians who have not taken the time to become more familiar with them. This book begins by giving a properly comprehensive explanation of the HBCU environment that provides the context for the academic, cocurricular, and social lives of its male students and then proceeds to enlighten readers to the intricacies of the issues of numerous subgroups within that population, including: high-achieving Black men; gay Black men; academically unprepared Black men; low-income Black men; Black men in science education; Black American immigrant students; Black male Millennial students; Black fathers; Black men affiliated with historically Black fraternities; Black male athletes; and academically gifted Black males in engineering. The book concludes with programmatic initiatives implemented on campuses across the nation to help retain Black male collegians, provides salient metalevel recommendations from chapter contributors, and offers directions for future research.

Such a review of these student characteristics and the impact they have on each other and on the colleges themselves provides an important view of the wonderful mosaic that is the Black male population on many of the campuses of our country's HBCUs. This picture would be most welcome at any time. It is particularly salient in 2011 as HBCUs and their tremendous impact continue to endure new threats to their existence like the one being proposed by the current governor of Louisiana, who is trying to merge one of his state's premier historically Black universities with a neighboring predominantly White school, and to eliminate one HBCU campus entirely. As more research like that presented in the present work is published, we can all learn to better appreciate the national treasure that our HBCUs still are and how they serve their students in a very important and critical way.

I also believe that the impact of this book can extend far beyond the campuses where this research material was collected. The critical work being done at HBCUs to support, retain, and graduate Black men can be significant "best practice" models for use at many of the PWIs across the country as well. Faculty, academic administrators, and student affairs practitioners at all institutions can all learn retention strategies for Black men from the material in this volume.

Bravo, Drs. Palmer and Wood!

Michael J. Cuyjet

Professor of College Student Personnel Program
Department of Educational and Counseling
University of Louisville

ACKNOWLEDGMENTS

This book was conceptualized in 2010 at the American Educational Research Association (AERA) Conference in Denver, Colorado and it is important to acknowledge the following individuals who helped bring it to completion. Collectively, we would to thank the contributors, who worked diligently to meet the many deadlines to get chapters submitted in a timely manner. Second, we would like to thank Michael Cuyjet for his wisdom, support, and guidance.

Robert T. Palmer would like to thank Marybeth Gasman, Terrell Strayhorn, James Earl Davis, and Marlyu McEwen for their mentorship and support, Dina C. Maramba for being a good colleague and friend, and J. Luke Wood for being a wonderful collaborative partner. This book is dedicated to Howard L. Simmons, Rosemary Gillet-Karam, Jason DeSousa, Brenda James, Cheryl Rollins, and Courtney Thrower—all of whom supported me as a PhD student at Morgan State University.

J. Luke Wood would like to thank God, his wife Idara, and his family. Immense gratitude is directed to Robert T. Palmer for his vision and leadership on this project as well as his fervent commitment to advancing the status of Black males in all educational settings. Appreciation is also extended to J. Luke Wood's mentors: Carlos Nevarez, Caroline Turner, Cecil Canton, and Lisa William-White as well as to his colleagues T. Kenyatta Jones, Adriel A. Hilton, and John D. Harrison.

1

SETTING THE FOUNDATION FOR BLACK MEN IN COLLEGES

Implications for Historically Black Colleges and Universities and Beyond

Robert T. Palmer and J. Luke Wood

In a monograph that Marybeth Gasman and colleagues authored for the Association for Higher Education Report (ASHE) series on historically Black colleges and universities (HBCUs), they characterized HBCUs as "unearthing promise and potential" (Gasman, Lundy-Wagner, Ransom, & Bowman, 2010). Given the history of HBCUs, this characterization is an appropriate fit. Indeed, these institutions were founded to provide Blacks with an opportunity for postsecondary education during an era when they were excluded from other institutions of higher education. Given the noble purpose for which they were established, HBCUs have served as critical facilitators of Black engagement and agency in political, social, and economic venues in American society. As such, these institutions have played a significant role in creating, sustaining, and advancing a Black middle class and the lives of Black professionals (Brown & Davis, 2001; Gasman, Baez, et al., 2007; Gasman, Lundy-Wagner, et al., 2010; Palmer & Gasman, 2008)

Upon their establishment, an overwhelming number of Blacks attended HBCUs (Allen, 1992; Fleming, 1984; Kimbrough & Harper, 2006; Sissoko & Shiau, 2005). However, over the years, fewer Blacks attended HBCUs because many opted to attend predominantly White institutions (PWIs). This is due largely to governmental initiatives and litigation designed to integrate the education of Blacks and Whites (e.g., *Adams v. Richardson,* 1972; *Brown v. Board of Education*, 1954; Civil Rights Act of 1964; and the implementation of federal aid programs). Indeed, as a result of litigation and legislation, the total number of Black college students enrolled in HBCUs declined from 18.18% in 1980 to 13.70% in 1998, while the number of Blacks enrolled in other institutions of higher education grew from 80.82% in 1980 to 86.3% in 1998 (Sissoko & Shiau, 2005). In 2007, the number of Black students attending HBCUs further declined to 10.63% while 89.37% now attend other postsecondary institutions (U.S. Department of Education, 2009a).

Several other factors may have contributed to the decline in the percentage of Blacks who attend HBCUs. Palmer, Maramba, and Lee (2010) conducted a qualitative study that investigated Black students' disinclination to consider attending HBCUs. Their findings were derived from the perceptions of 13 Black students enrolled in a PWI, who had not attended HBCUs themselves, but had relatives or friends who had done so. Findings from this study illustrated several important considerations. First, Palmer et al. (2010) found that the location of HBCUs served as a deterrent to college goers during their collegiate selection process. Specifically, the participants in the study were from New York, and they harbored a perception that all HBCUs were located below the Mason–Dixon Line. To this extent, participants feared that if they attended college out of state, they would be ineligible for any instate financial aid, and therefore, not be able to afford the cost of out-of-state tuition.

Second, some prospective students held the perception that HBCUs were "party" schools, lacking in academic rigor and achievement. These individuals perceived PWIs as offering a better education, believing that a degree from a PWI would be taken more seriously in the workplace when compared to one from an HBCU. Finally, participants broached that HBCUs lacked racial and ethnic diversity, and could not successfully prepare students to work in racially and ethnically diverse organizations following graduation. Interestingly, in a qualitative study that Dancy (2005) conducted with Black students about their perceptions of HBCUs, participants in his study echoed many of the same sentiments that were expressed by participants in Palmer et al.'s (2010) study.

Despite the change in HBCUs' student enrollment, the relevancy, importance, and contribution of HBCUs are unquestionable (Allen & Jewel, 2002; Brown, 1999; Brown, Bertrand, & Donahoo, 2001; Palmer, 2008, 2010). Numerous researchers have emphasized the prominent role that HBCUs have taken in educating Black students (Allen, Jewel, Griffin, & Wolf, 2007; Berger & Milem, 2000; Brown & Davis, 2001; Palmer & Gasman, 2008). These researchers noted that while HBCUs comprise 3% of all higher education institutions, they enroll 16% and graduate 20% of Black undergraduates (Allen et al., 2007; Gasman, Lundy-Wagner, et al., 2010). According to Palmer and Gasman (2008), students who attended HBCUs at the undergraduate level are more likely to continue their educational pursuits to graduate or professional schools than their PWI counterparts. In fact, Allen and colleagues (2007) reported that HBCUs awarded 20% of all first professional degrees to Black students.

Furthermore, Gasman, Lundy-Wagner, and colleagues (2010) noted that HBCUs prepare most of the nation's Black leaders in critical areas, such as science, mathematics, and engineering. More specifically, Perna and colleagues (2009) indicated that HBCUs comprised 17 of the top 20 leading producers of Black baccalaureate degrees in science, technology, engineering, and mathematics (STEM), and in 2004, produced 30% of the baccalaureate degrees awarded to Black students in STEM majors. Most impressively, HBCUs are able to achieve these outcomes while lacking resources comparable to those of their PWI counterparts (Gasman, Lundy-Wagner, et al., 2010; Kim & Conrad, 2006; Palmer, Davis, & Gasman, in press; Palmer & Griffin, 2009).

The supportive and nurturing climate of HBCUs and its impact on facilitating the academic growth and social development of Black students is another salient factor that makes HBCUs relevant to the higher education community. Indeed, many studies have consistently documented the supportive and family-oriented atmosphere of HBCUs, which are contrasted with the unwelcoming and individualistic climates of many PWIs (Allen, 1992; Allen et al., 2007; Berger & Milem, 2000; Bonous-Hammarth & Boatsman, 1996; Fleming, 1984; Flowers, 2002; Fries-Britt & Turner, 2002; Kim, 2002; Outcalt & Skewes-Cox, 2002). For example, in a seminal study that Gurin and Epps (1975) conducted from 1964 to 1970, with over 5,000 Black students enrolled in 10 HBCUs, they found that HBCUs provided Black students with positive self-images, strong racial pride, and facilitated their desire to continue their education beyond the undergraduate level.

Similarly, Fleming (1984) conducted a cross-sectional study on Black and White students attending HBCUs and PWIs. More specifically, her study involved approximately 3,000 freshmen and seniors across 15 colleges (8 PWIs and 7 HBCUs). The core question guiding this study was, "Who gets the most out of college?" Each of the participants in Fleming's (1984) study engaged in 4 to 8 hours of intensive testing, which involved measures of cognitive growth, participation in in-depth interviews, and an examination of their official transcripts. The results from her study were tantamount to the findings from the Gurin and Epps (1975) study. Fleming (1984) found that HBCUs fostered a well-rounded development, which included gains in academic outcomes, psychosocial functioning, intellectual self-confidence, and achievement motivation vis-à-vis their PWI counterparts. Further, she found that when compared to PWIs, HBCUs provided a more supportive interpersonal environment through caring personnel with whom Black students were able to discuss their concerns and stressors.

Another seminal study on HBCUs that produced findings similar to the Gurin and Epps (1975) and Fleming (1984) studies was conducted by Allen (1992). Using a cross-sectional approach, multivariate analysis, and data from 2,531 Black students (953 HBCUs and 1,578 PWIs), Allen reported that HBCUs provided Black students with an institutional climate that was supportive and nurturing. Similar to research from Gurin and Epps (1975) and Fleming (1984), he indicated that HBCUs valued Black students and fostered their intellectual growth and development. Further, Allen noted that HBCUs provided a positive social and psychological environment for Black students. Socially, he broached the view that HBCUs increased the likelihood and feasibility of Black students having extensive peer networks and other sources of support. Psychologically, Allen (1992) explained, HBCUs increased students' sense of belonging, encouraged empowerment, and facilitated their self-confidence and self-esteem.

While research about the role of HBCUs in affecting the social and academic development of Black students is necessary because it helps to justify the continued significance of these venerable institutions, there is a need for scholarship which advances understanding of student experiences by gender at HBCUs (Gasman, Lundy-Wagner, et al., 2010; Kimbrough & Harper, 2006; Lundy-Wagner & Gasman, 2011). Research is needed which critically interrogates the experiences, perceptions, and differential outcomes of gender groups. Indeed, many studies that examine students at HBCUs have not disaggregated the experiences of Black students by gender (Ehrenberg & Rothstein, 1994; Fries-Britt & Turner, 2002; Kim, 2002; Kimbrough, Molock, & Walton, 1996; Outcalt & Skewes-Cox, 2002). Given the questionable success of Black men documented in the contemporary literature on HBCUs (Geiger, 2006; Harper & Gasman, 2008; Nettles & Perna, 1997; Palmer, Davis, & Hilton, 2009; Palmer & Gasman, 2008; Provasnik, Shafer, & Snyder , 2004; Ross, 1998; Lundy-Wagner & Gasman, 2011), such research is crucial to enhanced understanding of and improved success within this group (Gasman, Lundy-Wagner, et al., 2010; Lundy-Wagner & Gasman, 2011). For instance, research findings reveal a gender disparity on the campus of HBCUs in enrollment, retention, and persistence to graduation (Allen, 1992; Geiger, 2006; Harper & Gasman, 2008; Kimbrough & Harper, 2006; Nettles & Perna, 1997; Palmer & Davis, in press; Palmer, Davis, & Hilton, 2009; Palmer, Davis, & Maramba, 2010, in press; Palmer, Maramba, & Dancy, in press; Palmer & Young, 2009; Provasnik et al., 2004; Ross, 1998; Lundy-Wagner & Gasman, 2011).

Gender disparities exist among other racial and ethnic groups, but they are more pronounced among Black students and persist at PWIs and HBCUs (Palmer et al., 2009). In fact, Kimbrough and Harper (2006) explained that Black women are graduating from HBCUs at rates that are two to three times higher than those of Black men. An article by Pope (2009) in *Diverse Issues in Higher Education* supported previous research findings regarding low graduation rates among Black men at HBCUs. Information from the article was derived from an analysis of government data by the Associated Press from 83 federally designated 4-year HBCUs. Findings illustrated that 37% of Black students at HBCUs graduate within 6 years, which is 4% lower than the national graduation rate for Black students. According to Pope (2009), Black men are a major reason for HBCU's dismal graduation rate, with 29% completing a baccalaureate degree within 6 years (Pope, 2009).

Further evidence, based on statistical data, from a 2007 report by the Thurgood Marshall College Fund (2008), a major organization representing 47 public HBCUs, substantiates low participation and graduation rates among Black men at HBCUs. Specifically, this report indicated that while female undergraduate enrollment increased 38% from 1986 to 2006, male undergraduate enrollment has progressed very little among these 47 institutions since the early 1990s. Furthermore, data from the U.S. Department of Education (2009b), illustrated that the percentage of Black males enrolled in HBCUs is gradually declining as the percentage of Black females is rising. For example, in 1990, Black males and females represented 32.23% and 48.91% of total fall enrollment, respectively. However, by 2007, these percentages had shifted to 31.42% and 51.25 %. These shifts mirror enrollment patterns for all males and females in HBCUs.

Furthermore, degrees that were conferred on males by HBCUs decreased by 6% from 1997 to 2007 while increasing 5% for females. Additional evidence indicates that this gender disparity is not endemic to the undergraduate population. According to the National Center for Educational Statistics (NCES), since 1991 more than 60% of associate, bachelor's, and master's degrees conferred at HBCUs have been earned by women (NCES, 2004). The percentage distribution of earned degrees conferred illustrates that Black females are outpacing Black males in HBCUs as follows: associate degree (12.91% male, 27.62% female); bachelor's (29.30% male, 57.0% female); master's (18.8% male, 55.50 female); professional (24.57% male, 40.43% female); and doctoral (24.64% male, 44.84% female) (U.S. Department of Education, 2009b).

Interestingly, HBCUs were once considered to be relatively immune from high attrition rates for Black students (Harper & Gasman, 2008; Kimbrough & Harper, 2006). Nevertheless, similar to PWIs, HBCUs are focused on investigating ways to increase retention and persistence rates for their Black male students. Some institutions have even implemented special programs aimed at increasing persistence among Black men (Chickering, Peters, & Palmer, 2006). These initiatives provide a platform for discourse on critical issues facing collegiate men and provide activities designed to facilitate male leadership and academic achievement. To put the experiences of Black men at HBCUs in context, the next section of this chapter will examine the literature on their experiences.

Review of Literature on Black Men at HBCUs

Historical evidence suggests that Black men at HBCUs have fared better than their female counterparts (Fleming, 1984; Gurin & Epps, 1975). A study Gurin and Epps (1975) conducted at 10 HBCUs with over 5,000 Black students indicated that, when compared to their female counterparts, Black men had considerably higher educational and career goals, were more likely to express an interest in enrolling in graduate and professional school, and were more attracted to prestigious careers in fields such as engineering, business, and the sciences.

Similarly, the results from Fleming's (1984) mixed-methods study on Black and White students at HBCUs and PWIs yielded comparable findings to the Gurin and Epps (1975) study. More specifically, Fleming (1984) noted that Black men tend to dominate HBCU campuses just as White men tend to dominate the campuses of PWIs. In fact, Fleming (1984) characterized college as a man's world. According to this study, despite some disenchantment with the classroom atmosphere, HBCUs help to facilitate the cognitive growth and social development of Black men. In particular, she indicated that

> males in Black colleges exhibit the happiest adjustment to college life that can be found. Despite some ambivalence surrounding their interactions with teachers, their experience is more strongly characterized by absorption with role models, greater satisfaction, and positive outcomes from the educational experience, and gains in assertiveness of self-expressions and in dealing with others.
>
> *(p. 168)*

Coincidentally, findings from Allen (1986) and Nettles (1988) regarding Black men at HBCUs are congruent with the Fleming (1984) and Gurin and Epps (1975) studies. Specifically, in a quantitative study that examined Black students' academic performance, racial attitudes, and college satisfaction at state supported PWI and HBCUs, Allen (1986) found that Black men at HBCUs had higher educational and career goals, had more positive relationships with faculty, and were more involved on campus than their female counterparts. Furthermore, Nettles' (1988) survey of college student academic and social experience revealed that Black men at HBCUs were more socially integrated, earned better grades, and perceived their college to be more supportive of their academic success.

Despite the positive experiences documented in research relating to Black men at HBCUs in particular, pertaining to involvement on campus, a study from Harper, Carini, Bridges, and Hayek (2004) revealed an interesting change among Black men and women at HBCUs regarding campus engagement. Specifically, using data from the National Survey of Student Engagement, which 1,167 Black students at 12 HBCUs completed, Harper and colleagues (2004) found that gaps in engagement between Black men and women at HBCUs had narrowed. In fact, on several measures of academic and social engagement (e.g., collaborative learning, affirming campus climates, and overall satisfaction), they found minimal differences between the experiences of Black men and women at HBCUs.

In a chapter that Kimbrough and Harper (2006) authored, they delineated findings from a focus group that provided insight into reasons for the disengagement among Black men at HBCUs. Participants offered five factors that contributed to Black male disengagement. First, participants suggested that Black men viewed sports and other forms of athleticism as more socially acceptable than leadership or purposeful engagement. Second, they explained that men typically encountered problems working collectively with others, which is a key factor in successful involvement in student organizations. Third, the participants indicated that many Black men are socialized to devalue purposeful engagement, even before coming to college. Fourth, participants noted a paucity of Black male role models and mentors who affirmed the importance of purposeful engagement. Fifth, participants stated that many Black men have difficulty earning a 2.5 grade point average (GPA)—the minimum grade average needed for membership in a historically Black fraternity. In addition to this critical insight into factors undergirding Black male disengagement at HBCUs, Kimbrough and Harper (2006) also observed that more contemporary research was needed on the experiences, issues, and conditions of Black men at HBCUs. More specifically, they indicated:

> The plight of [the Black] male collegian remains complex; fortunately, his needs and issues are making their way onto [the] higher education agenda. In spite of this increased momentum, in recent years we have acquired only limited insight into the experiences of African American men attending [HBCUs]. With much of the national attention being placed on issues facing [Black] students at [PWIs] ... the quality of life at HBCUs for [Black] men has gone virtually unnoticed.
>
> *(p. 190)*

Kimbrough and Harper's (2006) assertion that contemporary research on Black men at HBCUs was lacking and is needed may have served as an impetus for other scholars to be more attentive to the experiences and issues of Black men at HBCUs. For example, in a qualitative study that Palmer and Young (2009) conducted on key factors supporting the academic success of Black men at an HBCU, they found that participants felt campus involvement served as a critical linchpin for their success. However, consistent with research by Kimbrough and Harper (2006), their findings indicated that most of their male peers were disengaged on campus.

Further, other research on the experiences of Black men at HBCUs has shown that the conservative institutional climate of HBCUs may have a negative impact on Black male retention and persistence. For example, in a qualitative study with 76 Black men at 12 HBCUs, Harper and Gasman (2008) discovered that participants perceived the institutional climates of HBCUs to be too conservative, resulting in an unwelcoming environment. Moreover, they reported that conservatism was evident in expressions of sexuality and sexual orientation, self-presentation and expression, and ways in which faculty responded to students in the classroom. Harper and Gasman's (2008) findings are groundbreaking because they challenge HBCUs to reassess many of their conservative practices to provide a more welcoming environment to diverse cultural groups within the Black population.

Aside from Harper and Gasman's (2008) research, a study that Palmer and Gasman (2008) conducted with 11 Black men who were attending an HBCU explored the impact that social capital had on retention and persistence. Participants indicated that the social capital at this institution played a significant role in their academic success. In particular, the participants indicated that professors and administrators were accessible and displayed a willingness to form supportive relationships with students. These relationships encouraged persistence because they fostered a sense of belonging and affirmation. Participants realized that professors and administrators cared about them, their success at the university, and their future. Faculty and administrators mentored and served as role models to many of the students. They also directed and encouraged student participation in student support services, campus organizations, internships, and scholarship programs. In many ways, the interactions and experiences created a climate that the participants considered to be supportive and nurturing.

Similarly, Palmer and Strayhorn (2008) conducted a qualitative study on Black men to better understand factors crucial to their retention and persistence in HBCUs. They found that noncognitive variables (e.g., motivation, goal-oriented behavior, and exhibiting an affinity for one's major) coupled with support from institutional agents, played a vital role in the success of the participants. To this extent, while the studies by Palmer and Gasman (2008) and Palmer and Strayhorn (2008) provide contemporary insight into the experiences of Black men at HBCUs, they reinforce much of literature that has depicted HBCUs as being supportive environments that facilitate academic success and social development for Black students.

Moreover, a qualitative study by Palmer et al. (2009) revealed challenges to the retention and persistence for Black men at an HBCU that many researchers would characterize as predictors of attrition. Poor help-seeking behavior, lack of financial aid, and problems at home were each identified as salient challenges in the lives and experiences of undergraduate participants. While findings from this study provided beneficial information to HBCU administrators and other university personnel, one of the most prominent notions that emerged from this study was that participants characterized situations occurring in their homes or communities as a challenge to their persistence. Participants in the study delineated a variety of problems occurring in their homes or communities. These problems were not limited to issues of criminality; they included the need to financially support a family and other problems along those lines. The impact that students' homes or communities have on their academic performance is a phenomenon that researchers have recently begun to examine (Charles, Dinwiddie, & Massey, 2004). For example, using data from the National Longitudinal Survey of Freshmen, Charles et al. reported that underrepresented minorities living in segregated neighborhoods are more likely than White and Asian students to experience stressful events stemming from their home communities. Howard-Hamilton (1997) supported this finding, noting that Black male collegians tend to come from homes or neighborhoods where relatives and friends are more likely to engage in criminal activity or experience violent incidents. This occurs as a result of the sociopolitical and economic barriers facing Blacks in society in general. According to Charles et al. (2004), these experiences engender stressors that are negatively linked to academic success.

Palmer, Davis, and Maramba (in press) conducted a qualitative study of 11 Black men at an HBCU. The primary finding of this publication delineated ways in which family encouraged academic success among Black men. This finding is important because research suggests that Black students who attend HBCUs, specifically public HBCUs, tend to be first-generation college students (Allen, 1992; Allen et al., 2007; Ross, 1998). While literature on HBCUs has documented the prevalence of first-generation college students at HBCUs, a discussion about the abilities of these students' families to positively impact their college academic success is basically nonexistent. Consequently, institutional agents may not be fully cognizant of the extent to which students' families at public HBCUs have the cultural capital to facilitate their academic success. Although some students were first-generation college students in this current study and others were not, the participants' families played a critical role in their college success through the use of role modeling the importance of an education, providing messages of encouragement, sharing knowledge about their college experience, and helping the participants stay focused on achieving a college degree.

In a subsequent publication focused on Black men at HBCUs, Palmer and Davis (in press) discussed the impact of remedial education on helping to facilitate the social and academic integration of Black men entering a public HBCU. In this study, participants were engaged in the university's remedial program and persisted to graduation. This research is significant because it documented the important role that remediation continues to play in providing access to higher education for Black men, particularly at HBCUs. Given that Kimbrough and Harper (2006) and Davis and Palmer (2010) emphasized that 4-year public HBCUs and PWIs are being pressured by state officials to reduce the number of students admitted to their remedial programs or totally eliminate the programs because of lack of data and questions about their efficacy, Palmer and Davis' (in press) research provides some context about ways in which college remediation positively affects access, retention, and persistence for Black males at HBCUs.

Furthermore, in a qualitative study that Palmer, Maramba, and Davis (2010) conducted on Black men at HBCUs, they reported the critical influence of peer support on popularizing and encouraging the academic success of Black men who entered college academically unprepared and persisted to graduation. This finding is not consistent with previous research regarding the impact on academic success of Black males who have peers of the same race. Research has shown that Black males with same-race peers persuade their friends to disengage in activities that support academic success (Ford, Grantham, & Whiting,

2008). The findings from Palmer et al.'s (2010) study are consistent with Harper's (2006) study of 32 high-achieving Black males at six large public research PWIs. Despite the similarities between the two studies, it is important to note that Harper focused on high-achieving students whereas all participants in Palmer et al.'s study entered college as academically underprepared. Therefore, it is sensible to believe that many of Harper's (2006) participants entered higher education well-prepared and would have succeeded with or without peer encouragement. Given the Palmer et al. (2010) study's focus on academically underprepared students, it extends the body of knowledge on academic success for Black male college students by noting the role and importance of peers in popularizing academic achievement.

Finally, Palmer, Maramba, and Dancy (in press) delineated the impact of the Male Initiative on Leadership and Excellence (MILE), a program that an HBCU implemented to help increase the rate of retention and persistence among Black men. More specifically, MILE engaged participants in a variety of leadership development, values-building, and intentional learning strategies to promote their academic and personal success. The program provides an enriching educational experience that helps students become intentional, purposeful, and self-directed learners. According to Palmer et al. (in press), an evaluation of MILE that employed qualitative and descriptive statistics revealed that the program had a positive impact on Black male participants' retention and persistence. In his book, *African American Men in College*, Cuyjet (2006) listed other programmatic initiatives established at PWIs and HBCUs to help increase retention and persistence among Black male collegians. Similarly, these programs also were found to support Black male achievement in postsecondary education.

Despite the important contribution of this research to researchers and student affairs practitioners, consistent with Kimbrough and Harper's (2006) observation about the dearth of research on Black males at HBCUs, more research is needed to help practitioners, administrators, and faculty better understand the contemporary experiences and challenges of Black men at HBCUs. Furthermore, of the extant literature on Black men at HBCUs, Black male college students are treated as a monolithic group. Therefore, there is little to no consideration of the unique experiences and challenges that exist among the diverse academic and social subcultures of Black men. This dearth in the literature fails to interrogate the intricate commonalities and differences of the Black male experience in HBCUs, thereby glossing over important factors relevant to the experience, perceptions, and success of these men. With this in mind, the purpose of this book is to focus on the within group differences among Black men enrolled in HBCUs with respect to academic, sexual, and social contexts. Indeed, by focusing on specific subcultures, this book will provide practitioners, administrators, and other HBCU personnel with a more comprehensive understanding of the contemporary college experiences for the subcultures that will be discussed in the coming chapters, and best practices to implement to encourage these students' retention and persistence to degree completion. The next section will offer an in-depth view of each chapter.

Synopsis of the Book Chapters

In the present chapter, Robert T. Palmer and J. Luke Wood provide a compelling justification for this important volume on Black men in higher education in general and specifically at HBCUs. Using extant literature, they note that despite changes in Black male enrollment, retention, and persistence at HBCUs, little attention has been paid to their contemporary experiences. Moreover, there is a dearth of research that could provide institutional leaders with concrete strategies for better retaining Black men. Furthermore, they argue that the paucity of contemporary literature on Black males at HBCUs treats this subgroup as monolithic, assuming homogeneity of their experiences, challenges, and supports. As such, they call for more attention to be paid to investigations of within group differences among Black men at HBCUs.

In chapter 2, Marybeth Gasman and Dorsey Spencer consider the campus experiences and challenges of high-achieving Black men at HBCUs. In particular, their chapter offers insight into intrinsic and extrinsic motivational factors affecting the experiences, needs, challenges, and success of these Black men. Their contribution adds an important context to the literature on Black men at HBCUs as few studies have focused on the unique challenges and experiences of this population. Their chapter concludes by offering important implications for future research and institutional practice.

In chapter 3, Terrell Strayhorn and Jameel Scott examine the experiences of Black gay men at HBCUs. This chapter draws upon data from a larger, multiyear, qualitative research project that examined the perceptions and experiences of gay men of color in various campus contexts, including HBCUs. Strayhorn and Scott use participants' voices to provide rich, thick descriptions of their campus experiences. While studies frequently discuss the supportive campus climate of HBCUs, it is often assumed that all groups of students would characterize HBCUs as supportive. However, in a qualitative study that Patton (2011) conducted with 6 Black men attending an HBCU, they described how uncomfortable and oppressive the HBCU climate was because of their sexual orientation. Harper and Gasman (2008) reported similar findings about the unwelcoming climate that gay men experience at HBCUs. Given this situation, institutional leaders can use Strayhorn and Scott's chapter to help make the campus environment more supportive and inclusive for Black gay men at HBCUs.

In chapter 4, Tiffany Fountaine and Joelle Carter delineate the impact that the incorporation of a strength-based approach had on students' success, particularly that of Black males, who participated in a summer skill-building program to matriculate into college. They encourage institutional leaders to consider the inclusion of a strength-based approach in their curriculum to help facilitate academic success among students, especially those who enter college academically unprepared. Their chapter is particularly salient because there have been doubts raised about the efficacy of skill-building programs in helping students achieve success in college (Bahr, 2008; Boylan & Saxon, 1999; Levin & Calcagno, 2008; Perin & Charron, 2006). To this end, Parker (2007) explained that 22 states and systems of higher education have reduced or eliminated their skill-building programs, and similar considerations are being proposed elsewhere (Mazzero, 2002). Therefore, if colleges are questioning the efficacy of their skill-building programs, a strength-based approach might be one method to help improve academic outcomes among students who depend on these programs to access higher education.

In chapter 5, Jameel Scott draws from extant literature to provide context for the experiences and challenges of low-income Black men at HBCUs. He concludes by offering salient recommendations for institutional leaders to help increase academic success among this group of Black men at HBCUs.

In chapter 6, Sharon Fries Britt, Brian Burt, and Khadish Franklin draw from a larger, 5-year study that investigated the academic and social experiences of minority students who were successful in physics at HBCUs. They also make comparisons between Black students in physics at HBCUs and PWIs. One of the interesting findings discussed in their chapter is the importance of relationships with faculty, administrators, and peers and their influence on helping Black men achieve academic success in physics. They contend that these relationships are often absent for Black men who are in science programs at PWIs.

In chapter 7, Lorenzo DuBois Baber examines the experiences of second-generation Black male collegians and offers critical insight and recommendations for HBCU leaders about how they may rethink designing services and programmatic initiatives. In particular, Baber calls for campus leaders to take into consideration the heterogeneity among Black men on their campuses when conceptualizing, developing, and implementing services and initiatives.

In chapter 8, Fred Bonner addresses the challenges and opportunities facing millennial students within the context of HBCUs. To this end, he provides critical strategies and important recommendations for research applicable to institutional leaders as they work to support and retain this contemporary population of Black men on their campuses. To our knowledge, Bonner's chapter is one of the first chapters to provide context about Black male millennial students at HBCUs.

In chapter 9, T. Elon Dancy and Gralon Johnson explore how Black fathers negotiate multiple identities in postsecondary education by offering insight about their college experiences, particularly at HBCUs. Dancy and Johnson conclude by offering thoughts for higher education and society. The experiences of Black fathers at HBCUs have not been discussed in the literature, thus

Dancy and Johnson's chapter makes a particularly noteworthy contribution to this volume.

In chapter 10, Dorian McCoy provides an historical overview of Black Greek Letter Fraternities (BGLFs), delineates some of the challenges facing them, and provides recommendations for ways that administrators can respond to these issues. This chapter emphasizes the importance of BGLFs in facilitating academic and social development among Black male collegians.

In chapter 11, David Horton discusses the salience of focusing on Black male student athletes, particularly at HBCUs. In his chapter, he examines the relationship that student athletes have with their coaches and shows how it can be used to engender success. He concludes with practical recommendations and offers considerations for future research.

In chapter 12, Alonzo Flowers focuses on academically gifted Black males in engineering at HBCUs. His chapter provides rich insight into the experiences of academically gifted Black males in STEM. Flowers concludes by offering practical recommendations for faculty, administrators, and student affairs and considerations for future research on Black males in engineering disciplines.

In the concluding chapter to this volume, J. Luke Wood and Robert T. Palmer present four innovative programs implemented on various campuses to help facilitate Black male success. These programs provide critical information for researchers and practitioners interested in programmatic initiatives that engender academic success for Black males in higher education generally and in particular those at HBCUs. Following the presentation of these programs, the authors discuss metalevel recommendations derived from the implications for practice sections from chapters in this text. They conclude with several recommendations for future research.

This volume is significant because it emphasizes the diversity that exists among Black male collegians. Of course, there are some limitations to this edited book in that it does not focus on all the subcultures among Black male collegians. Nonetheless, this book is a template upon which future projects (e.g., articles, books) can build to advance the discourse on Black men in higher education. Despite its shortcomings, this volume makes a compelling contribution to the literature on Black male collegians.

This edited volume is applicable to practitioners, faculty, and researchers interested in the Black male experience in higher education, HBCUs, and gender identity. The content of each chapter and recommendations provided are grounded in extant theory and research relevant to the topical areas addressed. Thus, the multidimensional and dynamic relationship between theory, research, and practice and the implications of each are evident throughout. While this volume considers the context of HBCUs and the within group diversity of Black men, practitioners, faculty, and researchers at PWIs can use the critical information herein to create programs and implement strategies to increase retention and persistence among Black men on their campuses.

Finally, given the book's distinct approach, this volume is particularly useful for future researchers interested in exploring the varied experiences and challenges among the diverse types of Black men in higher education in general, specifically at HBCUs.

References

Adams v. Richardson, 351 f.2d 636 (D.C.Cir. 1972).

Allen, W. R. (1986). *Gender and campus differences in Black student academic performance, racial attitudes, and college satisfaction.* Atlanta, GA: Southern Education Foundation.

Allen, W. R. (1992). The color of success: African American college student outcomes at predominantly White and historically Black public colleges and universities. *Harvard Educational Review, 62*(1), 26–44.

Allen, W. R., & Jewell, J. O. (2002). A backward glance forward: Past, present and future perspectives on historically Black colleges and universities. *Review of Higher Education, 25,* 241–261.

Allen, W. R., Jewell, J. O., Griffin, K. A., & Wolf, D. S. (2007). Historically Black colleges and universities: Honoring the past, engaging the present, touching the future. *Journal of Negro Education, 76*(3), 263–280.

Bahr, P. R. (2008). Does mathematics remediation work? A comparative analysis of academic attainment among community college students. *Research in Higher Education, 49,* 420–450.

Berger, J. B., & Milem, J. F. (2000). Exploring the impact of historically Black colleges in promoting the development of undergraduates' self-concept. *Journal of College Student Development, 41*(4), 381–394.

Bonous-Hammarth, M., & Boatsman, K. (1996). *Satisfaction guaranteed? Predicting academic and social outcomes for African Americans college students.* Paper presented at the Annual Conference of the American Educational Research Association, New York.

Boylan, H. R., & Saxon, D. P. (1999). *Outcomes of remediation.* Boone, NC: National Center for Developmental Education.

Brown, M. C. (1999). *The quest to define collegiate desegregation: Black colleges, Title VI compliance, and post-Adams litigation.* Westport, CT: Bergin & Garvey.

Brown, M. C., Bertrand, R. D., & Donahoo, S. (2001). The Black college and the quest for educational opportunity. *Urban Education, 36,* 533–571.

Brown, M. C. & Davis, J. E. (2001). The historically Black college as social contract, social capital, and social equalizer. *Peabody Journal of Education, 76*(1), 31–49.

Brown v. Board of Education, 347 U.S. 483 (1954).

Charles, C. Z., Dinwiddie, G., & Massey, D. S. (2004). The continuing consequences of segregation: Family stress and college academic performance. *Social Science Quarterly, 85*(5), 1353–1373.

Chickering, A. W., Peters. K., & Palmer, R. T. (2006, March). *Assessing the impact of the Morgan male initiative on leadership and excellence (MILE).* Baltimore, MD: Morgan State University.

Civil Rights Act of 1964 (Title VII), 42 U.S.C. 2000e et. seq. 29 C.F.R. 1600-1610.

Cuyjet, M. J., & Associates (Eds.). (2006). *African American college men: Twenty first century issues and concerns.* San Francisco, CA: Jossey-Bass.

Dancy, T. E. (2005). Madness or elitism? African Americans who reject HBCUs. *Black Issues in Higher Education, 22*(5), 82.

Davis, R. J., & Palmer, R. T. (2010). The role and relevancy of postsecondary remediation for African American students: A review of research. *Journal of Negro Education, 76*(4), 503–520.

Ehrenberg, R. G., & Rothstein, D. S. (1994). *Do historically Black institutions of higher education confer unique advantages on Black students: An initial analysis* (NBER Working Paper Series, 4356). Cambridge, MA: National Bureau of Economic Research.

Fleming, J. (1984). *Blacks in college: A comparative study of student success in Black and White institutions.* San Francisco, CA: Jossey-Bass.

Flowers, L. (2002). The impact of college racial composition on African American students' academic and social gains: Additional evidence. *Journal of College Student Development, 43*(3), 403–410.

Ford, D. Y., Grantham, T. G., & Whiting, G. W. (2008). Another look at the achievement gap: Learning from the experiences of gifted Black students. *Urban Education, 43*(2), 216–239.

Fries-Britt, S., & Turner, B. (2002). Uneven stories: Successful Black collegians at a Black and a White campus. *Review of Higher Education, 25*(3), 315–330.

Gasman, M., Baez, B., Drezner, N. D., Sedgwick, K., Tudico, C., & Schmid, J. M. (2007). Historically Black colleges and universities: Recent trends. *Academe, 93*(1), 69–78.

Gasman, M., Lundy-Wagner, V., Ransom, T., & Bowman, N. (2010). *Unearthing promise and potential: Our nation's historically Black colleges and universities* (ASHE Higher Education Report). San Francisco, CA: Jossey-Bass.

Geiger, S. M. (2006). *Understanding gender at public historically Black colleges and universities: A special report of the Thurgood Marshall Scholarship Fund, Inc.* New York: Thurgood Marshall Scholarship Fund.

Gurin, P., & Epps, E. G. (1975). *Black consciousness, identity and achievement: A study of students in historically Black colleges.* New York: Wiley.

Harper. S. R. (2006). Peer support for African American male college achievement: Beyond internalized racism and the burden of "acting White." *Journal of Men's Studies, 14*(3), 337–358.

Harper, S. R., Carini, R. M, Bridges, B. K., & Hayek, J. (2004). Gender differences in student engagement among African American undergraduates at historically Black colleges and universities. *Journal of College Student Development, 45*(3), 271–284.

Harper, S. R., & Gasman, M. (2008). Consequences of conservatism: Black male undergraduates and the politics of historically Black colleges and universities. *Journal of Negro Education, 77*(4), 336–351.

Hill, S. T. (2002). *Science and engineering degrees by race/ethnicity of recipients*: 1995–2000. Arlington, VA: Division of Science Resource Statistics (NSF 07-308)

Howard-Hamilton, M. F. (1997). Theory to practice: Applying developmental theories relevant to African American men. *New Directions for Student Services, 80,* 17–30.

Kim, M. M. (2002). Historically Black vs. White institutions: Academic development among Black students. *Review of Higher Education, 45,* 385–407.

Kim, M. M., & Conrad, C. F. (2006). The impact of historically Black colleges and universities on the academic success of African American students. *Research in Higher Education, 47*(4), 399–427.

Kimbrough, W. M., & Harper, S. R. (2006). African American men at historically Black colleges and universities: Different environments, similar challenges. In M. J. Cuyjet & Associates (Eds.), *African American men in college* (pp. 189–209). San Francisco, CA: Jossey-Bass.

Kimbrough, R. M., Molock, S. D., & Walton, K. (1996). Perception of social support acculturation, depression, and suicidal ideation among African American college students at predominantly Black and predominantly White universities. *Journal of Negro Education, 65*(3), 295–307.

Levin, H., & Calcagno, J. C. (2008). Remediation in the community college: An evaluator's perspective. *Community College Review, 35*(3), 181-207.

Lundy-Wagner, V., & Gasman, M. (2011). When gender issues are not just about women: Reconsidering male students at historically Black colleges and universities. *Teachers College Record, 113*(5). Retrieved from http://www.tcrecord.org/library/content.asp?contentid=15936

Mazzero, C. (2002). Stakes for students: Agenda-setting and remedial education. *Review of Higher Education, 26,* 19–39.

National Center for Education Statistics (NCES). (2003). *Status and trends in the education of racial and ethnic minorities.* Washington, DC: Author.

Nettles, M. T. (Ed.). (1988). *Toward Black undergraduate student equality in American higher education.* New York: Greenwood Press.

Nettles, M. T., & Perna, L. W. (1997*). African American education databook: Vol. 1. Higher and adult education.* Fairfax, VA: Frederick D. Patterson Research Institute.

Outcalt, C. L., & Skewes-Cox, T. E., (2002). Involvement, interaction, and satisfaction: The human environment at HBCUs. *Review of Higher Education, 25*(3), 331–347.

Palmer, R. T. (2008). Promoting HBCUs: Black colleges provide a superior education; they just need to toot their horns a little louder. *Diverse Issues of Higher Education, 24*(26), 29.

Palmer, R. T. (2010). The perceived elimination of affirmative action and the strengthening of historically Black colleges and universities. *Journal of Black Studies, 40*(4), 762–776.

Palmer, R, T., & Davis, R. J. (in press). "Diamond in the Rough": The impact of a remedial program on college access and opportunity for Black males at an historically Black institution. *Journal of College Student Retention.*

Palmer, R. T., Davis, R. J., & Hilton, A. A. (2009). Exploring challenges that threaten to impede the academic success of academically underprepared Black males at an HBCU. *Journal of College Student Development, 50*(4), 429–445.

Palmer, R. T., Davis, R. J., & Maramba, D. C. (2010). Popularizing achievement: The role of an HBCU in supporting academic success for underprepared African American males. *Negro Educational Review, 61*(1–4), 85–106.

Palmer, R. T., Davis, R. J., & Maramba, D. C. (in press). The impact of family support for African American males at an historically Black University: Affirming the revision of Tinto's theory. *Journal of College Student Development.*

Palmer, R. T., & Gasman, M. (2008). "It takes a village to raise a child": The role of social capital in promoting academic success for African American men at a Black college. *Journal of College Student Development, 49*(1), 52–70.

Palmer, R. T., & Griffin, K. (2009). Desegregation policy and disparities in faculty salary and workload: Maryland's historically Black and predominantly White institutions. *Negro Educational Review, 60*(1–4), 7–21.

Palmer, R. T., Maramba, D. C., & Dancy, T. E. (in press). The magnificent "MILE": Impacting Black male retention and persistence at an HBCU. *Journal of College Student Retention.*

Palmer, R. T., Maramba, D. C., & Lee, J. M. (2010). Investigating Black students' disinclination to consider and attend historically Black colleges and universities (HBCUs). *National Association of Student Affairs Professionals Journal, 13*(1), 23–45.

Palmer, R. T., & Strayhorn, T. L. (2008). Mastering one's own fate: Non-cognitive factors with the success of African American males at an HBCU. *National Association of Student Affairs Professionals Journal, 11*(1), 126–143.

Palmer, R. T., & Young E. M. (2009). Determined to succeed: Salient factors that foster academic success for academically unprepared Black males at a Black college. *Journal of College Student Retention, 10*(4), 465–482.

Parker, T. L. (2007). *Ending college remediation: Consequences for access and opportunity* (ASHE/Lumina Policy Briefs and Critical Essays No. 2). Ames: Department of Educational Leadership and Policy Studies, Iowa State University.

Patton, L. (2011). Perspectives on identity, disclosure, and the campus environment among African American gay and bisexual men at one historically Black college. *Journal of College Student Development, 52*(1), 77–100.

Perin, D., & Charron, K. (2006). Lights just click on every day. In T. Bailey & V. S. Morest (Eds.), *Defending the community college equity agenda* (pp. 155–194). Baltimore, MD: John Hopkins University Press.

Perna, L., Lundy-Wagner, V., Drezner, N. D., Gasman, M., Yoon, S., Bose, E., & Gary. S. (2009). The contribution of HBCUs to the preparation of African American women for STEM careers: A case study. *Research in Higher Education, 50*, 1–23.

Pope, J. (2009). Men struggling to finish at Black college. Retrieved from http://diverseeducation.com/artman/publish/article_12432.shtml

Provasnik, S., Shafer, L. L., & Snyder, T. D. (2004). *Historically Black colleges and universities, 1976 to 2001* (NCES 2004-062). Washington, DC: National Center for Education Statistics.

Ross, M. (1998). *Success factors of young African American males at a historically Black college.* Westport, CT: Bergin & Garvey.

Sissoko, M., & Shiau, L.-R. (2005). Minority enrollment demand for higher education at historically Black colleges and universities from 1976 to 1998: An empirical analysis. *Journal of Higher Education, 76*(2), 181–208.

Thurgood Marshall College Fund (2008). Thurgood Marshall College Fund Demographic Report. Retrieved from http://www.thurgoodmarshallfund.net/images/demorep/demographic-report.pdf

U.S. Department of Education, National Center for Education Statistics. (2009a, August). *2006 through 2008 Integrated Postsecondary Education Data System (IPEDS), fall 2007, fall 2008, spring 2007, and spring 2008.* Washington, DC: Author.

U.S. Department of Education, National Center for Education Statistics. (2009b, August). *1990 through 2008 Integrated Postsecondary Education Data System, "Fall Enrollment Survey"* (IPED-SEF: 90), spring 2001, spring 2008, and fall 2008. Washington, DC: Author.

2

HIGH ACHIEVING BLACK MEN AT HISTORICALLY BLACK COLLEGES AND UNIVERSITIES

Marybeth Gasman and Dorsey Spencer, Jr.

In the past few years, the literature on Black men in higher education has grown at a great rate. Scholars, including Michael Cuyjet, Shaun R. Harper, Terrell L. Strayhorn, Robert T. Palmer, Jerlando Jackson, and Fred Bonner, II have written extensively on the subject. Many of our questions around issues of success and high achieving Black men have been answered due to the deep and consistent work of these scholars and others. In fact, given the resources that most possess, we would argue that a preponderance of majority institutions, in particular, have little excuse for the underperformance of the Black men that they enroll.

The situation for Black men at historically Black colleges and universities (HBCUs) is much less understood. Although some scholars, most prominently Robert T. Palmer, have done work related to these men, there are still many unanswered questions. HBCUs have fewer resources than their majority counterparts, yet they are purported to provide a more supportive, nurturing, and empowering learning environment for Black students (Palmer & Gasman, 2008). Still, research shows that this environment disproportionately benefits women. In the words of Gasman, Lundy-Wagner, Ransom, and Nelson (2010): "the reality of poor achievement, enrollment, and undergraduate degree completion by [Black] males at HBCUs suggests a gendered effect" (p. 32). Furthermore, Lundy-Wagner and Gasman (2011), Geiger, (2006), and Provasnik, Shafer, and Snyder (2004) claim that the significant gains in Black postsecondary enrollment at HBCUs can be almost exclusively attributed to gains made by Black women, given that Black male enrollment at HBCUs has essentially stagnated over the years.

The situation for Black men at HBCUs makes examining the reasons for the success of those who are high achieving even more relevant and important. In this chapter, we argue that the success of high achieving Black men at

HBCUs can be attributed to a combination of intrinsic and extrinsic factors. Intrinsic factors are those that motivate a high achieving Black male student from within. Extrinsic factors are those that motivate an individual but come from outside agents. We will discuss both sets of factors herein. In addition, we will make recommendations for practice that encourage the achievement of Black men and recommendations for future research to fill the gaps that currently exist.

Intrinsic Motivations for Achievement

The concept of the intrinsic motivators is primarily derived from Robert Palmer and Terrell Strayhorn's (2008) research on Black men at HBCUs. Palmer and Strayhorn identified four themes. They were: (a) personal responsibility, b) focus and direction, (c) management of time, (d) fervor for major. Religious beliefs have also been identified as having a significant impact on the success of Black men at HBCUs (Ross, 1998). Religion serves as a foundation and a sense of support for many young Black men.

Previous research depicts Black men at HBCUs as not being goal-oriented (Harper, Carini, Bridges, & Hayek, 2004). This is not the case with high achievers. High achieving Black men at these particular institutions are self-driven. They feel personally responsible for their academic success and persistence (Palmer & Strayhorn, 2008). High achievers make a conscious effort to wake in the morning and have a productive day. These individuals comprehend the seriousness and importance of doing well in college. These men understand that ultimately they are responsible for their success in college. High achievers are academically engaged, attend class consistently, and set academic goals that they work to attain (Kimbrough & Harper, 2006). These men understand the correlation between their academic career and their life after college, particularly with regard to graduate school and future employment (Kimbrough & Harper, 2006).

Some high achievers at HBCUs conduct daily self-analysis to motivate themselves to complete tasks and assignments. They exhibit an uncanny sense of fortitude and maturity in comparison to their peers. These students understand that dedication and hard work are the keys to success. Often Black men do not take advantage of campus resources such as tutoring and the writing center because of pride (Palmer, Davis, & Maramba, 2010). However, high achieving Black men understand the value of campus resources and make use of them. They also participate in extracurricular and cocurricular activities that enhance their academic experience (Palmer & Strayhorn, 2008). Research shows that participation in such activities enhances a student's affinity toward an institution, which results in heightened chances of success (Palmer et al., 2010). Finding the proper balance between academic and extracurricular activities is the key to the success of high achievers within the HBCU context.

For many college students the campus environment creates a myriad of potential distractions from academic work. Examples include relationships, intramural sports, student organizations, and parties. These distractions are not necessarily malevolent by nature, but they can be detrimental to one's academic career if they break concentration and focus. Even high achieving males often struggle with focus initially (Palmer & Strayhorn, 2008); maintaining focus is typically a skill that is developed over time. While focus is not one of the most easily acquired factors for success, it is one of the most vital. It is the glue that holds the other variables together. High achieving Black men at HBCUs understand that their main objective in being at an institution of higher education is to learn. They make productive use of nonclass time.

This is seemingly common sense, but many of the high achievers' peers do not completely grasp these ideals. For many of the average Black male students at HBCUs, academics takes a backseat to social life (Kimbrough & Harper, 2006). The leader of the Protestant Reformation, Martin Luther, once said, "How soon 'not now' becomes 'never'." High achieving Black male students at HBCUs understand the previous quote. Time management is another key to the academic success of these men, and it is a skill that has been designated as essential to academic success (Palmer & Strayhorn, 2008). Students often overlook this seemingly simple skill set that is required in an array of activities that require advance planning; for example, it affects going to class, studying, and even social time. For some males at HBCUs, being involved in athletics or extracurricular activities teaches them time management (Palmer & Strayhorn, 2008). These students balance their academic work with other commitments.

A participant in Palmer and Strayhorn's (2008) study describes the final intrinsic motivator for achievement as similar to the love one has for one's family, particularly one's parents. A passion for one's major is another important key to success. A passion for an academic major correlates with more investment in learning and comprehension of the necessary material that fosters learning (Palmer & Strayhorn, 2008). This is sometimes a difficult trait to acquire because it goes against a cultural norm. According to Brown and Davis (2001), education has always been a gateway to the American dream for Blacks. Oftentimes, Black people believe that education will save them from all of their socioeconomic issues (Brown & Davis, 2001). It is because of this mentality that many men at HBCUs choose a major that is likely to lead to financially lucrative employment after graduation rather than one in which they are truly interested (Palmer & Strayhorn, 2008). An issue then arises when students major in areas for which they may not have the skill sets (Clark, 1960). Without both the proper skill sets and a passion for the subject it becomes difficult to persist.

Extrinsic Motivations for Achievement

In addition to the intrinsic motivators, there are also extrinsic agents that allow for high achieving Black men at HBCUs to be successful. Extrinsic motivators for achievement are based around relationships and environment. According to Palmer and Gasman (2008), there are five central factors that enhance a Black male's ability to be a high achiever: relationships with faculty, campus administration, mentors and role models, peers, and the overall climate of campus. Students who engage with faculty inside the classroom and collaborate with administration through extracurricular organizations are able to successfully navigate the ins and outs of their college careers. Likewise Black men at HBCUs who have an active relationship with strong mentors and significant relationships with a positive peer group develop a solid support system that extends beyond their college life. This section of the chapter will explore high achieving Black males' relationships with faculty, campus administration, mentors and role models, peers, and the HBCU environment as a whole, highlighting the connections to their academic success.

High achieving men at HBCUs acknowledge the connection between their academic success and their faculty members. They see that their professors genuinely care about them and want them to succeed and they capitalize on these supportive relationships (Palmer & Gasman, 2008). They consider their relationships with professors to be advantageous and uplifting (Palmer & Gasman, 2008). High achievers believe faculty members are genuinely concerned about their academic and personal life and are often able to relate to them based on personal experiences. These men grasp the importance of meeting with professors during office hours (Palmer & Gasman, 2008). They understand that this action expresses attentiveness and sincerity in relation to their academics. Professors are viewed as being accessible and these students take advantage of this opportunity. They seek to build a relationship with the faculty. They take advantage of opportunities to work with faculty on research projects. In turn, these students are supported and challenged to meet high expectations. The perception of many of these high achievers is that faculty members see their potential and therefore are trying to assist them in reaching their optimal capacity.

Similarly, the HBCU administration is also an integral part of high achieving Black males' success: "These administrators are helpful, accessible, and demonstrate a caring attitude about student success" (Palmer & Gasman, 2008, p. 59). In addition to their job requirements, administrators often take on the function of mentors and role models. The difference between high achievers and average Black males at HBCUs is that high achievers acknowledge the importance of these relationships and take advantage of the administrators' willingness to help students.

High achieving Black males at HBCUs expressed that another noteworthy element in their academic success was their ability to access mentors and role models. They preferred to find an individual who possessed some similarities with them. These commonalties can be ethnic, socioeconomic, gender, or educational (Palmer & Gasman, 2008). The knowledge that there are other successful Black men serves as a source of motivation. The mentality of "if he can do it so can I" sets in. Mentors and role models can range from peers to alumni, although an older person is usually most desired. Current research supports having mentors and role models as being advantageous (Craig, 2006; Lavant, Anderson, & Tiggs, 1997). Mentors provide encouragement and advice. These individuals motivate students to persist and be successful.

According to Astin (1993), constructive peer interaction positively correlates with academic success. Recent research shows this is also true of high achieving Black men at HBCUs (Palmer & Gasman, 2008). These men attempt to surround themselves with peers who have similar aspirations. This cohort of high achieving men then maintains a symbiotic relationship that thrusts them toward academic success. A student in Palmer and Gasman's (2008) study stated that his peers who are high achievers "keep him invigorated and provide an outlet to relieve stress, as well as help him focus on his goals" (p. 61). Like minded men inspire high achieving men at HBCUs. They push each other to do well and support each other.

HBCUs provide a unique environment for Black students. The environment is perceived as nurturing and supportive (Fries-Britt & Turner, 2002). HBCUs also provide social capital (Brown & Davis, 2001). Both of these traits allow for students to be successful academically. High achieving Black men at these institutions are examples of this. HBCUs provide a "strong foundation" for Black students. The institutions enhance high achieving Black men's confidence and pride (Fries-Britt & Turner, 2002). High achieving Black men are able to harness the full potential of the energy that HBCUs generate for their students (Fries-Britt & Turner, 2002). They are able to foster a sense of confidence that translates into high academic performance, which is different for Black male students who attend predominantly White institutions (PWIs) who use energy that should be used on their studies to deal with the campus culture and environment. The racial homogeneity of HBCUs is also advantageous for high achieving Black men because they have an opportunity to see other Black men and women who are focused on being academically successful (Palmer et al., 2010). As institutions, HBCUs provide an entire system of support to aid students' academic success, mental well-being, and social development despite their conservative environment (Harper & Gasman, 2008).

Recommendations for Practice

High achievers at HBCUs are performing well, with HBCUs providing a positive, empowering environment for their success. However, there is much more that HBCUs could do in order to enable more of their Black male students to be high achievers. HBCUs need to provide additional opportunities for faculty interaction and undergraduate research, especially in the sciences. One way to do this is by applying for grants through the National Science Foundation (NSF) or the National Institutes for Health (NIH). The NSF and

NIH have funding available to foster better and more comprehensive mentoring relationships for Black men at HBCUs.

HBCUs need to track the performance of Black men. A few years ago, Philander Smith College started a Black Male Initiative that focuses on academic achievement of Black men. This program uplifts and supports Black men academically and socially. The college also monitors these men's performance and is intrusive in its advising of these individuals. In fact, President Walter Kimbrough intervenes himself when young men are falling behind. Black men are on the radar screen at Philander Smith and need to be at all HBCUs. This type of approach will create an environment ripe for more high achievers.

HBCUs provide wonderful role models and potential mentors to high achieving Black men. Yet, the provision of these mentors could be much more systematic. Imagine the results if each Black man attending an HBCU was assigned a mentor and met with him or her regularly. A program that provides a dual mentorship opportunity would be beneficial. Dual mentorship means the student has a peer mentor and an older mentor, preferably an alumnus, faculty, or administrator. Not only would the high achieving men be more successful, but mentoring could also assist those who are on the verge of being high achieving to possibly rise to the occasion.

Additionally, providing workshops for first year students during orientation or throughout the year is beneficial. Areas that these workshops should cover are time management, goal setting, productivity, and an explanation of vital campus and academic resources. Programs that exhibit and promote extracurricular involvement should also be considered.

Recommendations for Research

Although there is considerable research on HBCUs, a major study of students at these institutions has not been issued for decades. The last major studies were Fleming (1984) and Allen, Epps, and Haniff (1991). These studies provide important data about HBCUs, but no longer capture the current student body of these institutions. There is a substantial need for large scale, longitudinal study of Black students at HBCUs and Black men in particular. There are many unanswered questions that both qualitative and quantitative research could help us answer.

Studying the actions and strategies of high achieving Black men in a systematic way can help researchers and practitioners to apply successful approaches to other Black men with less motivation to succeed. There are ample unanswered questions. We know little about the family lives of these high achievers. What actions do their parents and siblings take to foster their success? We know little about the socioeconomic status of high achievers. Does coming from a higher socioeconomic status make it easier for Black men to succeed in college or are these high achievers able to overcome socioeconomic odds? What is the quality of the relationships these high achievers had with their high school teachers and guidance counselors and is this quality linked to their success? What kinds of adversities do these high achievers shoulder throughout college and do they possess coping skills that could be shared with other Black men? These are just a few of the research questions that remain unanswered, just waiting to be pursued by scholars, among them, it is to be hoped, some Black male scholars. More scholarship by Black men can serve as a source of empowerment for other Black men.

Concluding Thoughts

Too often, Black men at HBCUs are seen as underperforming and under-prepared for higher education. The fact is that some men at HBCUs fit this description. However, there are many Black men who are eager to pursue their education and know that they will benefit greatly from pursuing all avenues of support in college. They seek out resources, mentors, and research opportunities to bolster their performance in college. They also work diligently to promote the success of other Black men, realizing that their success is tied to the success of their peers. They see it as their role to build up the lives and experiences of other Black men. These young men should be held up as role models and celebrated because their success can serve as an inspiration for the performance of others.

References

Allen, W. R., Epps, E. G., & Haniff, N. Z. (Eds.). (1991). *College in Black and White*. Albany, NY: SUNY Press.

Astin, A. W. (1993). *What matters in college: Four critical years revisited*. San Francisco, CA: Jossey-Bass.

Brown, C. M., & Davis, J. E. (2001). The historically Black college as social contract, social capital, and social equalizer. *Peabody Journal of Education, 76*(1), 31–49.

Clark, B. R. (1960). The "cooling-out" function in higher education. *American Journal of Sociology, 65,* 569–576.

Craig. K. (2006). Factors that influence success for African American students. In F. W. Hale (Ed.), *How Blacks empower Black students: Lessons for higher education* (pp. 101–108). Sterling, VA: Stylus.

Fleming, J. (1984). *Blacks in college: A comparative study of student success in Black and White institutions.* San Francisco: Jossey-Bass.

Fries-Britt, S., & Turner, B. (2002). Uneven stories: Successful Black collegians at a Black and a White campus. *Review of Higher Education, 25*(3), 315–330.

Gasman, M., Lundy-Wagner, V., Ransom, T., & Bowman, N. (2010). *Unearthing promise and potential: Our nation's historically Black colleges and universities* (ASHE Higher Education Report). San Francisco, CA: Jossey-Bass.

Geiger, S. M. (2006). *Understanding gender at public historically Black colleges and universities: A special report of the Thurgood Marshall Scholarship Fund, Inc.* New York: Thurgood Marshall Scholarship Fund.

Harper, S. R., Carini, R. M., Bridges, B. K., & Hayek, J. C. (2004). Gender differences in student engagement among African American undergraduates at historically Black colleges and universities. *Journal of College Student Development, 45*(3), 271–284.

Harper, S. R., & Gasman, M. (2008). Consequences of conservatism: Black male undergraduates and the politics of historically Black colleges and universities. *Journal of Negro Education,* 77(4), 336–351.

Kimbrough, W. M., & Harper, S. R. (2006). African American men at historically Black colleges and universities: Different environments, similar challenges. In M. J. Cuyjet & Associates (Eds.), *African American men in college* (pp. 189–209). San Francisco, CA: Jossey-Bass.

Lavant, B. D., Anderson, J., & Tiggs, J. W. (1997). Retaining African American men through mentoring initiatives. In M. J. Cuyjet (Ed.), *Helping African American men succeed in college* (New Directions for Student Services, No. 80, pp. 43–52). San Francisco, CA: Jossey-Bass.

Lundy-Wagner, V., & Gasman, M. (2011). When gender issues are not just about women: Reconsidering male students at historically Black colleges and universities. *Teachers College Record,* 113(5). Retrieved from http://www.tcrecord.org/library/content.asp?contentid=15936

Palmer, R. T., Davis, R.J., & Maramba, D.C. (2010). Popularizing achievement: The role of an HBCU in supporting academic success for underprepared Black males. *Negro Educational Review,* 61(1–4), 85–106.

Palmer, R. T., & Gasman, M. (2008). "It takes a village to raise a child": Social capital and academic success at historically Black colleges and universities. *Journal of College Student Development,* 49(1), 1–19

Palmer, R. T., & Strayhorn, T. L. (2008). Mastering one's own fate: Non-cognitive factors associated with the success of African American males at an HBCU. *National Association of Student Affairs Professionals Journal,* 11(1), 126–143.

Provasnik, S., Shafer, L. L., & Snyder, T. D. (2004). *Historically Black colleges and universities, 1976 to 2001* (NCES 2004-062). Washington, DC: National Center for Education Statistics.

Ross, M. (1998). *Success factors of young African American males at a historically Black college.* Westport, CT: Bergin & Garvey.

3

COMING OUT OF THE DARK

Black Gay Men's Experiences at Historically Black Colleges and Universities

Terrell L. Strayhorn and Jameel A. Scott

> Today, Blacks are no longer the litmus paper or the barometer of social change. Blacks are in every segment of society and there are laws that help to protect them from racial discrimination. The new "niggers" are gays.... It is in this sense that gay people are the new barometer for social change.... The question of social change should be framed with the most vulnerable group in mind: gay people.
>
> *(Bayard Rustin, 2003, p. 275)*

Introduction

How does one open a chapter on Black gay men attending historically Black colleges and universities (HBCUs)? Do we begin with startling statistics, with historic and head-shaking headlines, or a review of what we know about Black [gay] men? Or do we begin with a laconic review of the literature on the rich history of HBCUs? And, if so, should we start at the beginning with Lincoln and Cheyney in Pennsylvania? Or, should we start at the end with Southern University in New Orleans or the University of the Virgin Islands? Maybe a smooth blend of all of them is appropriate.

Today there are over 4,200 degree-granting colleges and universities in the United States; together, they enroll over 18 million students including both undergraduate and graduate students. There are approximately 103 HBCUs located across 20 states, representing less than 3% of the total "system" of higher education in this country. HBCUs enroll approximately 300,000 students, the vast majority being Black students. And though a significant proportion of Black students now attend predominantly White institutions (PWIs), HBCUs enroll approximately 13% of all Black collegians and confer nearly one-fifth of all bachelor's degrees awarded to Black students annually (U.S. Department of Education, 2009). While national statistics are not readily available, it has been estimated that approximately 10 to 20% of all college students identify as gay, lesbian, bisexual, or transgendered (GLBT; Rankin, 2006), although estimates can be unreliable for some subpopulations such as Black men who may engage in same-sex sexual behaviors but not identify as gay or bisexual (Battle & Bennett, 2000). To be sure, Black gay men represent a respectable proportion of all Black men enrolled in higher education and, thus, they are worthy of scholarly attention.

Recent headlines also suggest the importance of a chapter on Black gay men at HBCUs. Consider the following: "Homos 101: Premier Black College is a Study in Anti-Gay Discrimination" and "Bat Beating at Morehouse Labeled Hate Crime," referring to Aaron Price's brutal attack against Gregory Love for glancing at him in the shower at Morehouse College. "Morehouse College Faces Its Own Bias—Against Gays" is another example. And people are still talking about Morehouse College's ban on effeminate Black men who wear "clothing associated with women's garb" (Windmeyer, 2009).

Turning again to the quote that opened this chapter, one could also highlight several historical figures who laid the foundation for civil rights politics for Blacks and gays. Consider Bayard Rustin, a close counselor and confidant of Dr. Martin Luther King, who played an almost singular "behind-the-scenes" role in organizing the 1963 March on Washington for Jobs and Freedom. Son of a single, unmarried teenage mother in West Chester, Pennsylvania, Bayard was a radical agitator for peace, anticipating the civil rights movement of the 1960s well before his time (D'Emilio, 1999). It is also well-documented that Rustin lived as an openly gay Black man whose sexuality made him an "embarrassment" to the Southern Christian Leadership Council and Dr. King's immediate cabinet of Black leaders (D'Emilio, 1996). Almost as unknown as Rustin himself is the fact that he attended Wilberforce University in Ohio and then Cheyney State Teachers College (now Cheyney University) in Pennsylvania, both HBCUs (D'Emilio, 2003). It is also rarely discussed that Bayard was a member of a historically Black fraternity. Indeed, Bayard Rustin represents an HBCU Black gay male who helped change the course of social history, although his gallant efforts were largely silenced (by others) or ignored given his precarious situation as a Black gay man (D'Emilio, 2003). And if he was right in his prophetic pronouncement, then perhaps the "question of social change" in higher education should be framed with one of the most vulnerable groups in mind: namely, Black gay men at HBCUs.

Whether measured according to their proportional representation among all college students, their life-threatening challenges as unprotected sexual minorities within American society, or historically underrepresented racial minorities within the gay community, studying the experiences of Black gay men at HBCUs is timely and critically important for those of us charged with supporting and enhancing the holistic development of college students. Yet, virtually little is known about the experiences of these students at HBCUs. This is the knowledge gap addressed by the present chapter. Before describing the studies that inform the present chapter, a brief review of the existing literature is offered in the next section.

What We Know about Black Gay Men at HBCUs

Three lines of scholarship relate to the focus of this chapter: theoretical research on GLBT identity development, studies on Black men in higher education, and a handful of studies on Black gay men in educational contexts. This section is organized around these three major foci.

GLBT Identity Development

Numerous scholars have studied the psychosocial development of GLBT people. Research in this area is largely theoretical with particular attention devoted to understanding the process by which individuals assume a gay or nonheterosexual identity, come to understand themselves as gay or homosexual, and subsequently reconcile such understandings with previously held perceptions of self (Cass, 1979, 1984; D'Augelli, 1994; Fassinger, 1991). For instance, Cass posited a stagelike model that explains gay identity development as a general movement away from awareness to an integrated sense of one's self as gay or lesbian. Her model consists of six stages through which gay individuals struggle to resolve developmental conflicts and tensions associated with knowing themselves in relation to others: (a) identity confusion, (b) identity comparison, (c) identity tolerance, (d) identity acceptance, (e) identity pride, and (f) identity synthesis.

A more recent theoretical model posits gay identity development as occurring through four stages along two separate, yet reciprocally catalytic processes: individual sexual identity and group membership identity (Fassinger, 1998; McCarn & Fassinger, 1996). The four stages are (a) awareness (i.e., feeling or being different, existence of alternative sexual orientations); (b) exploration (i.e., strong or erotic feelings for same sex, consideration of one's position about gays as a group); (c) deepening commitment (i.e., growing commitment to one's knowledge, values, and beliefs about sexuality; personal involvement in reference group); and (d) internalization/synthesis (i.e., synthesis of same-sex feelings and choices into personal identity, identification as a member of a [sexual] minority group). An initial phase of nonawareness precedes both processes of the model and "the four subsequent phases follow in the same progression for each branch [or process]" (McCarn & Fassinger, 1996, p. 521). Taken together, these models may be useful for explaining the process through which Black men assume a gay identity. To further our understanding of these issues, we found it necessary to review the literature on Black male collegians as well; the next section summarizes what we found.

Black Men in Higher Education

There has been a fairly recent shift toward examining the academic and social experiences of Black men in higher education (Cuyjet, 2006), and, sometimes, at HBCUs specifically (Palmer, Davis, & Hilton, 2009; Palmer & Gasman, 2008; Palmer & Strayhorn, 2008). For instance, some scholars have demonstrated that social integration positively affects Black male students at both 2- and 4-year colleges (Flowers, 2006; Harper, 2006; Strayhorn, 2008). Generally speaking, academic and social integration have been consistently linked with positive outcomes such as higher retention rates (Braxton, Milem, & Sullivan, 2000; Schwartz & Washington, 2002), acquisition of social and professional skills (e.g., time management and speaking skills; Harper, 2006), and enhanced self-efficacy (Strayhorn, 2010). Scholars have also studied causes for Black male student success at HBCUs (Palmer & Young, 2009). Their findings suggest that student engagement is correlated with academic success. Furthermore, faculty involvement at HBCUs helps to create nurturing environments for students, thereby promoting more social integration (Palmer & Gasman, 2008).

However, too often research regarding the lived experience of Black men in higher education has indicated poor social integration, lack of involvement on campus, feelings of isolation, and limited role models for support, without paying close attention to the ways in which specific subpopulations experience college in various contexts. Indeed, much of what has been written about Black men in higher education treats them as a monolithic group whose experiences are much more similar than different. Yet a growing body of research indicates that "they are not all the same" (Harper & Nichols, 2008) and much more information is needed about invisible Black male populations such as Black gay men who, unlike student athletes (Messer, 2006), may not enjoy the respect and admiration of some peers and faculty, as well as those who attend minority-serving institutions (Gasman, 2008). Thus, we searched for literature on the experiences of Black gay men in higher education generally, as well as studies on Black gay men at HBCUs specifically.

Black Gay Men in College

A small, but growing corpus of studies focuses on Black gay men in college. A review of the literature suggests at least three major conclusions. First, Black gay men at PWIs face social isolation from other Black or male students on campus (Washington & Wall, 2006). Second, apart from struggling to fit in, Black gay men face challenges with "coming out" for fear of losing friends and family, which can be detrimental to their development (Strayhorn, Blakewood, &

DeVita, 2010). Specifically, Strayhorn et al. (2010) posit that "coming out" is an ongoing process rather than a one-time event, and Black gay men tend to reveal their sexual orientation to a select group of friends before sharing that information with close family members. Lastly, the weight of evidence indicates that Black gay men struggle with feelings of depression, which D'Augelli (1994) put forth as a reason many are at-risk for mental health problems. Related to feelings of depression, some men in this group report feeling "multiple minority threat," which refers to the sense of having three strikes against them as targets of racism for being Black, and objects of homophobia for being gay (Strayhorn et al., 2010).

Another important line of inquiry consists of empirical studies that examine issues of sexual orientation and racial identity (C. E. Brown, 2008; Icard, 1986) and whether and how Black gay men identify sexually (E. Brown, 2005). For instance, E. Brown (2005) employed a case study approach to analyze qualitative data from 110 Black men in Atlanta. And although all of his male participants indicated that they have sex with men, relatively few identified as gay (37%); 13% identified as "down low bisexual," 9% as bisexual, 7% as homosexual, and even 17% as straight. He rightly concluded that Black gay men cannot accept a gay identity for at least three reasons: homophobia, heterosexism, and constructions of Black masculinity. We will return to this point again later in the chapter.

Given the importance of academic, social, and cultural factors to the healthy development of a gay identity (Cass, 1979; Fassinger, 1991), the academic success of Black male collegians (Cuyjet, 2006; Harper, 2006; Strayhorn, 2010), even at HBCUs (Palmer & Gasman, 2008), and the cognitive and psychosocial functioning of Black gay men in college (Strayhorn et al., 2010; Washington & Wall, 2006), there is a need for additional information to understand how these issues play out in the campus environment for Black gay men at HBCUs. This is the objective of the present chapter.

Chapter's Purpose

The expressed purpose of this chapter is to identify the challenges that Black gay men face at HBCUs and to offer recommendations for educational policies and practices that hold promise for enabling their success at HBCUs.

The Study

Since we were interested in understanding the academic and social challenges that Black gay men face at HBCUs, we drew upon data from a larger, multiyear, qualitative research project that examines the perceptions and experiences of gay men of color in various campus contexts (Strayhorn et al., 2010). Although the larger study consists of responses from various institutions, this chapter is based upon data from four HBCUs for which complete data were readily available. The campuses are best described as medium- to large-sized 4-year research universities located in the North- and Southeast regions of the country. Each campus offers multiple venues for student involvement on campus ranging from student government to athletics (e.g., varsity, intramural), from fraternities to professional societies (e.g., National Society of Black Engineers [NSBE]). A university-sponsored GLBT student organization was available on one campus only.

A total of nine participants provided information that formed the basis of this chapter. All participants were enrolled full-time; academic majors ranged from music to religious studies, engineering to social work. Participants were involved in a number of campus organizations: gospel choir, historically Black fraternities, social fraternities, political groups, professional societies, and honors clubs, to name a few.

To elicit information about Black gay men at HBCUs, the lead author worked with members of his research team to develop an interview protocol that consisted of several major questions and a few minor probes. For instance, participants were asked, "What has college been like for you?" Probes encouraged participants to "describe a time when..." or "tell me more about...," in consonance with techniques recommended by qualitative experts (Kvale, 1996). Semistructured one-on-one interviews were the primary method of data collection; each interview lasted 90 to 120 minutes, on average. Data analysis proceeded in several stages using the constant comparison method outlined by Glaser and Strauss (1999). In short , the analytic process consisted of identifying a preliminary set of codes using a form of open coding, comparing, and contrasting initial codes to determine whether different words or phrases could be combined or collapsed into similar categories, and then sorting categories and codes into major themes (for more see, Strayhorn, 2008). A summary of these major themes is reported in the next section.

Challenges of Black Gay Men at HBCUs

Several major findings were identified in the larger study (Strayhorn et al., 2010), using the analytic process outlined briefly in the previous section, although not all could be shared in this brief treatment of the subject; thus, four are discussed here as they relate to the challenges that Black gay men face at HBCUs.

Encounters with Homophobia and Harassment

Black gay men at HBCUs have relatively frequent encounters with homophobia and gay oppression, or what Kirk and Madsen (1989) referred to as "homo-hatred," on campus. Virtually all of the participants in the larger study had been verbally insulted (at least once), threatened with physical violence, or had their personal property damaged as a result of their perceived or actual sexual orientation. Verbal insults ranged from homophobic name calling (e.g., queer, sissy) to other derogatory terms (e.g., fag, b*tch). Enduring such insults and physical threats can take its toll on an individual; thus, it may be unsurprising, yet nonetheless problematic, that 100% of all men in the larger study reported having contemplated suicide or made at least one serious suicide attempt since entering college.

Perpetrators of such homophobic acts, interestingly, tend to be same-race male peers, faculty members, and even university staff. For instance, Black gay men at HBCUs identified the following individuals as typical offenders or harassers on campus: other Black male undergraduates, roommates, student athletes, resident assistants, professors, paraprofessional staff (e.g., administrative aides), and local or campus religious leaders. Sadly, almost 100% of participants expected to encounter future victimization on campus, especially since three of the four HBCUs in the larger study do not include sexual orientation in its university nondiscrimination policy. In fact, many of the men with whom we spoke talked about feeling unprotected, unvalued, and invisible on campus, which is another challenge.

Invisibility and Marginalization

Black gay men at HBCUs, especially those whose gay identity is more freely expressed, or central to their core self (Jones & McEwen, 2000), describe a life that places them at the margins of the dominant campus life. For instance, few Black gay men at HBCUs are actively involved in campus student clubs and organizations or social activities (e.g., parties). Instead, many report being involved in social or community organizations external to campus (e.g., grassroots GLBT activist agencies, GLBT youth centers) that, at times, focus specifically on the needs of gay men of color; several participants mentioned specific organizations such as Us Helping Us, Sexual Minority Youth Assistance League (SMYAL), Human Rights Campaign (HRC), Gay and Lesbian Alliance Against Defamation (GLAAD), and Stonewall Columbus, to name a few. In other words, they "elect" or are forced to live on the periphery of campus—sometimes literally (e.g., living off-campus away from campus residence halls)—and do not join mainstream student organizations or clubs such as the gospel choir, student association, or fraternities. As a result of living off-campus or being involved in organizations through the local community, friendships for Black gay men at HBCUs are often established with individuals from a select group in whom they are comfortable placing confidence and trust, most often individuals (e.g., students attending other colleges, community members, local residents) who share aspects of their racial or sexual background.

It can also be difficult for Black gay men at HBCUs to establish romantic relationships. There are at least two reasons for this that interviewees offered.

First, they report relatively few opportunities to forge meaningful relationships with other men in college, particularly other gay men on campus. Second, the campus climate at HBCUs tends to magnify the negative consequences of being "gay," especially since many HBCUs are religiously affiliated and predominantly Black (Gasman, 2008) and Blacks tend to subscribe to conservative views about gender and sexuality (Greene, 1994; Herek & Capitanio, 1995). So, some men at HBCUs go out of their way to avoid the "known homosexual[s]" on campus, although participants talk about how these same men make sexual advances to them privately through e-mail, text, Facebook, or face-to-face. As a result of limited opportunities to establish meaningful relationships with other men on campus, some Black gay men at HBCUs engage in unhealthy sexual practices (e.g., unprotected sex, random one-night hook-ups) or look elsewhere including church, gay clubs, bathhouses, and even online dating sites, although they frequently encounter race-based discrimination (e.g., "Not interested in Black guys" or "Whites and Latinos reply only") in such spaces (Adams & Kimmel, 1997; C. E. Brown, 2008).

In some ways, Black gay men at HBCUs resemble Horowitz's (1987) "outsiders," whose primary interests and involvements lie outside the academic and social realms of campus life. And though living at the margins of campus life in many areas, some Black gay men at HBCUs persist and excel academically. In fact, most of the men in the larger study maintained grade point averages (GPAs) above 3.0 and received scholarships from various sources. Previous scholars have explained academic success as a function of academic and social integration (Tinto, 1993), paying close attention to the way in which acceptance by one's peers and faculty members help validate students as knowers, affirm their experiences on campus, and enhance their confidence to succeed. Yet, for many Black gay men at HBCUs, neither their peers nor their faculty offer much validation, affirmation, or support to succeed. Instead they are forced to find success on their own, depending on support from external agents and a reasonable portion of resiliency and optimism to excel despite obstacles. There are other challenges that this group faces.

Lack of Family Support

Family is a central component of Black life in America and some researchers have stressed the supportive role that family members play in the success of Black students (Ahmeduzzaman & Roopnarine; Lareau, 2003; Mandara & Murray, 2007), but the family's role can be different for Black gay men at HBCUs. Several participants in the larger study reported losing contact with or support from their biological family members, especially parents, due to their sexual/affectional orientation; others described having to renegotiate or revise existing family relations (e.g., losing contact with siblings temporarily, talking to one parent through another). Biological family members were rarely identified as a major source of support or encouragement for Black gay men at HBCUs; when biological family members are mentioned they are typically mothers.

Instead, many GLBT students of color, including Black gay men at HBCUs, construct nonbiological family relationships with individuals, or *fictive kin*, who provide much-needed forms of support. Fictive kin refers to individuals "who are not related by blood, but by the imaginary ties of choice—they are 'adopted' family members who accept the affection, obligations, and duties of 'real' kin (Karner, 1998, p. 72) or "who embody the 'special characteristics' of family... those who provide care like family and do what family does; [they] are given the label of kin with its attendant affection, rights, and obligations" (Karner, 1998, p. 70). Many of the Black gay men in the larger study talked extensively about sharing "sisterlike" relationships with Black female peers, professors, and staff members; "brotherlike" relationships with Black men in the local community; and even mother- or fatherlike relationships with older gay people who "take them under their wings," offer advice about living productively as a Black gay man, encourage them to do well in college, and introduce them to other members of the gay community where possible. Without sufficient support from their biological families, Black gay men at HBCUs establish meaningful relationships with constructed families or fictive kin who supply various forms of emotional, social, and even financial support. Yet, not all Black gay men at HBCUs, or elsewhere for that matter, identify openly as gay; this leads to another challenge.

Issues of Identification

Similar to Peterson and his colleagues (1992), we want to point out that some Black gay men at HBCUs engage in repeated same-sex relations (ranging from kissing to sexual intercourse), yet do not identify as gay or bisexual but rather as heterosexual, straight, "messing around," "down-low (or DL)," "in the life," "queer," or "just me." Not only does this complicate our efforts to access and understand this population in terms of research, but it demonstrates the importance of language and adopting categories that distinguish between openly identified Black gay men and those who may engage in same-sex behaviors but identify differently. Just as E. Brown (2005) explained, we too believe that there are at least three reasons why Black men who have sex with men cannot accept a gay identity or label: homophobia, heterosexism, and constructions of Black masculinity.

Homophobia refers to the irrational fear, hatred, and intolerance of people who are gay, lesbian, and bisexual (Pharr, 1988). Obear (1991) further explains that "these intense prejudicial feelings often result in the belief in powerful negative stereotypes and discriminating actions against people who are gay, lesbian, or bisexual" (p. 39). Heterosexism, on the other hand, refers to belief in the inherent superiority and "naturalness" of heterosexuality, relegating anything nonheterosexual to lower, unnatural, or unacceptable status (Lorde, 1983). It is also true that stereotypes can lead to oppressive behaviors, especially when stereotypes are assumed and enacted by those in power to support prejudice. So, one reason why Black men who have sex with men may reject the label of "gay" is because "gay" has been stigmatized largely by negative stereotypes (e.g., flamboyant, feminine, sexual predator, AIDS as gay disease) upon which those in power (e.g., Whites, heterosexuals, men) often rely to discriminate against GLBT people. To avoid the stigma, some men reject the label altogether, although they engage in repeated same-sex behaviors. And to use Obear's (1991) comment about GLBT people in general, we found that Black gay men at HBCUs "experience homophobia and heterosexism on a daily basis" (p. 39). They may experience harassment, verbal abuse, physical assault, threats of violence, and even denial of membership to campus clubs and organizations (e.g., fraternities) as a result of their sexual/affectional orientation. Denying one's sexual orientation or "passing" as straight is frequently cited as a way of dealing with this challenge, although some evidence suggests that denying aspects of one's self may limit a person's ability to develop to their full potential (Pharr, 1988) and can cause serious health disorders, such as depression and suicidal thoughts (D'Augelli, 1994)

Masculinity also affects Black gay men's behaviors and activities, thereby reducing, if not eliminating the chances that they would identify as gay. For instance, Blacks, on average, subscribe to traditional notions of masculinity and gender expectations, which presume Black men as strong, stoic, unemotional, providers for their "family," procreators, conquerors of multiple women (sometimes simultaneously), and unrestrained fighters (Kimmel, 1996; Majors & Billson, 1992). Fear of being labeled as gay forces many Black gay men at HBCUs to adhere to traditional masculine roles and gender expectations, despite their natural propensity to assume healthy roles and identities that violate traditional expectations (e.g., some guys talked about choosing certain majors or dressing a certain way to avoid homophobic teasing). Indeed, homophobia "is great enough to keep 10 to 20% of the population living lives of fear (if their sexual identity is hidden) or lives of danger (if their sexual identity is visible) or both" (Pharr, 1988, p. 2).

Discussion of Findings

Recall that the purpose of this chapter was to identify the challenges that Black gay men face at HBCUs and to offer recommendations for educational policies and practices that hold promise for enabling the success of Black gay men at HBCUs. Here we identify four major challenges for this population at HBCUs:

(a) homophobia and harassment, (b) invisibility and marginalization, (c) lack of family support, and (d) issues of identification. Using these challenges as a guide, we offer the following recommendations for future policy, practice, and theory:

Implications for Practice

1. College student educators at HBCUs should work to create a campus environment that is perceived as warm, welcoming, and receptive to Black gay men. For instance, educators and student leaders should interrupt homophobic comments that are aired, intentionally or unintentionally, in classrooms, common spaces, or residence halls. Workshops and seminars can be offered that address issues of homophobia, homohatred, gay oppression, harassment, and productive ways of establishing community in residence halls.

2. Student activities professionals at HBCUs might establish new or revise existing campus clubs and organizations that appeal to the unique interests of Black gay men. For instance, only one campus in the larger study had a university-sanctioned GLBT student organization. More HBCUs should follow its lead by establishing such groups and other "safe zones" for gay students on campus. Actively encouraging GLBT students to be involved in campus activities is another way to promote the involvement and success of Black gay men at HBCUs.

3. Campus ministry staff members play an important role on HBCU campuses, particularly those that are private or religiously affiliated. Thus, campus ministry staff should keep in mind that the campus community is not all heterosexual and the gay community is not all nonreligious; there are important nuances. Outreach efforts should target the entire campus community without denying access to GLBT students; sermons, campus-published documents, and campus-sanctioned religious clubs (e.g., gospel choirs, intervarsity Christian groups) should avoid demonizing gay students on campus or promulgating heterosexist messages that render them as morally corrupt, homophobic messages that label them as dangerous predators, or homohatred messages that identify them as proper targets of unjustified mistreatment.

4. Campus administrators can look to partner with GLBT off-campus organizations to help bring their services on campus; this might also be an effective way of expressing the institution's desire to promote a more inclusive college environment for all students. Several of the students interviewed indicated that they joined clubs outside of campus, and were less involved with on-campus activities. Partnering with these off-campus organizations could nurture HBCU students' sense of connectedness with the campus, thereby increasing social integration.

Implications for Policy

1. Federal, state, and local policymakers should devise new or revise existing campus nondiscrimination policies to include sexual orientation as a protected class; for an explicit statement about GLBT discrimination (see D'Augelli and Rose, 1990).
2. Campus judicial officers or deans of student life should revise student conduct codes to prohibit homophobic and homohatred acts, as well as to explain explicitly how such offenses will be adjudicated.
3. Human resource professionals, provosts, deans, and department heads at HBCUs should conduct audits of campus human resource policies (e.g., health care benefits) to make sure that HBCU staff and student workers in domestic partnerships are not denied access to the same rights, benefits, and privileges afforded to heterosexual couples through compensation and benefits packages. For instance, some campuses require same-sex couples to demonstrate financial dependency over a 3- to 5-year period, although heterosexual couples are not required to do so. One equity-based question is: Why would an institution require this of some workers but not all?

Implications for Theory

1. Researchers and practitioners should increase the use of existing gay identity development theories (Cass, 1979, 1984; D'Augelli, 1994; Fassinger, 1991) in current research on GLBT students, particularly testing the efficacy of existing models of specific subpopulations such as Black gay men at HBCUs.
2. Researchers and practitioners should hypothesize new or revise existing gay identity development theories to account for the complexity of experiences among GLBT people of color, the nonlinearity of their "coming out" process, and the various ways in which an array of social identities (e.g., gay, Christian, fraternity member) and social locations (e.g., race, class, gender) intersect and simultaneously influence their lived experiences.
3. Done correctly, theory informs practice and practice, in turn, informs theory. So, we highly recommend that college student educators increase their use of extant theories when working with Black gay men at HBCUs. Similarly, educators would do well to reflect on their work with Black gay men at HBCUs when trying to understand the process through which individuals come to understand themselves as gay and adopt a healthy, productive gay identity. New approaches in practice may lead to new or different theoretical revelations, which can be incorporated into our current or future models.

All of these recommendations hold promise for promoting and improving the access, retention, and success of Black gay men at HBCUs. When considering these and other strategies for enhancing the campus conditions for this group at HBCUs, we urge educators, administrators, and leaders to follow Bayard Rustin's advice that began this chapter—to frame such discussions *with the most vulnerable group in mind: gay people of color.*

References

Adams, C. L., & Kimmel, D. C. (1997). Exploring the lives of older African American gay men. In B. Greene (Ed.), *Ethnic and cultural diversity among lesbian and gay men* (pp. 132–151). Thousand Oaks, CA: Sage.

Ahmeduzzaman, M., & Roopnarine, J. L. (1992). Sociodemographic factors, functioning style, social support, and fathers' involvement with preschoolers in African-American families. *Journal of Marriage and the Family, 54,* 699–707.

Battle, J., & Bennett, M. (2000). Research on lesbian and gay populations within the African American community: What have we learned? *African American Research Perspectives, 6*(2), 35–47.

Braxton, J. M., Milem, J. F., & Sullivan, A. S. (2000). The influence of active learning on the college student departure process: Toward a revision of Tinto's theory. *The Journal of Higher Education, 71*(5), 569–590.

Brown, C. E. (2008). *Racism in the gay community and homophobia in the Black community: Negotiating the gay Black male experience (*Unpublished master's thesis). Virginia Tech, Blacksburg, VA.

Brown, E. (2005). We wear the mask: African American contemporary gay male identities. *Journal of African American Studies, 9*(2), 29–38.

Cass, V. C. (1979). Homosexuality identity formation: A theoretical model. *Journal of Homosexuality, 4*(3), 219–235.

Cass, V. C. (1984). Homosexuality identity formation: Testing a theoretical model. *Journal of Sex Research, 9*(1–2), 105–126.

Cuyjet, M. J. (2006). African American college men: Twenty-first century issues and concerns. In M. J. Cuyjet & Associates (Eds.), *African American men in college* (pp. 3–23). San Francisco, CA: Jossey-Bass.

D'Augelli, A. R. (1994). Identity development and sexual orientation: Toward a model of lesbian, gay, and bisexual development. In E. J. Trickett, R. J. Watts, & D. Birman (Eds.), *Human diversity: Perspectives on people in context* (pp. 312–333). San Francisco, CA: Jossey-Bass.

D'Augelli, A. R., & Rose, M. L. (1990). Homophobia in a university community: Attitudes and experiences of heterosexual freshmen. *Journal of College Student Development, 31,* 84–91.

D'Emilio, J. (1996). Reading the silences in a gay life: The case of Bayard Rustin. In M. Rhiel & D. Suchoff (Eds.), *The seductions of biography* (pp. 59–68). New York: Routledge.

D'Emilio, J. (1999). Bayard Rustin: Civil rights strategist. *Harvard Gay and Lesbian Review, 6*(3), 12–15.

D'Emilio, J. (2003). *Lost prophet: Bayard Rustin and the quest for peace and justice in America.* New York: Free.

Fassinger, R. E. (1991). The hidden minority: Issues and challenges in working with lesbian women and gay men. *Counseling Psychologist, 19,* 157–176.

Fassinger, R. E. (1998). Lesbian and bisexual identity and student development theory. In R. L. Sanlo (Ed.), *Working with lesbian, gay, bisexual and transgender college students: A handbook for faculty and administrators* (pp. 13–22). Westport, CT: Greenwood.

Flowers, L. A. (2006). Effects of attending a 2-year institution on African American males' academic and social integration in the first year of college. *Teachers College Record, 108*(2), 267–286.

Gasman, M. (2008). Minority-serving institutions: A historical backdrop. In M. Gasman, B. Baez, & C. S. V. Turner (Eds.), *Understanding minority-serving institutions* (pp. 18–27). Albany, NY: SUNY Press.

Glaser, B. G., & Strauss, A. L. (1999). *The discovery of grounded theory: Strategies for qualitative research.* New York: Aldine De Gruyter.

Greene, B. (1994). Ethnic-minority lesbians and gay men: Mental health and treatment issues. *Journal of Consulting and Clinical Psychology, 62,* 243–251.

Harper, S. R. (2006). Enhancing African American male student outcomes through leadership and active involvement. In M. J. Cuyjet & Associates (Eds.), *African American men in college* (pp. 68–94). San Francisco, CA: Jossey-Bass.

Harper, S. R., & Nichols, A. H. (2008). Are they not all the same? Racial heterogeneity among Black male undergraduates. *Journal of College Student Development, 49*(3), 199–214.

Herek, G. M., & Capitanio, J. (1995). Black heterosexuals' attitudes towards lesbians and gay men in the United States. *The Journal of Sex Research, 32,* 95–105.

Horowitz, H. L. (1987). *Campus life: Undergraduate cultures from the end of the eighteenth century to the present.* New York: Knopf.

Icard, L. (1986). Black gay men and conflicting social identities: Sexual orientation versus racial identity. *Journal of Social Work and Human Sexuality, 4*(1–2), 83–93.

Jones, S. R., & McEwen, M. K. (2000). A conceptual model of multiple dimensions of identity. *Journal of College Student Development, 41*(4), 405–414.

Karner, T. X. (1998). Professional caring: Homecare workers as fictive kin. *Journal of Aging Studies, 12*(1), 69–82.

Kimmel, M. S. (1996). *Manhood in America: A cultural history.* New York: Free.

Kirk, M., & Madsen, H. (1989). *After the ball: How America will conquer its fear and hatred of gays in the 90s.* New York: Doubleday.

Kvale, S. (1996). *InterViews: An introduction to qualitative research interviewing.* Thousand Oaks, CA: Sage.

Lareau, A. (2003). *Unequal childhoods: Class, race, and family life.* Berkeley: University of California Press.

Lorde, A. (1983). There is no hierarchy of oppressions. *Interracial Books for Children, 14*(3–4), 9.

Majors, R., & Billson, J. (1992). *Cool pose: The dilemmas of Black manhood in America.* New York: Touchstone.

Mandara, J., & Murray, C. B. (2007). How African American families can facilitate the academic achievement of their children: Implications for family-based interventions. In J. F. L. Jackson (Ed.), *Strengthening the African American educational pipeline: Informing research, policy, and practice* (pp. 165–186). Albany, NY: SUNY Press.

McCarn, S. R., & Fassinger, R. E. (1996). Revisioning sexual minority identity formation: A new model of lesbian identity and its implications for counseling and research. *Counseling Psychologist, 24*(3), 508–534.

Messer, K. L. (2006). African American male college athletes. In M. J. Cuyjet & Associates (Eds.), *African American men in college* (pp. 154–173). San Francisco, CA: Jossey-Bass.

Obear, K. (1991). Homophobia. In N. J. Evans & V. A. Wall (Eds.), *Beyond tolerance: Gays, lesbians, and bisexuals on campus* (pp. 39–66). Alexandria, VA: ACPA.

Palmer, R. T., Davis, R. J., & Gasman, M. (in press). A matter of diversity, equity and necessity: The tension between Maryland's higher education system and its historically Black institutions over the OCR agreement. *Journal of Negro Education.*

Palmer, R. T., Davis, R. J., & Hilton, A. A. (2009). Exploring challenges that threaten to impede the academic success of academically underprepared African American male collegians at an HBCU. *Journal of College Student Development, 50,* 429–445.

Palmer, R. T., & Gasman, M. (2008). "It takes a village to raise a child": The role of social capital in promoting academic success of African American men at a Black college. *Journal of College Student Development, 49*(1), 52–70.

Palmer, R. T., & Strayhorn, T. L. (2008). Mastering one's own fate: Non-cognitive factors associated with the success of African American males at an HBCU. *National Association of Student Affairs Professionals Journal, 11*(1), 126–143.

Palmer, R. T., & Young, E. M. (2009). Determined to succeed: Salient factors that foster academic success for academically unprepared Black males at a Black college. *Journal of College Student Retention, 10*, 465–482.

Peterson, J. L., Coates, T. J., Catania, J. A., Middleton, L., Hilliard, B., & Hearst, E. (1992). High-risk sexual behavior and condom use among gay and bisexual African American men. *American Journal of Public Health, 82*, 1490–1494.

Pharr, S. (1988). *Homophobia: A weapon of sexism.* Little Rock, AR: Chardon.

Rankin, S. R. (2006). LGBTA students on campus: Is higher education making the grade? *Journal of Gay and Lesbian Issues in Education, 3*(2/3), 111–117.

Rustin, B. (2003). The new "niggers" are Gays. In D. W. Carbado & D. Weise (Eds.), *Time on two crosses: The collected writings of Bayard Rustin* (pp. 275–276). Berkeley, CA: Cleis Press.

Schwartz, R. A., & Washington, C. M. (2002). Predicting academic performance and retention among African American freshmen men. *NASPA Journal, 39*, 354–370.

Strayhorn, T. L. (2008). Fittin' In: Do diverse interactions with peers affect sense of belonging for Black men at predominantly White institutions? *NASPA Journal, 45*(4), 501–527.

Strayhorn, T. L. (2010). Buoyant believers: Resilience, self-efficacy, and academic success of low-income African American collegians. In T. L. Strayhorn & M. C. Terrell (Eds.), *The evolving challenges of Black college students: New insights for policy, practice, and research* (pp. 49–65). Sterling, VA: Stylus.

Strayhorn, T. L., Blakewood, A. M., & DeVita, J. M. (2008). Factors affecting the college choice of African American gay male undergraduates: Implications for retention. *National Association of Student Affairs Professionals Journal, 11*(1), 88–108.

Strayhorn, T. L., Blakewood, A. M., & DeVita, J. M. (2010). Triple threat: Challenges and supports of Black gay men at predominantly White campuses. In T. L. Strayhorn & M. C. Terrell (Eds.), *The evolving challenges of Black college students: New insights for policy, practice and research* (pp. 85–104). Sterling, VA: Stylus.

Tinto, V. (1993). *Leaving college: Rethinking the causes and cures of student attrition* (2nd ed.). Chicago, IL: University of Chicago Press.

U.S. Department of Education, National Center for Education Statistics. (2009, June). *The condition of education 2009* (NCES Report No. 2009-081). Washington, DC: U.S. Government Printing Office.

Washington, J., & Wall, V. A. (2006). African American gay men: Another challenge for the academy. In M. J. Cuyjet & Associates (Eds.), *African American men in college* (pp. 174–188). San Francisco, CA: Jossey-Bass.

Windmeyer, S. L. (2009, October 23). There's no one way to be a Morehouse man: Why can't a Morehouse man wear a fierce pair of Jimmy Choos to class? *Advocate.com.* Retrieved from http://www.advocate.com/Society/Education/Theres_No_One_Way_to_Be_a_Morehouse_Man/

4

"YES, I CAN!"

Strengths-Based Approaches for Engaging and Empowering Academically Underprepared Black Men

Tiffany P. Fountaine and Joelle Carter

Since the late 1980s, several researchers have explored college access, experiences, outcomes, and implications for academically underprepared Black men (Allen, 1992; Cuyjet & Associates, 2006; Fleming, 1984; Hale, 2006; Palmer, Davis, & Hilton, 2009; Palmer & Gasman, 2008). Research has shown that Black men are attending college at significantly disproportionate rates than their White, as well as their Black female counterparts. According to a report by the National Center for Education Statistics (NCES; 2010), the gender gap for enrollment between male and female Black students has increased significantly over the last 30 years. In 1976, nearly 54% of Black undergraduates were female. By 2008, women accounted for 64% of the total Black undergraduate enrollment. Further, Black men continue to fall behind Whites (Bernanke, 2007; McDaniel, DiPrete, Buchmann, & Shwed, 2010) and their Black women counterparts in college completion rates. In 2008, Black women represented 68% of degree recipients and received more than twice as many degrees (219,200) as Black men (104,300). Data reported by NCES (2010) show that this pattern was apparent across all levels of degrees, with about twice as many degrees conferred on Black women as Black men at each level. In fact, national data show that nearly 68% of Black men who begin college do not persist to graduation within 6 years (Harper, 2006).

Researchers have outlined several factors that serve as barriers to and impede the success of Black men in college. Poor retention and persistence rates and active disengagement on campus have been linked with systemic discrimination in the educational pipeline (Palmer et al., 2009; West, 2001); lack of or minimal family involvement (Lewis & Middleton, 2003; Palmer, Davis, & Maramba, in press); perceived cultural attitudes of "acting White" (Fordham & Ogbu,

1986; Lundy, 2005); conservative institutional climates at historically Black colleges and universities (HBCUs; Harper & Gasman, 2008); inadequate financial assistance (Thomas, Farrow, & Martinez, 1998); perceived incongruence of academic success and masculinity (Davis, 2003); and academic preparation (Davis & Palmer, 2010; Klopfenstein, 2004; Palmer & Davis, in press; Perna, Redd, & Swail, 2003; Riegle-Crumb, 2006, Zamani, 2000). Although none of those factors individually has been cited as the fundamental cause of decreased retention and poor persistence rates, Fleming, Tezeno, and Zamora (2008) contended that academic underpreparedness may be a more significant retention issue for Black students, particularly those who are enrolled in HBCUs. Even when controlling for comparable abilities, Black students have been reported to experience more academic problems than their White counterparts (Sherman, Giles, & Williams-Green, 1994). Further, it has been reported that the overall academic preparation of Black students attending HBCUs lags behind that of students at other institutions (DeSousa, 2001).

The implications for Black students' academic underpreparedness are vast, but perhaps none is more critical than the consequences for Black males, especially considering the gravity of the gap between Black women and men in college, and, given the relationship between college degree attainment and social mobility, the significant economic and social repercussions (Bush & Bush, 2005). In response, scholars and stakeholders (Hoffman, Liagas, & Snyder, 2003; Hrabowski, 2002) have offered countless strategies including academic courses, special programs, and support services to assist academically underprepared Black men. These activities, designed to stimulate and strengthen students' intellectual competencies and enhance students' engagement, have demonstrated promising advances for academic improvement and success. For example, research seminars offered in the first year of college have been touted for building personal confidence and enhancing engagement for students who might not have had such experiences in high school (Copeland, 2006). Likewise, multicultural content based and culturally relevant courses (Fleming et al., 2008); interactive pedagogical methods and classroom experiences (Fleming et al., 2008; Ford & Harris, 1995); perceived higher expectations from teachers and peers (Oakes, 2005); peer tutorial programs (Glenn, 2007; Osman, 2007); and peer and faculty mentorship programs (Howard–Hamilton, 1997) have also been linked with the increased academic performance of underprepared students. Black male initiatives (Cech, 2007; Lavant, Anderson, & Tiggs, 1997; Palmer, Maramba, & Dancy, in press; Roach, 2003; Suddeth & Miller, 2009), and participation in Black Greek-letter fraternal organizations (Harper, 2007; Pascarella et al., 1996), have also played a vital role in the academic success of Black men in college. Lastly, summer bridge programs, often designed for high-risk students during the summer before they enroll in college, have been shown to positively impact the success of academically underprepared Black men by providing rigorous academic work, generally in mathematics and

English, to better prepare them for college level coursework in the fall (Copeland, 2006; Davis & Palmer, 2010; Palmer & Davis, in press).

Maximizing the Resources, Maximizing the Impact

For years, HBCUs have been forced to do more with less. Despite their pleth-
ora of challenges, including inadequate budgets, aging infrastructures, frequent
leadership changes, and opponents' criticism of their relevancy and necessity,
these institutions have remained steadfast and continued to produce more with
less resources while managing to outpace predominantly White institutions
(PWIs) in preparing and producing the majority of the nation's Black professionals (Gasman, 2009; Gasman et al., 2007; Hawkins, 2004; Palmer & Gasman, 2008). Notwithstanding, HBCU administrators, faculty, and other vested
stakeholders must be creative and innovative in exploring, developing, and
implementing strategies to promote their students' success despite the aforementioned challenges. One additional strategy that may warrant consideration by
HBCUs is the infusion of the strengths-based educational model—a paradigm
which emphasizes the positive aspects of student effort and achievement, as
well as human strengths—into academic courses, programs, and other support
services. There has been relatively little research on the effects of these models
on Black students, and virtually no research studies that focus on the impact of
these approaches within the context of HBCUs, specifically. This chapter discusses the impact of a strengths-based approach to teaching and learning, which
one HBCU employed to facilitate the academic development and enhance the
engagement of students enrolled in a precollege remedial education summer
program. The positive initial outcomes, particularly for Black men, suggest
that strengths-based approaches may be a viable strategy for grappling with the
challenges associated with precollege academic underpreparedness as well as a
factor for improved academic performance and increased engagement for Black
male collegians.

HBCU Profile

This chapter discusses the impact of a strengths-based program at a public,
doctoral research, historically Black university located in the mid-Atlantic
region of the United States. According to the University's Office of Institutional Research, the undergraduate enrollment at the time of this program
was 6,114. A little over 90% of the undergraduate student population is Black.
White, Hispanic, Asian, and Native American students comprised 2.8%, 0.9%,
0.7%, and 0.2% of the undergraduate student population, respectively. Thirty-
five percent of the undergraduate students are classified as out of state students,
many from the neighboring states in the mid-Atlantic and Northeast regions
of the United States. The most popular and highest producing majors at the

university include engineering, architecture, and nursing. The student–faculty ratio is 18:1. The outcomes from the most recent data collected from the University's placement exam indicated that nearly 70% of the freshman class is placed into one or more developmental or remedial courses in mathematics, English, and reading comprehension—thereby indicating that the majority of incoming students were academically underprepared for college work.

Core Assumptions and Practices of the Strengths-Based Model

Grounded in theories and practices of positive psychology, strengths-based educational approaches and models stress the positive aspects of student effort and achievement (Lopez & Louis, 2009). Positive psychology is the science of optimal human functioning. Essentially, positive psychology is the scientific study of the strengths and virtues that enable individuals and communities to thrive. It comprises the examination of positive emotions, positive individual traits, and positive institutions (Seligman & Csikszentmihalyi, 2000). The application and functions of positive psychological concepts in the field of education, in particular higher education, have been increasing as a means to address the learning needs of today's students (Conoley & Conoley, 2009; Lopez, 2006). Through various forms of educational reform (e.g., high-stakes testing, the progressive evolution of public charter schools and the like), the relevance and importance of student motivation and strong perceptions of self-worth are two concepts that are closely aligned with positive psychology. Although rooted in historical practices of psychological science and basic principles of teaching and learning, strengths-based educational approaches also draw from contemporary educational conceptions including the measurement of achievement (Carey, 2004), strengths, and determinants of positive outcomes (Lopez, 2004), as well as individualization, or the process by which teachers and educational practitioners think about and act upon the needs of each student and systematically make strides to personalize the intellectual experience of those students (Levitz & Noel, 2000).

Strengths-based educational approaches involve a process of assessing, teaching, and designing experiential learning activities to help students identify their greatest talents—naturally recurring patterns of thoughts, feelings, or behaviors that can be productively applied (Anderson, 2004). Using students' innate talents as a framework, the strengths-based model is designed to develop and apply strengths to those talents in an effort to enhance learning, intellectual growth, and academic achievement to levels of personal excellence. Drawing from the lens of positive psychology, this approach assumes that an individual's greatest opportunity for development lies in leveraging his or her natural talents rather than solely remediating his or her areas of weakness. Within the context of higher education, the strengths-based model has been primarily used to develop intervention programs to empower students to capitalize upon their talents to succeed in college rather than placing a comparable focus on over-coming personal weaknesses and deficiencies (Clifton & Harter, 2003).

Traditional approaches to student development and teaching learning have often employed a deficit remediation education model. These approaches often include evaluation and assessment, identification of strengths and weaknesses, and weakness remedying, and can result in academic tracking. Those who use this process are dedicated to helping students by first diagnosing their needs, problems, and deficits and then developing programs and services to help students improve in areas where they are underprepared. In essence, the deficit remediation education model presupposes the most important aspect is to "fix" the student (Clifton, Anderson, & Schreiner, 2006, p. xiii). Typically, this model does not allow students to focus on their interests until their deficits are corrected. This process essentially sorts students, often by their scores on standardized tests, based on perceived academic abilities, and has been a major factor in school organizations (Williams & Land, 2006). Researchers have argued that high stakes testing frameworks are disadvantageous to Black students especially because achievement is narrowly measured and recognized only through testing. Incoming first year students at this HBCU, including summer program participants, were initially evaluated based on their high school cumulative grade point averages and earned scores from the SAT and ACT standardized examinations (Williams & Land, 2006). Essentially, for this HBCU, a student's failure to earn the required minimum test scores resulted in an automatic academic tracking at the postsecondary level and placement into a remediation program. While the authors of this chapter acknowledge the predominance of deficit models in education as well as the benefits of this practice (i.e., students are provided with additional and needed remediation to strengthen their skills in areas of weaker performance), they contend it is important to consider alternative strategies when approaching student learning and assessing student achievement. There may be additional models to help students maximize academic performance.

With sole reliance on deficit model perspectives, an individual's strengths can be missed and often go unnoticed. In contrast, a strengths-based approach evaluates talent to identify strengths and weaknesses such that one can "integrate activities of one's life around talents, and manage around weaknesses" (Clifton & Harter, 2003, p. 120). Lopez and Louis (2009) proposed that education aimed at developing strengths should consist of measuring strengths and positive psychological outcomes; tailoring the learning experience to the needs of the individual student; creating positive support networks which appreciate and capitalize on the diversity of strengths; and applying and developing strengths. Strengths-based education models have been implemented on hundreds of campuses across the nation (Lopez & Louis, 2009) and these models have been linked with greater self-confidence and greater academic efficacy (Austin, 2005); well-being and positive behavior (Mahoney, 2009);

leadership development (Brodersen, 2008; Lehnert, 2009); retention (Gomez, 2009; Swanson, 2006); persistence (Cantwell, 2005); student success and achievement (Gomez, 2009); and positive outcomes for student engagement (Tyler, 2006).

Participants and Program Context

The exemplar HBCU provided a summer academy as an alternative admission program designed to ease the transition from high school to college for students whose academic profile and performance suggest the need for early intervention to improve their potential for success in college. The institution identified this student population as at-risk because their high school grade point averages (GPAs) and lower standardized test scores deemed them academically underprepared for the rigors of college work. Offered as a 6 week residential program in the summer before entering the first year of college, the program required participants to enroll and successfully complete a sequence of three remedial courses designed to strengthen the students' skills in English, mathematics, reading comprehension, and vocabulary development. In addition, participants were provided with supplemental instruction through peer tutorial services and were helped with navigating the college process through a peer mentorship program as well as various academic, personal, and leadership development seminars. The program consisted of approximately 300 students who were divided into 15 sections or cohorts of 20. There were five faculty members for each of the remedial areas—English, mathematics, reading comprehension, and vocabulary—and each facilitated instruction for three class sections. Additionally, there was one peer tutor and two peer mentors assigned to each cohort.

Infusion of a Strengths-Based Model

In the summers of 2009 and 2010, program coordinators implemented a strengths-based educational model as a pilot for students participating in the University's summer transition academy with the intent to facilitate academic development through remedial education courses and to enhance student engagement during students' summer transition experience. For the purposes of this pilot program, academic development was conceptualized as the use of intentional and proactive pedagogical methods promoting an active and collaborative learning environment. Essentially this means, using their strengths as a framework, faculty encouraged students to take ownership of their learning through interactive classroom discourse, peer interaction, and assignments that reinforce critical thinking and analytical skills. Traditional measures of achievement, such as cumulative scores on tests and homework assignments, were employed in the classroom. Thus, academic achievement was determined by the number of students who completed each remedial course with a grade of C or better.

As stated earlier, the other primary goal of the incorporation of a strengths-based approach was to enhance the engagement of program participants. According to Kuh (2009), student engagement is a broadly defined concept that represents the time and effort students devote to activities that are empirically linked to desired outcomes of college and to what extent institutions promote student participation in these activities. Engagement includes activities ranging from time spent preparing for class to talking with students of a different race or ethnicity. In this program, student engagement was characterized by students' participation in structured cocurricular activities, peer interactions, and students' ability to identify and to apply strengths in their transition into the collegiate environment. Multiple strategies were used to assess student engagement during the program. These informal and formal strategies included individualized mentor/mentee meetings, cocurricular program evaluations, participant observation, and pre- and postsurveys designed to assess students' understanding and application of strengths.

The strengths-based model was incorporated into all components of the program including curriculum, delivery of instruction, peer tutorial services, peer mentorship, and transition and leadership activities. In general, the strengths-based model begins with educators discovering what they do best and then developing and applying their strengths as they assist students in identifying and applying their strengths in the learning process, all in an effort to reach previously unattained levels of personal excellence and success (Lopez & Louis, 2009). Therefore, all program staff, summer academy faculty members, peer tutors, and peer mentors completed the StrengthsFinder© assessment, which is the nucleus of the strengths-based education framework. In Web based survey format, the assessment is designed to identify talent themes from high performing individuals in a variety of professional fields (Lopez, Janowski, & Wells, 2005). The results of the assessment are a cluster of themes referred to as signature themes that describe an individual's dominant innate abilities and tendencies (Clifton & Anderson, 2002). For example, the signature themes for a student may be *Communication, Woo, Positivity, Activator*, and *Ideation*. The StrengthsFinder results also provide additional information and guidance to enhance one's strengths. For example, a recommendation for course selection techniques for a student possessing a strong communication theme may be to "take classes from professors who encourage students to interrupt lectures to share stories or offer examples that amplify a concept" (Clifton et al., 2006, p. 157), or a study skills technique for a student possessing a strong activator theme may be to "jot down one or two key thoughts as he or she reads an article, story, or the directions from a project and to use those insights to shape the study group discussions" (p. 171).

Within the context of higher education, the StrengthsFinder assessment and strengths-based education techniques have been used with students in various academic settings, such as freshmen orientation seminars and mentoring sessions facilitated by counselors, academic advisors, and faculty members (Bowers & Lopez, 2010). In this case, the StrengthsFinder assessment was first used by summer academy team members to identify their natural talents and provide each with recommendations for leveraging strengths and specific action items for applying strengths. Each team member participated in a 1- to 3-day training and orientation to strengths application for the summer program. This was a critical step in that it is imperative for practitioners and faculty to acquire their self-knowledge and awareness of their strengths before designing and implementing curriculum and programs to help students build upon their own strengths (Braskamp, 2006).

Curriculum and Program Enhancement

To gain maximum understanding of the impact of the strengths-based model, program administrators made efforts to ensure pilot programs had minimal deviation from the 2008 program. The 2009 and 2010 program structure, course content and materials, course times and locations, supplemental resources, selection of faculty, and cocurricular and student development activities were consistent with that of the program in 2008. However, in addition to three remedial courses in English, mathematics, and reading comprehension and vocabulary, the pilot summer program curriculum was modified to include a fourth course—a strengths-based orientation seminar facilitated by program staff and faculty.

Through a traditional first-year student orientation course framework, strengths facilitators engaged students in a 6-week seminar. Initially, each student participant completed the StrengthsFinder assessment and identified his or her dominant talents, that were subsequently referred to as the student's top five themes. Strengths facilitators helped students to explore their key themes and talents, link those talents to students' personal goals and objectives, apply those talents to college orientation skill development in areas such as time management, study strategies, and group dynamics, and then document and exercise approaches to application both in and outside of the classroom. For example, peer mentors encouraged students to explore leadership opportunities through campus organizations and community outreach programs to cultivate their strengths. Other examples included faculty emphasizing the importance of strengths application in seeking support through campus resources such as academic advisement, tutoring, and career coaching. Strengths seminar facilitators also encouraged students to capitalize on the diversity of strengths by assigning group activities and tasks, and mediating reflective dialogue about the benefits of team building and peer engagement.

In addition, seminar facilitators administered success plans to help guide students in linking their themes to action. The success plan is a precursor and intermediary tool which enables students to set and review personal goals based on their dominant themes. It is comprised of three core components. The first component is student information—student's name, scheduling of appointment, and advisor. The second aspect contains questions to probe students' perspectives about what they enjoy doing and their academic and career interests. Other questions challenge students to identify a person who has had a positive influence on their life and to reflect on two successes they are most proud of. Combined, these questions serve as guided reflection to enable students to consider things they do innately well, skills where they have evidenced maximum potential, and to target factors that influence their motivation, specifically their ability to sustain motivation and encourage resiliency. The third and final component—the success plan chart—includes four categories: (a) Goals, (b) Strengths to Help Me Excel, (c) Partners Needed for Support, and (d) Measures to Identify Goal Achievement. The success plan is profoundly instrumental when working with Black students in that researchers have argued that in general, Black college students are more negative about their ability to academically succeed than their White counterparts when setting their academic goals (Hackett, Betz, Casas, & Rocha-Singh, 1992; Laar, 2000). The administration of the success plan encourages students to think critically and independently about their innate gifts and abilities and to use those talents as a utility to reach their academic career and goals.

Student Success Outcomes

Academic Development

The 2009 and 2010 overall program success rates—students earning a letter grade of C or better—increased to 91% from 2008 (see Table 4.1). Black men specifically, showed marked improvement as well. In 2009, 92.9%, and in 2010, 88.3% of Black men earned a letter grade of C or better in each course—an increase from 81% in 2008. In addition, nearly half of the program participants earned a GPA of 3.0 or better, signifying a letter grade of B or higher in each of the three courses in 2009; slightly more than 40% achieved this same feat in 2010. Both measures show significant progress from 2008, where 31% of participants earned a letter grade of B or better in each of the courses. Furthermore, Black men represented more than 30% of all students who earned a 4.0 GPA in the summers of 2009 and 2010, a significant percentage increase from that of students in 2008. It is important to note that the average high school GPA, cumulative math and verbal scores on the SAT, and composite scores on the ACT were relatively consistent among participants across all 3 years.

TABLE 4.1 Enrollment, Trends, and Outcomes for Summer Program Participants, 2008-2010

	2008 Cohort	2009 Cohort	2010 Cohort
Total Enrollment	305	292	308
Males	104	113	120
Females	201	179	188
Average High School GPA	2.6	2.7	2.6
Average SAT/ACT Score	770/15	790/15	790/15
Success Rate Overall	87.2%	91%	91%
Males	81.7%	92.9%	88.3%
Females	89%	89.3%	92%
Achievement 3.0+ GPA	31%	49%	41%
Black Male Achievement 4.0 GPA	17%	31%	31%

Student Engagement

Feedback from the individualized mentor–mentee meetings, responses to cocurricular program evaluations, discovery from informal participant observation, and the findings from pre- and postsurveys revealed that summer program participants were able to identify and better articulate their strengths to others. Student survey responses also demonstrated that participants developed a "deeper" understanding and application of their strengths. Further, participants reported increased use of their strengths during the program and indicated that the application of strengths allowed them to remain positive, build new relationships, and work effectively in groups during the transition experience. More importantly, students believed their strengths would influence their focus and engagement during the academic year and articulated ways they would apply strengths in negotiating some of the challenges in the first year faced by many academically underprepared students. For example, students were able to describe how they might use their strengths to communicate early and regularly with faculty, seek out and utilize academic resources and other support services, capitalize on the diversity of strengths among peer groups, and leverage strengths to become more involved and engaged on campus.

Discussion and Implications

The outcomes from incorporating a strengths-based approach to this remedial program revealed several benefits. Not only did Black men demonstrate significant boosts in academic performance, they also bolstered the efficacy of a strategy many HBCUs already employ to address the needs of academically underprepared students—summer remedial education programs. In general, college summer remedial education, often referred to as summer bridge programs, have been a critical nexus to college access and have been particularly helpful for Black students (Attewell, Lavin, Domina, & Levey, 2006; Davis & Palmer, 2010; Good, Halpin, & Halpin, 2002; Kimbrough & Harper, 2006; Palmer & Davis, in press). However, some opponents have called for the elimination of college remediation because of the lack of documentation evaluating the efficacy of remedial education (Attewell et al., 2006; Merisotis & Phipps, 2000), and questions about the effectiveness of college remediation on promoting students' academic success (Adelman, 2004). Given that part of the reason for the elimination of such programs is predicated on the lack of efficacy of college remediation, the preliminary results from the initiative discussed in this chapter may offer a useful strategy for HBCU administrators, policymakers, and institutional leaders to enhance the educational effectiveness of college remediation.

Further, the engagement outcomes of Black men were consistent with characteristics of positive engagement. In this program, Black men exhibited behaviors that are akin to benchmarks associated with positive student engagement. The National Survey for Student Engagement (NSSE) offers five benchmarks for student engagement: (a) academic challenge, (b) student–faculty interaction, (c) active collaborative learning, (d) supportive campus environment, and (e) enriching educational experiences (Kuh, 2003). The results of this strengths-based program resembled several of the activities, conditions, and learning outcomes associated with student engagement benchmarks. For example, the level of academic challenge and active collaborative learning benchmarks were most paramount among Black male students. In several instances, students indicated that the mandatory tutoring sessions coupled with being tutored and coached by their strengths-trained peers, heightened their understanding of complex and difficult mathematical concepts and reading assignments. Further, Black male students often shared with program staff and administrators that the encouragement to ask pertinent questions during class discussions and lectures, as well as intentional grouping by strengths facilitators for assignments outside of class increased their confidence and understanding of academic material.

In general, academic achievement is a multifaceted construct that can be defined and conceptualized in various ways. In this program, traditional measurements of academic achievement for Black men were used due in part to the limitations of the program structure and time-constraints. Practitioners and faculty interested in developing or establishing similar programs for Black males may consider alternative ways to measure the impact of strengths on academic achievement to gain a better understanding of how factors such as increased confidence, peer interactions, and interactions with faculty inside and outside of the classroom influence academic success.

Summary

There are inherent institutional challenges facing HBCUs—from continued lack of resources and funding (Gasman, 2009; Gasman et al., 2007; Hawkins, 2004) to recent criticism about their current relevancy and overall quality (Fryer & Greenstone, 2007; Riley, 2010). These challenges, coupled with the educational and societal factors affecting Black men, make for a daunting mission for concerned scholars, faculty, and administrators who attempt to improve the academic achievement of Black men attending HBCUs. However, despite the difficulty of the challenge, special priority must continue to be given to the promotion of academic excellence and graduation of Black men, particularly those who are academically underprepared.

Despite years of research and some recommendations for best practices, no long-term practical solutions exist regarding retaining and graduating academically underprepared Black men. Given that the success of Black men in college has broader implications across family, social, economic, and political lines, there is a question as to why relatively little research has been dedicated exclusively to academically underprepared Black men, and even less has been studied within the context of an HBCU. Nonetheless, it is hoped that the practices and outcomes discussed in this chapter continue to stimulate dialogue and reflection on what we have done, what we are currently doing, and provide guidance as to how we should move forward to most effectively interface and empower our academically underprepared Black male students.

References

Adelman, C. (2004). *Principal indicators of student academic histories in post-secondary education, 1972–2000.* Washington, DC: U.S. Department of Education, Institute of Education Sciences.

Allen, W. R. (1992). The color of success: African American college student outcomes at predominantly White and historically Black public colleges and universities. *Harvard Educational Review, 62,* 26–44.

Anderson, E. C. (2004). *What is strengths-based education? A tentative answer by someone who strives to be a strengths-based educator.* Unpublished manuscript.

Attewell, P., Lavin, D., Domina, T., & Levey, T. (2006). New evidence on college remediation. *Journal of Higher Education, 77,* 886–924.

Austin, D. B. (2005). The effects of a strengths development intervention program upon the self-perceptions of students' academic abilities. *Dissertation Abstracts International, 66*(05A). (UMI No. ATT 16311722)

Bernanke, B. S. (2007). *The level and distribution of economic well being.* Speech. Retrieved from http://www.federalreserve.gov/newsevents

Bowers, K. M., & Lopez, S. J. (2010). Capitalizing on personal strengths in college. *Journal of College and Character, 11*(1), 1–1.

Braskamp, L. (2006). *The StrengthsQuest guidebook: Introducing strengths-based development and StrengthsQuest to higher education leaders.* Princeton, NJ: Gallup.

Brodersen, D. J. (2008). *Predictors of peer leader success as strengths counselors in a first-year seminar* (Doctoral dissertation). Available from ProQuest Dissertations and Theses Database. (UMI No. AAT 3308536)

Bush, E. C., & Bush, L. (March 10, 2005). Black male achievement and the community college. *Blacks Issues in Higher Education, 22*(2), 44.

Cantwell, L. D. (2005). *A comparative analysis of strengths-based versus traditional teaching methods in a freshman public speaking course: Impacts on student learning and academic engagement* (Doctoral Dissertation). Available from ProQuest Dissertations and Theses Database. (UMI No. AAT 3207574)

Carey, K. (2004). *A matter of degrees: Improving graduation rates in four-year colleges and universities.* Washington, DC: Education Trust.

Cech, S. J. (2007) Georgia touts push to send more Black males to college, *Education Week, 27*(15), 9.

Clifton, D. O., & Anderson, C. E. (2002). *StrengthsQuest: Discover and develop your strengths in academics, career, and beyond.* Washington, DC: Gallup.

Clifton, D. O, Anderson, E. C., & Schreiner, L. A. (2006). *StrengthsQuest: Discover and develop your strengths in academics, career, and beyond.* New York: Gallup Press.

Clifton, D. O., & Harter, J.K. (2003). Strengths investment. In K. S. Cameron, J. E. Dutton, & R. E. Quinn (Eds.), *Positive organizational scholarship* (pp. 111–121), San Francisco, CA: Berrett-Koehler.

Conoley, C. W., & Conoley, J. C. (2009). *Positive psychology and family therapy: Creative techniques and practical tools for guiding change and enhancing growth.* Hoboken, NJ: Wiley.

Copeland, E. J. (2006). Creating a pathway: The role of historically Black institutions in enhancing access, retention, and graduation. In F. Hale (Ed.), *How Black colleges empower Black students* (pp. 51–61), Sterling, VA: Stylus.

Cuyjet, M. J., & Associates. (Eds.). (2006). *African American men in college.* San Francisco, CA: Jossey-Bass.

Davis, J. E. (2003). Early schooling and academic achievement of Black males. *Urban Education, 38*(5), 515–537.

Davis, R. J., & Palmer, R. T. (2010). The role and relevancy of postsecondary remediation for African American students: A review of research. *Journal of Negro Education, 76*(4), 503–520.

DeSousa, D. J. (2001). Reexamining the educational pipeline for African American students. In L. Jones (Ed.), *Retaining African Americans in higher education: Challenging the paradigms for retaining students, faculty, and administrators* (pp. 21–44), Sterling, VA: Stylus.

Fleming, J. (1984). *Blacks in college: A comparison study of students' success in Black and White institutions.* San Francisco, CA: Jossey-Bass.

Fleming, J., Tezeno, A., & Zamora, S. (2008). The retention planning process at Texas Southern University: A case study. In M. Gasman & C. L. Tudico (Eds.), *Historically Black colleges and universities: Triumphs, troubles, and taboos* (pp. 163–186). New York: Palgrave Macmillan.

Ford, D. Y., & Harris, J. J. (1995). Underachievement among gifted African American students: Implications for school counselors. *School Counselor, 42*, 196–203.

Fordham, S., & Ogbu, J. U. (1986). Black students' school success: Coping with the "burden of acting White." *The Urban Review, 18*(3), 176–206.

Fryer, R. G., & Greenstone, M. (2007). *The causes and consequences of attending historically Black colleges and universities* (Working Paper Series, 13036, ALL). Washington, DC: National Bureau of Economic Research.

Gasman, M. (2009). Historically Black colleges and universities in a time of economic crisis. *Academe, 95*(6), 26–30.

Gasman, M., Baez, B., Drezner, N. D., Sedgwick, K., Tudico, C., & Schmid, J. M. (2007). Historically Black colleges and universities: Recent trends. *Academe, 93*(1), 69–78.

Glenn, F. S, (2007). The retention of Black male students in Texas public community colleges. In A. Siedman (Ed.), *Minority student retention: The best of the Journal of College Student Retention: Research, Theory, and Practice* (pp. 59–77). Amityville, NY: Baywood.

Gomez, M. (2009). *Effects of integrating a strengths-based curriculum into a freshman seminar for at-risk college freshmen.* (Doctoral dissertation). Available from ProQuest Dissertations and Theses Database. (UMI No. AAT 3366113)

Good, J. M., Halpin, G., & Halpin, G. (2002). A promising prospect for minority retention: Students becoming peer mentors. *Journal of Negro Education, 69*(4), 375–383.

Hackett, G., Betz, N. E., Casas, J. M., & Rocha-Singh I. A. (1992). Gender, ethnicity, and social cognitive factors predicting the academic achievement of students in engineering. *Journal of Counseling Psychology, 39*(4), 527–538.

Hale, F. W. (2006). *How Black colleges empower Black students.* Sterling, VA: Stylus.

Harper, S. (2006). *Black male students at public universities in the US: Status, trends and implications for policy and practice.* Washington, DC: Joint Center for Political and Economic Studies.

Harper, S. (2007). The effects of sorority and fraternity membership on class participation and African American student engagement in predominantly White classroom environments. *College Student Affairs Journal, 27*(1), 94–116.

Harper, S. R., & Gasman, M. (2008). Consequences of conservatism: Black male undergraduates and the politics of historically Black colleges and universities. *Journal of Negro Education, 77,* 336–351.

Hawkins, D. B. (2004). Doing more with less. *Black Issues in Higher Education.* Retrieved from http://diverseeducation.com/article/3759/

Hoffman, K., Liagas, C., & Snyder, T. (2003). *Status and trends in the education of Blacks.* Washington, DC: National Center for Education Statistics.

Howard-Hamilton, M. F. (1997). Theory to practice: Applying developmental theories relevant to African American men. In M. J. Cuyjet (Ed.), *Helping African American men succeed in college* (New Directions for Student Services, No. 80, pp.17–30). San Francisco, CA: Jossey-Bass.

Hrabowski, F. A. (2002). Postsecondary minority student achievement: How to raise performance and close the achievement gap. *College Board Review, 195,* 40–48.

Kimbrough, W., & Harper, S. R. (2006). African American men at historically Black colleges and universities: Different environments, similar challenges. In M. J. Cuyjet & Associates (Eds.), *African American men in college* (pp. 189–209). San Francisco, CA: Jossey-Bass.

Klopfenstein, K. (2004). Advanced placement: Do minorities have equal opportunity? *Economics of Education Review, 23,* 115–131.

Kuh, G. D. (2003). The National Survey on Student Engagement: Conceptual framework and overview of psychometric properties. Retrieved from http://nsse.iub.edu/pdf/conceptual_framework_2003.pdf

Kuh, G.D. (2009). Understanding campus environments. In G. McClellan & J. Stringer (Eds.), *Handbook on student affairs administration* (3rd ed., pp. 59–80). San Francisco, CA: Jossey-Bass

Laar, C. V. (2000). The paradox of low academic achievement but high self-esteem in African American students: An attributional account. *Educational Psychology Review, 12*(1), 33–61.

Lavant, B. D., Anderson, J., & Tiggs, J. W. (1997). Retaining African American men through mentoring initiatives. In M. J. Cuyjet (Ed.), *Helping African American men succeed in college* (New Directions for Student Services, No. 80, pp. 43–52). San Francisco, CA: Jossey-Bass.

Lehnert, A. B. (2009). *The influence of strengths-based development on leadership practices among undergraduate college students* (Doctoral dissertation). Available from ProQuest Dissertations and Theses Database. (UMI No. AAT 3377758)

Levitz, R., & Noel, L. (2000). The earth-shaking, but quiet revolution, in retention management. Retrieved from http://www.cobleskill.edu/strategic/Revolution.pdf

Lewis, C. W., & Middleton, V. (2003). African Americans in community colleges: A review of research [Special issue]. *Community College Journal of Research and Practice, 27*(9–10), 787–798.

Lopez, S. J. (2004). *Naming, nurturing, and navigating: Capitalizing on strengths in daily life.* Paper presented at the National Conference on Building a Strengths-Based Campus: Best Practices in Maximizing Student Performance, Omaha, NE.

Lopez, S. J. (2006). *Positive psychology and higher education.* Omaha, NE: Gallup Press.

Lopez, S. J., Janowski, K. M., & Wells, K. J. (2005). *Developing strengths in college students: Exploring programs, context, theories, and research.* Lawrence: University of Kansas Press.

Lopez, S. J., & Louis, M. (2009). The principles of strengths-based education. *Journal of College & Character, 10*(4), 1–8.

Lundy, G. F. (2005). Peer relations and school resistance: Does oppositional culture apply to race or gender? *Journal of Negro Education, 73*, 233–245.

Mahoney, M. W. (2009). *Re-examining alcohol use among intercollegiate athletes, from a strengths-based perspective: The case study of an athletics program* (Doctoral Dissertation). Available from Pro-Quest Database for Dissertations and Theses. UMI No. (AAT 3350347)

McDaniel, A., DiPrete, T. A., Buchmann, C., & Shwed, U. (2010). The Black gender gap in educational attainment: Historical trends and racial comparisons. *Demography.* Retrieved from http://ssrn.com/abstract=1567515

Merisotis, J. P., & Phipps, R. A. (2000). Remedial education in colleges and universities: What's really going on? *Review of Higher Education, 24*, 67–85.

National Center for Education Statistics (NCES). (2010). *Status and trends in the education of racial and ethnic minorities.* Washington, DC: Author.

Oakes, J. (2005). *Keeping track: How schools structure inequality* (2nd ed.). New Haven, CT: Yale University Press.

Osman, G. D. (2007). *Student perceptions of the effectiveness of a mandatory remedial tutorial program in a developmental program at a historically Black university* (Doctoral Dissertation). Available from ProQuest Dissertations and Theses Database. (UMI No. AAT 3286867)

Palmer, R, T., & Davis, R. J. (in press). "Diamond in the Rough": The impact of a remedial program on college access and opportunity for Black males at an historically Black institution. *Journal of College Student Retention.*

Palmer, R. T., Davis, R. J., & Hilton, A. A. (2009). Exploring challenges that threaten to impede the academic success of academically underprepared Black males at an historically Black institution. *Journal of College Student Development, 50*, 429–445.

Palmer, R. T., Davis, R. J., & Maramba, D. C. (in press). The impact of family support on the success of Black men at an historically Black university: Affirming the revision of Tinto's theory. *Journal of College Student Development.*

Palmer, R. T., & Gasman, M. (2008). "It takes a village to raise a child": The role of social capital in promoting academic success for African American men at a Black college. *Journal of College Student Development, 49*(1), 52–70.

Palmer, R. T., Maramba, D. C., & Dancy, T. E. (in press). The magnificent "MILE": Impacting Black male retention and persistence at an HBCU. *Journal of College Student Retention.*

Pascarella, E. T., Edison, M., Whitt, E. J, Nora, A., Hagedorn, L. S., & Terenzini, P. T. (1996). Cognitive effects of Greek membership during the first-year of college. *NASPA Journal, 33*, 242–259.

Perna, L. W., Redd, K. E., & Swail, W. S. (2003). *Retaining minority students in higher education: A framework for success.* San Francisco, CA: Jossey-Bass.

Riegle-Crumb, C. (2006). The path through math: Course sequences and academic performance at the intersection of race and gender. *American Journal of Education, 113*, 101–119.

Riley, J. (2010). Black colleges need a new mission. *The Wall Street Journal.* Retrieved from http://online.wsj.com/article/SB10001424052748704654004575517822124077834.html

Roach, R. (2003). Georgia on the mind. *Black Issues in Higher Education, 20*(18), 32.

Seligman, M. E., & Csikszentmihalyi, M. (2000.) Positive psychology: An introduction. *American Psychologist, 55*(1), 5–14.

Sherman, T. M., Giles, M. B., & Williams-Green, J. (1994). Assessment and retention of Black students in higher education. *Journal of Negro Education, 63*(2), 164–180.

Suddeth, T., & Miller (2009). African American male retention success at Ohio State University. Retrieved from http://26866a52b05332f6335894de1aa50843cd2cfcef.gripelements.com/pdf/BRC/brc-college-board-presentation.pdf

Swanson, J. (2006). *Success in the first year: Impact of alternative advising on students at a liberal arts college* (Doctoral dissertation). Available from ProQuest Dissertations and Theses Database. (UMI No. AAT 3246327)

Thomas, E. P., Farrow, E. V., & Martinez, J. (1998). A TRIO program's impact on participant graduation rates: The Rutgers University Student Support Services Program and Its Network of Services. *The Journal of Negro Education, 67*(4), 389–403.

Tyler, J. O. P. (2006). *The impact of strengths-based development on student engagement.* Available from ProQuest Dissertations and Theses Database. (UMI No. AAT 3218187)

West, C. (2001). *Race matters.* New York: Vintage Books

Williams, D. G., & Land, R. R. (2006). The legitimation of Black subordination: The impact of color-blind ideology on African American education. *Journal of Negro Education, 75*(4), 579–588.

Zamani, E. M. (2000). Sources and information regarding effective retention strategies for students of color. *New Directions for Community Colleges, 112,* 95–104.

5

"REACHING OUT TO MY BROTHERS"

Improving the Retention of Low-Income Black
Men at Historically Black Colleges and Universities:
A Critical Review of the Literature

Jameel A. Scott

Higher education serves as a vehicle for social and economic mobility, particularly for Blacks (Gasman, 2008; Harper, Patton, & Wooden, 2009). Historically, historically Black colleges and universities (HBCUs) have contributed to this mobility by ushering in the Black middle class and advancing the number of Black degree holders, despite social and academic impediments (Allen & Jewell, 2002; Drewry & Doermann, 2004; Kim, 2002). Today, questions emerge from policymakers and academics about the relevance of HBCUs and their ability to retain and graduate low-income Black men (Riley, 2010). Ironically, this population has the worst statistics nationally regarding college retention and degree attainment. Data from the U.S. Department of Education indicate that over the past 35 years, Black male college graduation rates have not increased more than 5%. Moreover, graduation rates differ by socioeconomic status (SES), and this gap is exacerbated when race is included. The SES gap is wide between those who earn a college degree: during the past 35 years, 25% of students from low-income families graduated from postsecondary education, 40% of students from middle-income families graduated, and 58% of students from high income families completed degree programs (New Data, 2004). Further, there is a 7% difference in graduation rate between Blacks and Whites (BPS:04/09). Given the aforementioned data, it is clear that more attention needs to be paid to low-income college students, and to this end, this chapter focuses on low-income Black men.

HBCUs are one type of institution that is making efforts to increase success among low-income Black men. Despite their efforts, many HBCUs have low graduation rates for this population. Scholars have noted that SES is a statistically significant indicator for whether a student graduates from college

(Hearn, 2001; Strayhorn, 2010; Titus, 2010). In an effort to better understand and improve retention and persistence among low-income Black men, I examined literature and retention theories to provide recommendations for HBCUs. To achieve this goal, I provide a synopsis of the literature on low-income students, giving particular attention to students at HBCUs, and use this context to delineate a picture of the challenges facing this population. I then examine retention theories and provide a framework for analyzing Black men at HBCUs. I conclude this chapter with recommendations for HBCU faculty and administrators to increase retention and graduation rates of low-income Black male students. But first, the theoretical framework through which the literature is analyzed is discussed in the next section.

Theoretical Framework

A culturally sensitive research approach is used as a lens through which to analyze the literature. This approach highlights the sensitivities of minority students under study (Tillman, 2002), and allows researchers to take into consideration the cultural and historical distinctions of individuals at HBCUs. The culturally sensitive approach attempts to avoid, denial, or neglect the cultural norms and histories of the group being studied, and thus I can focus on the nuances of the particular group being studied. Rather than that group's cultural norms being neglected or overlooked, they are highlighted, brought into context, and used to further the understanding of the issue being studied.

Further, a culturally sensitive approach allows cultural norms and histories to be sufficiently represented in the research. Similar to Harper and Nichols (2008), I argue that scholars need to recognize that Black men are not a monolithic group; in contrast, this group is diverse in numerous ways. Harper and Nichols (2008) identified variance socioeconomic status, noting differences between low-income and high-income students and their interactions on campus. They contended that students should therefore be investigated for their unique differences.

Other scholars have found several challenges for low-income students, such as lower graduation rates (Strayhorn, 2006; Titus, 2010), poor academic preparation for college (Cabrera & La Nasa, 2001), and high dropout rates (Bailey & Moore, 2004). In using this cultural sensitivity framework, I pay particular attention to the cultural nuances found in the literature with regard to low-income Black male students.

Literature Review

There is a dearth of empirical research on low-income Black students in the higher education literature generally, specifically in the literature on HBCUs. In an attempt to unravel the current literature, I divided the literature into two sections: first, I will review literature on Black men as it relates to their academic persistence, paying particularly attention to the effects of student participation in clubs and organizations. Second, I will discuss the applicability of a revised Tinto's theory to HBCUs. Discussing these bodies of literature is important because research has found that these are salient factors that determine the retention of all students (Braxton, Hirschy, & McClendon, 2004; Fries-Britt, Gardner, Low, & Tinto, 2002; Milem & Berger, 1997; Pascarella & Terenzini, 2005; Tinto, 1993). Notwithstanding, I will begin with a brief history of HBCUs to provide a context for the institutions I am focusing on here.

HBCU Context

HBCUs emerged during a period when Blacks were denied access to education. Blacks' desire for education served as the impetus (with the support of White abolitionists) to establish HBCUs. Black families and communities often worked and saved nickels and dimes to send deserving students to college (Drewry & Doermann, 2004). HBCUs at one point educated a majority of Black students, particularly from 1865 to the 1960s (Palmer & Gasman, 2008). Despite the inequitable state and federal funding that HBCUs receive (Sav, 1997), they have educated a large number of Black students. These institutions are known for enrolling, educating, and graduating students who typically would not have been accepted into predominantly White institutions (PWIs) because of institutional racism or lack of academic preparation (Harper et al., 2009; Kim & Conrad, 2006). Additionally, HBCUs have disproportionately enrolled students who were from low SES backgrounds and were able to educate them to a greater extent than their PWI counterparts (Allen, 1987; Coaxum, 2001). After several federal policies and government initiatives (e.g., *Adams v. Richardson* 1972; *Brown vs. Board of Education,* 1954; Civil Rights Act of 1964, and affirmative action laws), PWIs opened their doors to Black students, and HBCUs gradually experienced a precipitous drop in enrollment of Black students, especially those from middle- and upper-income families (Allen & Jewell, 2002; Sissoko & Shiau, 2005).

Currently there are 103 HBCUs, which represents only 3% of higher education institutions in America. These institutions enroll 12.9% of all Black students (National Center for Education Statistics, 2010), which dropped from over 90% in 1984 (Fleming, 1984). The United Negro College Fund (UNCF) reported in 2011 that despite the drop in enrollment at HBCUs, these institutions still graduate 20% of all Black students who earn bachelor's degrees; are responsible for graduating over 50% of all Black professionals and public school teachers; and 70% of Black dentists. At present, HBCUs continue to educate a population that is often of low SES and that generally has poor academic preparation prior to starting college (Minor, 2004).

Participation in Clubs or Organizations

Researchers have given substantial attention to the effects on their academic performance of student involvement in clubs or other organizations. Students' participation in a club or organization is an additional avenue through which students learn from their peers, faculty, and staff (Braxton et al., 2004; Pascarella & Terenzini, 2005). Many scholars have concluded that student involvement increases persistence and graduation rates (Fries-Britt et al., 2002; Milem & Berger, 1997; Tinto, 1993). For example, Jackson and Swan (1991) suggested that Black students' grades improved significantly as a result of their involvement on campus. They noted that a possible explanation for this relationship is that students' involvement on campus leads to greater confidence and increased academic expectations. Harper (2006) suggested that campus involvement positively impacts students, providing them with leadership and time management skills, learning to work with a team (or as a team player), gaining public speaking skills and political savvy.

Regarding HBCUs, Kimbrough and Harper (2006) challenged HBCUs to address the declining retention and graduation rates of their students. They acknowledged the noteworthy legacy of HBCUs and their history of having similar and at times higher retention and graduation rates than their PWI counterparts. However, they asserted that HBCUs no longer have higher graduation rates than PWIs. They added that only 7 of the nation's 103 HBCUs have graduation rates above 50% for their male students. Although their research does not specify some of the reasons for these numbers, such as increased levels of low SES at HBCUs and lack of resources, it does further our understanding of the impact of college involvement on Black males. One of the challenges noted in Kimbrough and Harper's (2006) study is the unwillingness of Black men to ask for help. They argued that schools have a responsibility to provide an environment for the students to learn and excel, which includes faculty and staff reaching out to these young men, despite students' reluctance to do so.

One way students can become acclimated to the college environment and receive resources (e.g., tutoring, mentorship) is by getting involved in college activities. Strayhorn's (2010) national study found that SES was the most significant predictor for academic achievement for Black male students. He also found that low-income Black men significantly benefited from college involvement, meaning that it is a significant predictor of graduation. To this end, Strayhorn (2010) recommended that schools actively find ways to improve recruitment efforts to target Black male student participation in college organizations.

In addition to the positive advantages of student involvement on campus, some scholars have found some potentially negative consequences. For example, Strayhorn's (2010) and Harper and Harris' (2006) studies found that joining a Black Greek-letter organization (BGLO) negatively impacted Black male students' GPAs. Harper and Harris (2006) contended, however, that there are several benefits to joining a BGLO, such as it having "a significant positive effect on the racial identity development of [Black] men because of the emphasis they place on social and cultural awareness and collectivism" (p. 136). It is interesting to note that Harper and Wolley (2002) argued for colleges to provide more outlets (clubs and organizations) for males. They stated that many organizations are avoided by Black male students because they do not have a masculine reputation. Nevertheless, Jones (2004) and Harper and Harris (2006) argued that joining a fraternity is viewed as very masculine among Black male students. Despite this, many schools provide minimal support to BGLOs, possibly due to their poor reputation regarding participants' GPAs. However, these organizations have the potential to improve graduation rates for Black male collegians, particularly low-income Black men (Harper, 2006).

Persistence to Graduation

It is clear from the research that postsecondary retention and graduation rates are lowest among low-income Black men when compared to any racial/ethnic or gender group (National Center for Education Statistics, 2010; Kahlenberg, 2004; Strayhorn, 2008). Peng and Fetters (1978) and Ishitani (2003) indicated that students from low-income families were at higher risk of dropping out in their first year of college than those from more affluent backgrounds. Titus' (2010) study, albeit not focused on low SES, suggested that the more employment hours students work during their first year of college, the less likely it is that they will graduate within 6 years. His study also indicated that low-SES students have a higher chance of working more hours during their first year of college, which potentially affects their academic standing. This study reinforced Walpole's (2003) findings, which also indicated that low-income students work more hours than high-income students. The specific reasons why students work so many hours has yet to be understood. Some scholars assume that students work many hours in college in order to offset college costs (Perna, 2010; Riggert et al., 2006; Stern & Nakata, 1991); however, this assumption is incomplete since students work for varied reasons (e.g., to gain experience, network). It is understood by scholars (e.g., Furr & Elling, 2000; Light, 2001; Riggert et al., 2006) that working in college can reduce the time that could be devoted to developing healthy relationships with faculty, studying, and participating in college activities/organizations. Given that HBCUs tend to serve more low-income students, they are more inclined to enroll students who may work more than 20 hours a week (Palmer, Davis, & Hilton, 2009).

Arguably the most widely used retention theory is Tinto's (1993), which argues that students need to be socially and academically integrated into the college campus—a theory that has been criticized by many (Braxton & Lee, 2005; Guiffrida, 2006; Kuh & Love, 2000). A closer examination of Tinto's theory and the criticism it elicits will be discussed later in this chapter. Strayhorn

(2008) used Tinto's theory in order to evaluate low-income students' retention patterns in an article titled after Ralph Ellison's groundbreaking novel *The Invisible Man*. Strayhorn (2008) used this title to acknowledge the paucity of research that addresses low-income Black male students, which thereby causes them to be invisible. Findings from Strayhorn's (2008) study emphasized that "low-income Black males who are more socially integrated into campus life also are more likely to be retained than those with little to no social integration" (p. 80). His study also suggested that Black men who attended HBCUs had higher chances of being retained than Black men at PWIs.

An additional component of persistence often examined is students' motivation. Studies have indicated that colleges giving more attention to improving Black students' graduation rates will facilitate higher graduation rates for those students (Townsend, 1994). More specifically, if schools make a more concerted effort to increase graduation rates by increasing faculty involvement, providing mentorship and tutoring on campus, and being attentive to the student's financial aid needs, there is a greater likelihood that their graduation rates will increase (Townsend, 1994). For example, Townsend (1994) indicated that Grambling State University has relatively low financial resources yet enrolls a high number of low SES students and graduates them in large proportions compared to their HBCU peers. Townsend (1994) indicated that the university president has given significant attention to ensuring that every student, regardless of SES, has the resources needed to improve his or her likelihood of graduating. Similarly Lynch and Engle (2010) suggested that some postsecondary institutions are graduating large numbers of Black students. They claim that beginning with the president, they have been able to increase the Black graduation rates by everyone taking on a mission that is focused strategically on increasing the number of minorities who graduate. Their study suggested that, "when colleges focus on student success, all students benefit greatly—particularly students of color" (p. 2). To this end, if HBCUs put greater effort into ensuring that low SES students have access to mentors, tutors, school activities, and engaged faculty, their potential to gain a greater sense of confidence and belonging on campus may significantly increase, resulting in higher retention and graduation rates (Braxton et al. 2004).

Applicability to HBCUs of a Revised Tinto's Theory

Arguably the most cited retention theorist is Tinto (1975, 1982, 1988). Tinto's student departure theory has been the center of heated debate for the past three decades. His theory relied on earlier sociological research by Spady (1970) who posited that the social integration of students on campus increases their commitment to the institution, which consequently decreases the likelihood of student departure. Tinto (1982) expanded this theory to include academic integration. Tinto (1982) believed that a student's integration to the academic life and social life of the college campus was indicative and a predictor of the student's likelihood of graduation. He emphasized the need for students to break away from their previous culture and adopt the culture of the college campus. In doing so, he contended that the student would be more cognizant of campus resources, have increased campus involvement, and development of productive relationships with faculty and peers would be facilitated, which are all vital for college completion (Tinto, 1993).

Although receiving notable attention, Tinto's (1993) scholarship has been vigorously criticized for its lack of empirical evidence and cultural sensitivities (Braxton & Lee, 2005; Braxton, Sullivan, & Johnson, 1997; Rendón, Jalomo, & Nora, 2000). Braxton and Lien (2000) suggested that there is little evidence to support Tinto's theory. Additionally, other scholars have claimed that the theory was designed for White men on predominately White college campuses, and is not applicable to minority students (Hurtado & Carter, 1997; Kuh & Love, 2000; Guiffrida, 2005). Scholars further this claim by adding that Tinto's theory encourages students to deny their cultural traditions and supportive relationships in order to adopt those of the PWI. This approach is problematic for Black students especially given their history of oppression and racism in America (Moore & Upcraft, 1990; Tierney, 1992).

Cabrera, Castaneda, Nora, and Hengstler (1992) also criticized Tinto's theory and offered a new one, by combining Tinto's (1988) theory with Bean's (1986) theory which asserted that attitudes and intentions are correlated with behavior. Bean (1986) argued that a student's attitude and intentions in college reflect the likelihood of that student graduating. Cabrera et al. (1992) suggested that Tinto (1988) and Bean's (1986) retention theories should not be utilized in isolation, but rather in concert. However, their theories are problematic because they are rooted in Western assimilation culture and do not address the needs of minority students (Guiffrida, 2006). The challenge with accepting Tinto's theory as it stands is that in isolation the theory prescribes universal answers to "the problem" of retention, which lacks consideration of minority students. Scholars have argued that were a fuller appreciation for the experiences of minority students included with Tinto's theory it would help to increase the retention (and graduation) rates of minority students (Guiffrida, 2006; Rendón et al., 2000).

Guiffrida (2006) is one scholar who has made Tinto's theory more applicable to minorities, particularly those at HBCUs. He examined Tinto's theory with the goal of enhancing its applicability to minorities. Guiffrida (2006) incorporated two new variables into Tinto's theory, self-determination theory and job involvement theory. In doing this, he acknowledged that Tinto incorporated family background and precollege commitment as retention factors. However, he enhanced the theory by asserting that students who come from a collectivist framework should not break away from their families and support system, but rather recognize that retention could be enhanced if students embrace their families and external support systems. More specifically, Guiffrida (2006) recommended the term *integration* be replaced with *connection*. He stated, "connection recognizes students' subjective sense of relatedness without implying the need to break ties with one's former community" (p. 457).

Another point that Guiffrida (2006) raised is that by and large Black students are collectivist-oriented (they value group involvement and relatedness) versus their White peers on whom Tinto's theory was based. A challenge many Black students face is their increased likelihood to fulfill their intrinsic nature of relatedness at the expense of autonomy and competitiveness which have extrinsic rewards (e.g., high GPA). As low-income Black men find ways to transition, by having blended connectedness to their home environments and college campuses, HBCUs must find ways to ensure their persistence and college survival.

HBCUs

Although the previous studies primarily focused on minority students at PWIs, the findings have relevance for HBCUs. Scholars such as Allen and Jewell (2002), Gasman (2008), and Hope (1996) have suggested that there is a distinct culture at most HBCUs. This notion suggests that the culture at HBCUs is different from that of PWIs. Nevertheless, like Black students who attend PWIs, students at HBCUs enter college with cultural histories and traditions which may be different from those present on their campus. It should not be assumed that Black students, particularly those from low socioeconomic backgrounds, are a monolithic group. These students may experience culture shock and isolation when they enter college (Rendón et al., 2000). However, low-income students may also enter college having family and associates who support their pursuit of a college degree (Palmer, Davis, & Maramba, in press). As Guiffrida (2006) suggested, schools should support students in their nurturing and supportive relationships on and off campus. Likewise, as discussed in this chapter, students who are active on campus often have higher retention rates than those who are less active. Therefore, an application of Guffrida's (2006) version of Tinto's (1993) theory could help HBCUs increase the retention rates of low-income Black students.

Suggestions for Implementation

Scholars have noted that one of the most significant predictors of a student's graduation is SES (Kahlenberg, 2004; Strayhorn, 2008; Tinto, 1993). The lower the student's SES, the less likely he is to graduate. The vast majority of students who attend HBCUs are students from low SES backgrounds, many of whom are Black men (Allen & Jewell, 2002). This fact is significantly different from the situation with PWIs, which disproportionately educate non-Blacks and students from middle- to high-income groups. However, HBCUs are asked by politicians and academics to compete with PWIs, often using student retention and graduation rates as proxies to determine how well they are performing. It is important to note that HBCUs have had success in graduating low SES students; however, there is still is room for improvement. What follows are nine suggestions for HBCUs to help them increase retention and persistence among low-SES Black students. This list of suggestions is not exhaustive, and may not apply to all HBCUs.

Potential Remedies for Improving Retention Rates

1. It is vital that schools take on strategic initiatives to increase the retention and graduation rates of their students, which includes low-income Black men. This initiative has to be embraced by the institutions' executive leadership, faculty, and staff. This means, that the overall campus community should facilitate a culture of excellence by having its members (e.g., faculty, staff, and administration) support the goal of retaining their students. To do this, faculty can increase office hours and reach out to those students who need additional support. Administrators and staff can provide encouraging words to students and provide enhanced opportunities for mentorship. HBCU faculty, staff, and administration should make a strategic plan, discussing their efforts to improve retention among low-income students.

2. HBCUs should provide workshops and seminars throughout the year, which include financial aid seminars. Because many low-income students may be unfamiliar with the financial aid process, it is important that HBCU administrators provide adequate support to these students. Perna (2008) conducted a qualitative study, asking parents and students about their familiarity with the financial aid process. She found, that disproportionately, low-income students were misinformed or simply were unaware of the financial aid process. Administrators should take steps to ensure that every student is provided with information on financial aid. This could be done with one-on-one consultation and in seminars.

3. Working while in college often has negative effects on academic performance. However, many low-income students must work to pay for college, and at times other expenses (e.g., many have to support their families). HBCU faculty and staff should examine ways to work with students who are employed to best determine the most appropriate work schedule and courses of action for the students. This could include, helping the students make a schedule which is tailored around their work schedule, or even encouraging students to take lighter course loads. Some students may need to increase their loans, or even apply for scholarships. HBCUs administrators should make sure that their students are well informed about their options and have support in making these decisions.

4. HBCU faculty should try and find avenues to get students involved in class. One way to get students involved is by incorporating group exercises during class. It is important that students feel a part of the college, and this can be encouraged by utilizing various teaching techniques such as group activities; doing this will help students feel more connected to their institutions. Additionally, if faculty use different teaching techniques, students' learning and their grades may increase as well. hooks (1994), contends that a student's education is enhanced when students are brought into the learning process, and feel they are empowered to learn as well as teach. One way to achieve this goal is through group activities because students have a high potential to feel they are playing an active role in learning and teaching. Additionally, if they gain confidence as a result of their learning experience, their grades will improve, bringing them closer to graduation.

5. HBCUs should create or enhance their mentorship programs on their campuses. This would aid students in feeling welcomed and connected to the campus. Mentors can help students become acclimated to campus, provide information on internships, campus involvement opportunities, and provide guidance through college. These mentors could be in the form of peer and faculty/staff mentorship.

6. Many schools make it the student's responsibility to join clubs and get active. HBCU administrators should be responsible for ensuring not only that students have viable options for organizations to join, but also play an active role in getting students connected to these organizations. This does not mean that administrators are responsible for students' active participation in these organizations, but for encouraging and supporting their participation. This could be done by holding seminars in the residence halls and addressing the benefits of getting active on campus.

7. HBCUs should create partnerships with business and organizations in the surrounding community, if they do not already exist. These partnerships could increase avenues for student involvement, provide mentorship opportunities, and offer opportunities for students to give back to their local campus communities.

8. HBCUs should also seek to develop learning communities among diverse students with similar interests. For example, premed or engineering students should be grouped together in residence halls to form a support structure. This could serve as a mechanism for enhancing student retention rates. Student Affairs can also plan activities to strengthen student engagement that involve these communities of learning.

9. Faculty and administrators at HBCUs should examine ways to work with BGLOs in order to find ways to improve students' retention and graduation rates. By working with BGLOs in this endeavor, campus personnel will be using an entity that already attracts the male population. Administrators in particular should meet with BGLO leaders to discuss potential

ways to increase student involvement and learn how their activities could help foster academic success.

References

Adams v. Richardson, 351 f.2d 636 (D.C.Cir. 1972).

Allen, W. R. (1987). Black colleges vs. White colleges: The fork in the road for Black students. *Change, 19*(3), 28–34.

Allen, W. R. & Jewell, J. O. (2002). A backward glance forward: Past, present, and future perspectives on historically Black colleges and universities. *Review of Higher Education, 25*(3), 241–261.

Astin, A. W. (1999). Involvement in learning revisited: Lessons I have learned. *Journal of College Student Personnel, 40*(5), 587–598.

Bailey, D. F., & Moore, J. L. (2004). Emotional isolation, depression, and suicide among African American men: Reasons for concern. In C. Rabin (Ed.), *Linking lives across borders: Gender-sensitive practice in international perspective* (pp. 186–207). Pacific Grove, CA: Brooks/Cole.

Bean, J. P. (1986). Assessing and reducing attrition. In D. Hossler (Ed.), *Managing college enrollment* (53 ed., pp. 47–61). San Francisco: Jossey-Bass.

Braxton, J. M., Hirschy, A. S., & McClendon, S. A. (2004). *Understanding and reducing college student departure* (ASHE-ERIC Higher Education Report, *30*,[3]). San Francisco, CA: Jossey-Bass.

Braxton, J. M., & Lee, S. D. (2005). Toward reliable knowledge about college student departure. In A. Seidman (Ed.), *College student retention: Formula for success* (pp. 61–88). Westport, CT: Greenwood.

Braxton, J. M., Sullivan, A. V., & Johnson, R. M. (1997). Appraising Tinto's theory of college student departure. In John C. Smart (Ed.), *Higher education: Handbook of theory and research* (Vol. 12, pp. 102–122). New York: Agathon Press.

Brown v. Board of Education, 347 U.S. 483 (1954).

Cabrera, A., & La Nasa, S. (2001). On the path to college: Three critical tasks facing America's disadvantaged. *Research in Higher Education, 42*(2), 119–150.

Civil Rights Act of 1964 (Title VII), 42 U.S.C. 2000e et seq. 29 C.F.R. 1600-1610.

Coaxum, J. (2001). The misalignment between the Carnegie classification and Black colleges. *Urban Education, 36*(5), 572–583.

Drewry, H. N. & Doermann, H. (2004). *Stand and prosper: Private Black colleges and their students.* Princeton, NJ: Princeton University Press.

Fleming, J. (1984). *Blacks in college: A comparative study of students' success in Black and in White institutions.* San Francisco, CA: Jossey-Bass.

Fries-Britt, S., Gardner, J. N., Low, L., & Tinto, V. (2002). Retaining students: New questions and fresh perspectives (video teleconference print resource packet). Columbia, SC: National Resource Center for the First-Year Experience and Students in Transition, University of South Carolina.

Furr, S., & Elling, T. (2000). The influence of working on college student development. *NASPA Journal, 37*(2), 454–470.

Gasman, M. (2008). Minority-serving institutions: An historical backdrop. In M. Gasman, B. Baez, & C. S. Turner (Eds.), *Understanding minority-serving institutions.* (pp. 8–27). Albany, NY: SUNY Press.

Guiffrida, D. A. (2005). To break away or strengthen ties to home: A complex question for African American students attending a predominantly White institution. *Equity and Excellence in Education, 38*(1), 49–60.

Guiffrida, D. (2006). Towards a cultural advancement of Tinto's theory. *Review of Higher Education, 29*(4), 451–472.

Harper, S. R. (2006). Enhancing African American male student outcomes through leadership and active involvement. In M. J. Cuyjet & Associates (Eds.), *African American Men in College* (pp. 68–94). San Francisco, CA: Jossey-Bass.

Harper, S. R., & Harris, F. (2006). The role of Black fraternities in the African American male undergraduate experience. In M. J.Cuyjet (Ed.), *African American men in college* (pp. 128–153). San Francisco: Jossey-Bass.

Harper, S. R., & Nichols, A. H. (2008). Are they not all the same? Racial heterogeneity among Black male undergraduates. *Journal of College Student Development, 49*(3), 199–214.

Harper, S. R., Patton, L., & Wooden, O. (2009). Access and equity for African American students in higher education: A critical race historical analysis of policy efforts. *Journal of Higher Education, 80*(4), 389–414.

Harper, S. R., & Wolley, M. A. (2002). Becoming an "involving college" for African American undergraduate men: Strategies for increasing African American male participation in campus activities. *Association of College Unions International Bulletin, 70*(3), 16–24.

Hearn, J. C. (2001). Assess to postsecondary education: Financing equity in an evolving context. In M. B. Paulsen & J. C. Smart (Eds.), *The financing of higher education: Theory, research, policy and practice* (pp. 439–460). New York: Agathon Press.

hooks, b. (1994). *Teaching to transgress: Education as a practice of freedom.* New York: Routledge.

Hope, R. O. (1996). Revitalizing minority colleges and universities. In R. O. Hope & L. I. Rendón (Eds.), *Educating a new minority: Transforming America's educational system for diversity* (pp. 390–402). Hoboken, NJ: Wiley.

Hurtado, S., & Carter, D. F. (1997). Effects of college transition and perceptions of the campus racial climate on Latino college students' sense of belonging. *Sociology of Education Journal, 70*, 324–345. .

Ishitani, T. T. (2003). A longitudinal approach to assessing attrition behavior among first-generation students: Time-varying effects of pre-college characteristics. *Research in Higher Education, 44*(4), 433–449.

Jackson, K. W., & Swan, L. A. (1991) Institutional and individual factors affecting Black undergraduate student performance: Campus race and student gender. In W. R. Allen, E. G. Epps, & N. Z. Haniff (Eds.), *College in Black and White: African American students in predominantly White and in historically Black public universities* (pp. 127–141). Albany, NY: SUNY Press.

Jones, R. L. (2004). *Black haze: Violence, sacrifice, and manhood in Black Greek-letter fraternities.* Albany, NY: SUNY Press.

Kahlenberg, R. D. (2004). *America's untapped resource: Low-income students in higher education.* New York: Century Foundation Press.

Kim, M. (2002). Historically Black vs. White institutions: Academic development among Black students. *Review of Higher Education, 25*(4), 385–407.

Kim, M., & Conrad, C. F. (2006). The impact of historically Black colleges and universities on the academic success of African American students. *Research in Higher Education, 47*(4), 399–427.

Kimbrough, W. M., & Harper, S. R. (2006). African American men at historically Black colleges and universities: Different environments, similar challenges. In M. J. Cuyjet (Ed.), *African American men in college* (pp. 189–209). San Francisco, CA: Jossey-Bass.

Kuh, G. D., & Love, P. G. (2000). A cultural perspective on student departure. In J. M. Braxton (Ed.), *Reworking the student departure puzzle* (pp. 196–212). Nashville, TN: Vanderbilt University Press.

Light, A. (2001). In-school work experience and the returns to schooling. *Journal of Labor Economics, 19*, 65–93.

Lynch, M., & Engle, J. (2010). *Big gaps, small gaps: Some colleges and universities do better than others in graduating African-American students.* Washington, DC: The Education Trust.

Milem, J. F., & Berger, J. B. (1997). A modified model of college student persistence: Exploring the relationship between Astin's theory of involvement and Tinto's theory of student departure. *Journal of College Student Development, 38*(4), 387–400.

Minor, J. T. (2004). Decision making in historically Black colleges and universities: Defining the governance context. *Journal of Negro Education, 73*(1), 40–52.

Moore, L. V., & Upcraft, M. L. (1990). Theory in student affairs: Evolving perspectives. In L. V. Moore (Ed.), *New directions for student services: No. 51: Evolving theoretical perspectives on students* (pp. 3–24). San Francisco: Jossey-Brass.

National Center for Education Statistics. (2010). *Projections of education statistics to 2010.* Washington, DC: Author.

Palmer, R. T., Davis, R. J., & Hilton, A. A. (2009). Exploring challenges that threaten to impede the academic success of academically underprepared Black males at an HBCU. *Journal of College Student Development, 50*(4), 429–445.

Palmer, R. T., Davis, R. J., & Maramba, D. C. (in press). The impact of family support for African American males at an historically Black university: Affirming the revision of Tinto's theory. *Journal of College Student Development.*

Palmer, R. T., & Gasman, M. (2008). "It takes a village to raise a child": The role of social capital in promoting academic success of African American men at a Black college. *Journal of College Student Development, 49*(1), 52–70.

Pascarella, E. T., & Terenzini, P. T. (2005). *How college affects students: Vol. 2. A third decade of research.* San Francisco, CA: Jossey-Bass.

Peng, S. S., & Fetters, W. B. (1978). Variables involved in withdrawal during the first two years of college: Preliminary findings from the National Longitudinal Study of High School Class of 1972. *American Educational Research Journal, 15,* 361–372.

Perna, L. (2008). Understanding high school students' willingness to borrow to pay college prices. *Research on Higher Education, 49,* 589–606.

Rendón, L. I., Jalomo, R. E., & Nora, A. (2000). Theoretical considerations in the study of minority student retention in higher education. In J. M. Braxton (Ed.), *Reworking the student departure puzzle* (pp. 127–156). Nashville, TN: Vanderbilt University Press.

Riggert, S. C., Boyle, M., Petrosko, J. M., Ash, D., & Rude-Parkins, C. (2006). Student employment and higher education: Empiricism and contradiction. *Review of Educational Research, 76,* 63–92.

Riley, J. (2010). Black colleges need a new mission. *The Wall Street Journal.* Retrieved from http://online.wsj.com/article/SB10001424052748704654004575517822124077834.html

Sav, G. T. (1997). Separate and unequal: State financing of historically Black colleges and universities. *Journal of Blacks in Higher Education, 15,* 101–104.

Sissoko, M., & Shiau, L. (2005). Minority enrollment demand for higher education at historically Black colleges and universities from 1976 to 1998: An empirical analysis. *Journal of Higher Education, 76*(2), 181–208.

Spady, W. G. (1970). Dropouts from higher education: An interdisciplinary review and synthesis. *Interchange, 1,* 64–65.

Strayhorn, T. L. (2006). Factors influencing the academic achievement of first generation college students. *NASPA Journal, 43*(4), 82–111.

Strayhorn, T. L. (2008). The invisible man: Factors affecting the retention of low-income African American males. *NASAP Journal, 11*(1), 66–87.

Strayhorn, T. L. (2010). When race and gender collide: Social and cultural capital's influence on the academic achievement of African American and Latino males. *Review of Higher Education, 33*(3), 307–332.

Stern, D., & Nakata, Y. (1991, January/February). Paid employment among U.S. college students. *Journal of Higher Education, 62*(1), 25–43.

Tierney, W. G. (1992). An anthropological analysis of student participation in college. *Journal of Higher Education, 63*(6), 603–618.

Tierney, W. G. (1999). Models of minority college-going and retention: Cultural integrity versus cultural suicide. *Journal of Negro Education, 68*(1), 80–91.

Tillman, L. (2002). Culturally sensitive research approaches: An African American perspective. *Educational Researcher, 31*(9), 3–12.

Tinto, V. (1975) Dropout from higher education: A theoretical synthesis of recent research. *Review of Education Research, 45*(1), 89–125.

Tinto,V. (1982) Limits of theory and practice in student attrition. *Journal of Higher Education, 53*(6),.687–700.

Tinto, V. (1987). *Leaving college: Rethinking the causes and cures of student attrition.* Chicago, IL: University of Chicago Press.

Tinto, V. (1988). Stages of student departure: Reflections on the longitudinal character of student leaving. *Journal of Higher Education, 59*(4), 438–455.

Tinto, V. (1993). *Leaving college: Rethinking the causes and cures of student attrition* (2nd ed.). Chicago, IL: University of Chicago Press.

Titus, M. (2010). Understanding the relationship between working while in college and future salaries. In L. Perna (Ed.), *Understanding the working college students: New research and its implications for policy and practice* (pp. 261–282). Sterling, VA: Stylus.

Townsend, L. (1994). How universities successfully retain and graduate Black students. *Journal of Blacks in Higher Education, 4,* 85–89.

United Negroe College Fund. (2011). Data retrieved from http://www.uncf.org/members/aboutHBCU.asp

Walpole, M. (2003). Socioeconomic status and college: How SES affects college experiences and outcomes. *Review of Higher Education, 27*(1), 45–73.

6

ESTABLISHING CRITICAL RELATIONSHIPS

How Black Males Persist in Physics at HBCUs

Sharon Fries-Britt, Brian A. Burt, and Khadish Franklin

Introduction

The educational achievement of Black males is in decline and scholars indicate that disparities between this group and other groups begin early. In elementary school and continuing into high school, Black males lead all other racial/ethnic and gender groups in suspensions, expulsions, behavioral problems, and referral to special education services (Harper, 2006; Jackson & Moore, 2006; Palmer, Davis, & Hilton, 2009; Strayhorn, 2008; White & Cones, 1999). By the time Black males reach college age, they are more likely to be incarcerated than enrolled in postsecondary education (Harrison & Beck, 2005). Given that students of color are projected to comprise 50% of the U.S. population by 2050 (Museus, Palmer, Davis, & Maramba, 2011), the disproportionate rates of death, incarceration, unemployment, and comparatively low levels of college graduation rates among Black males raise imminent concerns for the nation's future (Harper, 2006; Jackson & Moore, 2006; Palmer et al., 2009; Strayhorn, 2008).

Notwithstanding these challenges, the higher education community must recognize the within-group differences between Black males in order to provide a more expansive portrait of their status. This is especially important because not all Black males are failing (Fries-Britt, 1998; Harper, 2005; Hrabowski, Maton, & Greif, 1998). Further, this approach will allow educators to have a better understanding of "what works" in helping Black males to succeed.

This chapter will shed light on what works in helping Black males succeed in higher education. More specifically, this chapter discusses the experiences of Black males majoring in physics and related science, technology, engineering, and mathematics (STEM) fields. Given the nation's need for talent in the STEM fields, this population represents an important segment of the U.S. talent pool. If the United States seeks to change the trajectory of Black males and invest in their educational success, a more critical understanding of barriers and factors of support for this group is needed. The authors suggest that no group is better positioned to provide insight into what works for Black males than these males themselves, especially those who are persisting to degree completion.

The completion of a college degree has important individual and societal benefits (Swail, Redd, & Perna, 2003). For individuals, these benefits accrue in monetary form, as college graduates earn annual incomes which are twice those of high school graduates (Harper, 2006; Swail et al., 2003). Moreover, individuals who complete an undergraduate degree are qualified to compete for access to graduate programs. Ultimately, these individuals may be hired to fill professional positions needed to advance a highly technological society. The considerable advantage of a formal education has made college an attractive goal for many students (Swail et al., 2003). However, Black men have not been able to benefit from these advantages at the same rate as their peers (Harper, 2006; Strayhorn, 2008).

The chapter starts with a brief review of the literature on the academic and social challenges Black males face prior to and upon matriculation. The emphasis is on factors that shape their experience in higher education with a particular focus on historically Black colleges and universities (HBCUs). We also identify themes within the extant literature on the collegiate experiences of Black men (precollege experiences of Black men, Black men in college, Black men at HBCUs, and Black men in STEM). Then, we discuss the study methodology followed by the findings and discussion. We conclude with recommendations for research and practice.

Literature

Precollege Experiences of Black Men

Precollege experiences have long-term implications for college-bound Black men (Cuyjet, 1997, 2006; Pascarella & Terenzini, 2005). Black men are more likely to attend secondary schools that are underresourced and perform at lower academic levels than the schools their white peers attend (Jackson & Moore, 2006; Palmer et al., 2009; Perna, 2002; Strayhorn, 2008). Several indicators, such as high school rank and scores on standardized tests, serve as predictors for college participation and retention of Black men (Hood, 1992). Those who have positive precollege experiences are more likely to persist in college (Hood, 1992; McDonough, 2005); and those who have negative precollege experiences (i.e., suspensions, expulsions, behavioral problems, and referral to special education services) are less likely to be successful in college (Palmer et al., 2009; Strayhorn, 2008; White & Cones, 1999).

The academic preparation that Black males receive significantly influences college participation in STEM majors (Hrabowski & Pearson, 1993; Moore, Madison-Colmore, & Smith, 2003; Russell & Atwater, 2005). For instance, at the K-12 level, parental involvement (Perna & Titus, 2005; Qian & Blair, 1999) and teachers' early identification of student interest in science and mathematics (Hrabowski & Pearson, 1993), are critical factors that promote interest in academic and career opportunities in STEM fields for Black men. When those interventions are lacking, Black men are less likely to pursue STEM majors.

Black Men in College

The low and disproportionate number of Black men succeeding in higher education is alarming. At the collegiate level, Black men lag behind their peers in degree attainment. For example, more than two-thirds of Black men who enter college will not graduate within 6 years (Ryu, 2010). Between 1988 and 2008, Black male enrollment grew from 18% to 29%, whereas, Black female rates rose from 24% to 40% (Ryu, 2010). This rate of increase represents the largest gap amongst all racial and ethnic groups. Cross and Slater (2000) contends that the graduation rate for Black men in college is so ominous that:

> if we project into the future the past 20-year trend in college degree attainments of [B]lack men, we would find that by the end of this century [B]lack men would be out of higher education all together and [B] lack women would earn all of the bachelor's degrees awarded to [Blacks]. The dire result is not likely to occur, but the trend is a matter of serious concern.
>
> (p. 82)

Some researchers have offered insight into some of the factors associated with the low access, retention, and persistence among Black men in college. For example, Horn and Berger (2004) indicated that Black male attrition may be a byproduct of external factors such as decreases in federal aid, increases in student debt, and a greater number of Black students who work throughout their undergraduate careers. Harper (2006) argued that the absence of mentors, small numbers of Black students in large classes, a lack of institutional accountability, and the need to devote more resources to programs and student organizations are specific factors contributing to the attrition of Black men at higher education.

Black Men at HBCUs

Data suggest that Black students who attend HBCUs have more positive collegiate experiences (Fries-Britt & Turner, 2002; Kim, 2002; Kim & Conrad, 2006) and graduate with higher psychosocial outcomes than their Black peers who attend predominantly White institutions (PWIs) (Allen, 1992; Perna, Lundy-Wagner et al., 2009). Black students at HBCUs are also purported to be more satisfied with their college experiences (Allen, 1992; Kim & Conrad, 2006; Palmer & Gasman, 2008). Research has shown that students who are more satisfied with their college experience are more likely to persist (Astin, 1993; Tinto, 1993). More recently, in a study aimed at providing a more nuanced understanding of the Black male experience at an HBCU, Palmer and Gasman (2008) found that the supportive environment at the HBCU contributed to participants' persistence in college. Students described a climate where faculty members and staff were accessible and served as mentors. Their Black peers served as sources of motivation and helped to play a critical role in creating and sustaining a supportive climate.

Black Men in STEM

For Black men who attend HBCUs, many of the barriers to persisting in college, pursuing a STEM major, and graduating with a baccalaureate degree are mitigated. HBCUs are rich with sources of support for Black students. For instance, peer interactions play a major role in the persistence of Black males in college because they enable students to "meet the need for belonging, feedback, and new learning experiences" (White & Cones, 1999, p. 214). In the same vein, a growing body of literature highlights the impact of positive peer interactions in both social and academic terms among Black men in college (Fries-Britt, 1997, 1998; Hood, 1992; Hrabowski & Maton, 1995; Palmer, Davis, & Maramba, 2010).

The supportive climate at HBCUs that facilitates the success of Black men in STEM are often absent at PWIs. In fact when Black men arrive on the campus of PWIs, there may be assumptions that they are academically unprepared, which contributes to their inability to succeed in STEM fields (Hrabowski, 2003; Museus et al., 2011). Interestingly, Maton, Hrabowski, and Schmitt (2000) posited that when institutions are not committed to providing a supportive environment for Black men, they "lose qualified ... students to other majors, or from higher education totally" (p. 632). This untapped resource of possible students is another potential cause of underrepresentation. Although HBCUs graduate fewer Black men than PWIs, HBCUs play a pivotal role in graduating Black men within STEM fields (Museus & Liverman, 2010; Perna, Gasman, Lundy-Wagner, & Dresner, 2010; Perna, Lundy-Wagner et al., 2009), because they provide a supportive campus climate which is a salient factor in determining whether students will stay in a STEM major or transfer to another major (Seymour & Hewitt, 1997).

There are a number of factors that deter students from studying for STEM majors (Maton et al., 2000). For example, classroom competition is a factor that contributes to Black men leaving STEM fields (Gasman et al., 2009). The introductory STEM courses are perceived to be weed-out courses rather than cultivating students' interest in STEM (Green & Glasson, 2009; Seymour & Hewitt, 1997). STEM courses in PWIs are often comprised of a majority of nonminority students and faculty members who tend to utilize a Eurocentric perspective, which contributes to a chilly classroom climate (Green & Glasson, 2009). Consequently, the classroom composition adds to feelings of isolation or otherness (Maton et al., 2000). Moreover, the lack of Black role models in STEM fields further perpetuates the feeling of displacement for Black men (Green & Glasson, 2009; Hrabowski, 1991).

At HBCUs, Black faculty members and same-race peers serve as role models and mentors to Black collegians (Kimbrough & Harper, 2006; Palmer & Gasman, 2008; Perna, Lundy-Wagner et al., 2009). This support helps reduce the feeling of being an outsider that many Black students experience (Perna, Lundy-Wagner et al., 2010). In addition, the supportive environment increases students' belief that they are capable of achieving in science (Perna, Lundy-Wagner et al., 2009). This sense of self-efficacy is often reduced for students at PWIs who have to prove they are good enough to remain in STEM (Seymour & Hewitt, 1997). Finally, HBCUs provide additional training to students interested in STEM instead of making them feel inadequate about their knowledge in math and science (Palmer & Gasman, 2008). The attention devoted to students' STEM development at HBCUs increases their foundational knowledge in STEM subjects. As a result, many STEM students graduate with competitive academic records and content knowledge to enter prestigious graduate programs (Palmer & Gasman, 2008; Pearson & Pearson, 1985; Solórzano, 1995).

Methodology

This chapter is the product of a larger investigation of minority students in physics. In published (see Fries-Britt, Younger, & Hall, 2010a, 2010b) and forthcoming work (e.g., Fries-Britt & Holmes, forthcoming), we describe aspects of the larger research project. In this current study we focus on the experiences of the Black men who attended HBCUs or predominately Black institutions (PBIs) for all or part of their education. In keeping with the practices of the National Science Foundation (NSF) and the National Association for Equal Opportunity in Higher Education's (NAFEO), we have combined both types of institutions (e.g., PBIs, HBCUs) and refer to them throughout the chapter as HBCUs.

Two research questions guided this work: (a) How do Black men majoring in physics characterize their experiences at HBCUs? (b) What unique opportunities and challenges do they encounter on HBCU campuses?

Conceptual Framework

We utilized several bodies of literature to serve as a theoretical guide for this study. First we examined the general literature on Black males in education to understand the factors impacting their experience (Allen, 1992; Cross & Slater, 2000; Cuyjet, 1997; Fleming, 1984). This work provides an overview of the issues impacting Black males and points to the barriers and struggles that Black males encounter in education. We then turned to minorities in science and engineering (Busch-Vishniac & Jarosz, 2004; Cabrera, Colbeck, & Terenzini, 2001; National Action Council for Minorities in Engineering [NACME], 2008; Seymour & Hewitt, 1997) to understand the specific barriers that impact minority student success in STEM fields. Much of this work points to the weeding out process, faculty interactions in the classroom, academic preparation, and experiences of isolation. Additionally, the growing research on minority high achievers offered yet another dimension to understanding factors that impact successful students (Fries-Britt, 1998; Fries-Britt & Griffin, 2007; Fries-Britt & Turner, 2002; Griffin, 2006; Harper, 2005; Hrabowski et al., 1998). This body of work was important because the students in the current study represented an important segment of the Black male population that is "beating the odds" and succeeding despite the challenges Black males face in education. From these various bodies of literature, we developed a set of factors that we identified as important to underrepresented students in STEM.

Data collection occurred annually at the joint meeting of the National Society of Black Physicists (NSBP) and the National Society of Hispanic Physicists (NSHP) from 2005 to 2009. The primary source of data consisted of individual interviews 60 to 90 minutes in length and focus groups of 6 to 12 participants for 90 to 120 minutes each. All individual interviews and focus groups were audiotaped and transcribed verbatim. Collecting data at the joint annual meeting ensured that we would have a diverse group of students reflective of multiple institutional types. Each year the research team interviewed approximately 25 to 30 students resulting in a database of approximately 159 students. We have completed files which were comprised of interview and demographic data on 133 students, of which 95 identified as Black, 10 identified as Caribbean/African, 6 students identified as Latino, and 22 students identified as other. From a sample of 95 Black students, 56 were Black males and approximately 44 of these males had some or all of their postsecondary school educational experiences at an HBCU. The majority of the 133 students were at the junior level and above with 50% of the sample at the master's and doctoral or postgraduate level. The entire sample consisted of students from a variety of postsecondary institutions including public and private, predominantly White, historically Black, and Hispanic serving institutions from across the United States.

The interview protocol was developed based on the major themes in the literature (e.g., interactions with faculty, peers, academic preparation, science exposure, role models, and parents). Using the interview protocol as a guide, we developed themes/codes and organized and prepared the data for analysis by reading through each transcript individually to get a general sense of the data collected. A three-member coding team then met and compared notes as we began organizing the data into categories. This process is consistent with Creswell's (2003) three-step process of data analysis and interpretation. Nvivo software was used to code and manage the data. Nvivo is a qualitative data analysis software package used for coding, retrieving, and reviewing textual data.

Findings and Discussion

We begin with a brief explanation of the educational experiences and background of the participants. We then discuss two major themes: (a) establishing relationships: a main ingredient for success at HBCUs, and (b) peers: an important link in academic success and persistence. We conclude with a brief discussion of several challenges and barriers that Black males in STEM identified at HBCUs.

Participant Background and Educational Experiences

Although we were interested in having diverse institutional representation in the study, it came as a surprise to learn during the analysis of the data that participants' individual educational experiences included attendance at multiple institution types. The diversity of institutional experience exists for several reasons. First, approximately 50% of the sample were undergraduate and graduate students respectively. Many of the graduate students completed their undergraduate degree at an HBCU and at the time of the study they were enrolled at a PWI for graduate work. Some participants transferred from a PWI during their undergraduate work to complete their degree at an HBCU and vice versa. Another category included Black men who were enrolled in collaborative programs between HBCUs and PWIs, and they attended classes at both types of institutions. Finally, there were some participants in the sample who only attended HBCUs. While the findings focus primarily on what students shared about their HBCU experience, entangled in their stories are comparisons to PWIs. Thus, we offer these observations when appropriate and when we believe that the contrasting view helps to illustrate a point and extends the strength and importance of the finding.

The majority of participants in this study were second-generation collegians. Most participants had at least one parent who had earned a college degree and in some cases both parents had earned a degree. "My family has always been very supportive. Both of my parents are school teachers and they graduated from a 4-year college." This observation by one male was fairly representative of the participants, although parents' occupations varied. It was not unusual for some of the parents to have a graduate degree in some areas of STEM fields, but not always. This finding is similar to other studies (Maton & Hrabowski, 1995, 2004; Hrabowski et al. 1998), which found parents to be highly educated.

Not surprisingly, first-generation students shared different stories about their parents' educational experiences: "my mom stopped in eighth grade. She already had a kid at 13. My dad stopped at sixth or seventh grade.... Sixth grade was the last time either of my parents ever saw my report cards ... they were always there at events when I [had] things to do." This student explained that while his parents could not help him academically he did obtain support from other individuals. For instance, his study was aided by his basketball coach who was also his math teacher. Interestingly, his math teacher/coach would not let him play ball unless he earned an "A" in math. Many of the first-generation students felt supported by their family but they often turned to other mentors who helped them academically.

Establishing Relationships: A Main Ingredient for Success at HBCUS

Overwhelmingly, the HBCU campus climate was perceived in very positive terms. This finding is well documented in the literature (Allen, 1992; Fleming, 1984; Fries-Britt & Turner, 2002; Kim, 2002; Kim & Conrad, 2006). The participants talked about their HBCU experiences with a sense of confidence and candor. Similar to works from Bonner and Bailey (2006) as well as Palmer and Gasman (2008), what stood out about the HBCU campus was the establishment of relationships. Students described connecting right away with faculty, administrators, and peers on campus. The *ease* at which relationships were established at HBCUs was very important and the *care* that individuals extended to help students succeed was perceived as different from what they encountered at PWIs.

Students discussed the importance of key administrative staff, including administrative assistants, program directors, and faculty. Administrators and support staff provided important information on the inner workings of the department and on campus. Similarly, Palmer and Gasman (2008) found that administrative staff provided students with support and encouragement. In this current study, office staff looked out for students, aided them with course registration, provided access to supplies and study space, and on occasion supplied them with a home-cooked meal. These individuals were described in familial terms and with endearments. An example of this is illustrated by a student, who noted,

> There was one women who I know has been very influential through my entire academic career ... she was the Administrative Assistant to the Dean of Math and Science ... right out of high school ... leaving home for the first time, she was a very, I will say nurturing influence. And I

mean, not to the point of, like, mothering but at the same time, you know she was kind of the person that I know I could go to.

Students really appreciated the help that they would receive from the staff. Another student shared,

> [Y]ou'd have to know the campus to know that some departments you get lackluster responses from secretaries. So you know you develop a relationship with Ms. Cain [pseudonym]...simple things like making a copy or stapling some papers together, little things that you don't even think is important that she allows, really helps.

In most cases these individuals were described as helpful; however, there were instances where students described some staff as problematic if you got on their "bad side." Being on a staff member's "bad side" could prevent students' paperwork from being processed as quickly or lead to things getting "lost." In sharing their stories, students often made comments like, "in physics you have to treat Mrs. Johnson (pseudonym) right or you will not graduate." The small size of many of the departments gave these individuals important roles outside of their formal job classification making relationship building important. When the students talked about these relationships, they often laughed but they always returned to a level of seriousness to say how important these individuals were to their success.

Widely cited in the literature is the importance of students' relationships with faculty. Nonetheless, the participants described distinctly different experiences in establishing relationships with faculty at HBCUs and PWIs. This is illustrated by a student who was comparing his experience of connecting with faculty at both types of institution; each was similar in size and prestige; however, his immediate ability to establish relationships with faculty was different on the HBCU campus.

> [F]rom day one when I stepped in a physics major at [X HBCU] I interacted with faculty members. At [X PWI] it's a little bit different, even though the size of the schools are the same, the only time that I talked to a faculty member was when I needed to work on a research proposal. Not saying that they weren't accessible because they always say that their door is open, but there was no real need to talk to them in my mind.

As this student commented in "his mind" there did not seem to be a real reason to talk to faculty even though he said that their door was open. The participant's experiences would suggest that the relationships are more nuanced. Notwithstanding, many of the participants talked about a "vibe" that they picked up in their interactions with faculty on PWI campuses. Often this vibe is perceived as negative and faculty did not seem willing to engage them in conversation. However, when faculty did, students often felt put down. This finding may not be surprising, as PWIs are often described as hostile environments where Black students face discrimination and feelings of isolation (Allen, 1992; Cabrera, Nora, Pascarella, Terenzini, & Hagedorn, 1999; Fries-Britt 1997; Fries-Britt & Turner, 2002; Museus, Nichols, & Lambert, 2008; Smedley, Myers, & Harrell, 1993). For instance, some scholars have found that Black men encounter discrimination that perpetuates negative stereotypes and many of these stereotypes impact students' interactions with faculty (Bonner & Bailey, 2006; Majors & Billson, 1992). Even when White faculty have an open door policy, many students did not feel comfortable seeking help or going to them as mentors unless they had to, or as another student described, "the mentorship is there but you also have to take the initiative to go and approach the faculty."

At HBCUs faculty often approached students first. They tended to reach out to students, engaging them in conversations that motivate them to do their best and to work hard. Some of the students described the faculty at HBCUs as "having your back." A male student shared that his professors at an HBCU always provided him and his peers with feedback and advice about how to do well:

> And one thing that he taught us while we were going through our undergraduate and graduate courses was that, you know, you have to realize that regardless of what you are doing right now, someone else is doing 10 times that and more ... so you always have to keep on progressing yourself ... and trying to move forward instead of staying stagnant.

This student perceived that the professor supported him because he was "always giving feedback" and mentoring the student. Literature points to the critical role that mentoring plays in the collegiate experience of Black men (Harper, 2006; Palmer & Gasman, 2008; Strayhorn, 2008). It is often through these mentoring relationships and ongoing conversations that students establish strong bonds with professors. The development of a strong relationship occurs over time. As one student observed:

> As I've grown in physics, my relationships with my advisors at [X HBCU] [have gotten stronger]. They've also grown outside of just talking physics. They ask me about [my] personal life and if I'm spending too much time in the lab [they ask about] my well-being.

First, the student noted that as he "grew in physics" his relationship with his advisor developed. His "growth" in part referred to the success that he experienced working in the lab and in class with his advisor. Over time, this academic relationship naturally evolved and developed into other nonacademic areas of conversation and interests. Aside from this student sharing, other students noted that professors on HBCU campuses understood them culturally and related to the types of activities taking place on campus. For instance, one student was impressed that his professor was attending homecoming and that he encouraged the class to think about managing their coursework to prepare for homecoming. In this regard, this student stated:

> I had a math professor … and he would remind us homecoming is in 3 weeks. "I'm not going to want to do this, neither are you. Therefore, you need to prepare." Therefore, that kind of helped along the course as opposed to a White professor that didn't understand why his class didn't show up on Friday.

This example illustrates how students can relate to faculty in nonacademic areas. Clearly faculty understood the student culture and valued the traditions of the campus, which added to the sense of connection that students felt.

Students also had the opportunity to establish relationships with a diverse group of faculty including women and international faculty in STEM fields at HBCUs. In general, students described women faculty as nurturing and accessible. Students had mixed reactions to working with international faculty. The majority of the students took courses with international faculty members from a number of different countries. Some students commented that international faculty expected them to be further along in their understanding of the subject matter; students also noted that some international faculty tended to view U.S. students as not willing to work as hard as students from other countries. Several students described international faculty as "rude" and yet others felt like these faculty pushed them harder to succeed and provided them with professional opportunities.

Peers: An Important Link in Academic Success and Persistence

Participants described the critical role of peer interaction in their academic success in physics. In some cases, peers were described as indispensable and they played an important role in helping students study and understand concepts from class. One student who considered himself to be smart in high school later described himself as a "slacker" and not really motivated in college. He faced challenges in college, and he questioned his self-efficacy when he had to go up against other bright students. Because he realized that he did not know as much as others, he relied on his peers to "carry" him for a while. The support he received from his peers really sustained him.

> Like, for me, I'm learning a lot, I was a slacker to the core. But if it wasn't for them [peers] I wouldn't have done my homework. If it wasn't for them asking for help I wouldn't have done nothing … my high school our motto was it wasn't due until it was due … and I went to a … magnet school … everybody there they knew that they were smart … it's just a different thing to go to a place where you know you are the top 10 to being 0 and then having to show yourself what you can do.

Academically, the transition from high school to college can be challenging. Peers who share academic experiences and work together can be instrumental in each other's success. In conversations with peers, students learned from their experiences and were able to advise one another on navigating coursework and campus processes. Several students said that when upperclassmen shared with them that they had failed an exam or were forced to retake a class, it enabled the students to be "easier" on themselves because they felt "normal" and validated in some of their own challenges. Padilla, Trevino, Gonzalez, and Trevino (1997) noted that in order for students to be successful on a campus they must have theoretical and heuristic knowledge. While theoretical knowledge is knowledge students receive from engaging in their studies and listening to their professors' lecture, heuristic knowledge is the practical knowledge that students need to function on campus. It is this type of knowledge that comes from peers and the informal domains of the campus. Through peer interactions, important pieces of information are passed along about a wide range of topics, and this helps students succeed.

Other scholars also noted the important role of peers to students' college experience. Harper (2006), in a study of Black male peer relationships, found that peers were very important to the collegiate success of Black men. Students commented on the important role of their peers in supporting them. One participant noted, "There is no way I would have been nearly as successful at Ohio State were it not for the support of other [Black] students here. They have applauded everything I have done so far" (p. 347). In Harper's study, most of the support that the students talk about centered on their social connections and engagement in organizations. In this current work students focused more on their peer relationships in academic contexts.

Not all students felt like their interactions with peers aided them academically. These students tended to serve as "unofficial tutors," helping their peers with their coursework. In fact, students described gaining minimal benefits from peer interactions and in some cases teaching their peers meant that they were not focusing on their own academic concerns:

> I'd say the time I spent gaining knowledge from peers is much, much less than the time I spent trying to impart knowledge to them ... this is not only in physics classes and math classes, I've also done it in chemistry classes, I spend a lot of my free time trying to get other people to understand what we have to do in class ... so I spend a lot of time just working stuff out over, and over, and over again, which it does help me, but it's not necessarily what I would be doing if I were working on the stuff that I would want to be working on.

While this student served an important role in helping his peers he spends less time focusing on his own work. The student explained that his peers would rather spend 3 hours with him than with the professor. More specifically, the student shared,

> with the professor you run the risk of them knowing that you are really [do not know the material well] especially if they have to keep explaining a concept or problem. If you, … still don't get it, then the professor is gonna start to … either think negatively of you or the class in general … start dumbin' stuff down, so they [students] would much rather deal with other students who are gonna help them than professors.

Seymour and Hewitt (1997) found STEM faculty, "are often represented as unapproachable or unavailable for help with either academic or career-planning concerns" (p. 34). If students perceive faculty as unavailable or insensitive, they may feel uncomfortable seeking out these relationships and interactions with them. Consequently, they may be more inclined to ask peers for help as opposed to faculty. This illustrates the important role that peer to peer interactions have on the collegiate experiences of students, particularly Black students in STEM (Astin, 1993; Harper, 2006).

Challenges at HBCUs

Even with tremendous opportunities to develop strong relationships with faculty and staff, and opportunities to work in supportive ways with peers, participants identified challenges with attending HBCUs. Having access to state-of-the-art equipment in the sciences remained a challenge. Students who attended partnership programs between HBCUs and PWIs were aware of these differences as they took courses on both campuses. Many students attending HBCUs described having to "ask" or "negotiate" the use of equipment at a private lab or PWI campus. These experiences caused discomfort for students who felt like "visitors" rather than "residential" scientists who had a sense of "ownership" with their lab. Students who later enrolled at PWIs for graduate school noted that without a state-of-the-art lab, they were not fully prepared to compete with peers who had this access earlier in their academic careers.

Resource challenges have been longstanding issues at HBCUs since their inception (Anderson, 1988). HBCUs continue to lack parity in funding compared to their PWI counterparts, which poses a disadvantage for these institutions (Palmer & Griffin, 2009). Although HBCUs play an important role in degree attainment for Blacks and other populations, Minor (2008) argued that governmental agencies and the private business sector seem less willing to financially support HBCUs in a similar manner to PWIs. The lack of resources at HBCUs will continue to be a challenge until measures are taken to evaluate funding trends and state formulas.

In this study we endeavored to understand how Black men majoring in physics characterized their experiences at HBCUs and the unique opportunities and challenges they encountered on campus. Our findings suggest that Black men characterized their experiences at HBCUs around the establishment of relationships with faculty, administrators, and peers. Participants spoke about the ease they felt in making connections with peers and the importance of having peers who they can rely on for academic support. While students encountered some challenges with the bureaucracy, the relationships with administrators and staff on campus often help to ease these challenges. Perhaps the most challenging issue students identified was having access to state-of-the-art resources and opportunities to engage in research.

Conclusion

HBCUs are integral to the success of Black men in the academy, particularly in STEM. Every participant in this study had part, and in some cases all of their educational experience at an HBCU. The mission of HBCUs to serve students from diverse academic backgrounds is reflected in the demographics of the participants. Although the majority of the students were second generation, and some might have argued that they would succeed on their own, research affirms how the collaborative classroom environments enhance learning gains in STEM (Terenzini, Cabrera, Colbeck, Parente, & Bjorklund, 2001). These supportive environments are likely to occur in HBCUs where relationships are easily fortified and students work together to succeed. Students attending HBCUs tend to be socialized into understanding that they must work together to ensure not only their success, but the success of others as well.

Second, since there are so few physics students, relationships with peers, administrative staff and faculty are critical. At HBCUs, it is typical for faculty to be highly engaged with students in physics (Whitten, Foster, & Duncombe, 2003). Despite this current study's findings, research must continue to understand the best ways to cultivate success for Black men. As the nation continues toward the goal of increasing the number of college graduates, and in particular growing interest in STEM fields, it is critical to note the importance of HBCUs in facilitating the success of Black men.

References

Allen, W. R. (1992). The color of success: African-American college student outcomes at predominantly White and historically Black colleges and universities. *Harvard Educational Review, 62,* 26–44.

Anderson, J. D. (1988). *The education of Blacks in the South 1860–1935.* Chapel Hill: University of North Carolina Press.

Astin, A. W. (1993). *What matters in college: Four critical years revisited.* San Francisco, CA: Jossey-Bass.

Bonner, F. A., & Bailey, K. (2006). Assessing the academic climate for African American men. In M. Cuyjet (Ed.), *African American men in college* (pp. 24–46). San Francisco, CA: Jossey-Bass.

Busch-Vishniac, I. J., & Jarosz, J. P. (2004). Can diversity in the undergraduate engineering population be enhanced through curricular change? *Journal of Women and Minorities in Science and Engineering, 10*(3), 255–282.

Cabrera, A. F., Colbeck, C. L., & Terenzini, P. T. (2001). Developing performanceindicators for assessing classroom teaching practices and student learning: The case of engineering. *Research in Higher Education, 42*(3), 327–352.

Cabrera, A. F., Nora, A., Terenzini, P. T., Pascarella, E., & Hagedorn, L. S. (1999). Campus racial climate and the adjustment of students to college: A comparison between White students and African-American students. *Journal of Higher Education, 70*(2), 134–160

Creswell, J. W. (2003). *Qualitative inquiry and research design: Choosing among five traditions.* Thousand Oaks, CA: Sage.

Cross, T., & Slater, R. B. (2000). The alarming decline in the academic performance of African American men. *Journal of Blacks in Higher Education, 27*, 82–87.

Cuyjet, M. J. (1997). African American men on college campuses: Their needs and their perceptions. In M. J. Cuyjet & Associates (Eds.), *Helping African American men succeed in college* (New Directions for Student Services, No. 80, pp. 5–16). San Francisco, CA: Jossey-Bass.

Cuyjet, M., J. (Ed.). (2006). *African American men in college.* San Francisco, CA: Jossey-Bass.

Fleming, J. (1984). *Blacks in college: A comparative study of students' success in Black and in White institutions.* San Francisco, CA: Jossey-Bass.

Fries-Britt, S. L. (1997). Identifying and supporting gifted African American men. In M. J. Cuyjet & Associates (Eds.), *Helping African American men succeed in college* (New Directions for Student Services, No. 80. pp. 65–78). San Francisco, CA: Jossey-Bass.

Fries-Britt, S. L. (1998). Moving beyond Black achiever isolation: Experiences of gifted Black collegians. *Journal of Higher Education, 69*(5), 556–576

Fries-Britt, S., & Griffin, K. (2007). The black box: How high-achieving Blacks resist stereotypes about Black Americans. *Journal of College Student Development, 48*(5), 509–524.

Fries-Britt, S. L., & Holmes, K. (forthcoming). Prepared and progressing: Black women in physics. In C. Chambers (Eds.), *Black American female undergraduates on campus: Successes and challenges.*

Fries-Britt, S.L., & Turner, B. (2002). Uneven stories: The experiences of successful Black collegians at a historically Black and a traditionally White campus. *Review of Higher Education, 25*(3), 315–330.

Fries-Britt, S.L., Younger, K. T., & Hall, W. (2010a). Lessons from high achieving minorities in physics. In S. R. Harper & C. B Newman (Eds.), *Students of color in STEM* (pp. 75–84). San Francisco, CA: Jossey-Bass.

Fries-Britt, S. L., Younger, K. T., & Hall, W. (2010b). Underrepresented minorities in physics: How perceptions of race and campus climate affect student outcomes. In E. T. Dancy (Ed.), *Managing diversity: (Re)Visioning equity on college campuses* (pp. 181–198). New York: Peter Lang.

Gasman, M., Perna, L.W., Yoon, S., Drezner, N. D., Lundy-Wagner, V., Bose, E., & Gary, S. (2009). The path to graduate school in science and engineering for underrepresented students of color. In M. F. Howard-Hamilton, C. L. Morelon-Quainoo, S. D. Johnson, R. Winkle-Wagner, R., & L. Santiague (Eds.), In *Standing on the outside looking in: Underrepresented students' experiences in advanced degree programs* (pp. 63–81). Sterling, VA: Stylus.

Green, A., & Glasson, G. (2009). African Americans majoring in science at predominantly White universities (A review of the literature). *College Student Journal, 43*(2), 366–374.

Griffin, K. (2006). Striving for success: A qualitative exploration of competing theories of high-achieving Black college students' academic motivation. *Journal of College Student Development, 47*(4), 384–400.

Harper, S. R. (2005). Leading the way: High-achieving African American male students. *About Campus, 10*(1), 8–15.

Harper, S. R. (2006). *Black male students at public flagship universities in the U.S.: Status, trends and implications for policy and practice.* Washington, DC: Joint Center for Political and Economic Studies.

Harrison, P. M., & Beck, A. J. (2004). *Prisoners in 2003*. Washington, DC: U.S. Department of Justice, Office of Justice Programs, Bureau of Justice Statistics. Retrieved from http://www.ojp.usdoj.gov/bjs/abstract/p03.htm

Hood, D. W. (1992). Academic and noncognitive factors affecting the retention of black men at a predominantly white university. *Journal of Negro Education, 61*(1), 12–23.

Horn, L., & Berger, R. (2004). *College persistence on the rise? Changes in 5-year degree completion and postsecondary persistence rates between 1994 and 2000* (NCES 2005-156). Washington, DC: U.S. Department of Education, National Center for Education Statistics.

Hrabowski, F. A. (1991). Helping gifted Black males succeed in science. *Journal of Health Care for the Poor and Underserved, 2*(1), 197–201.

Hrabowski, F. (2003). Raising minority achievement in science and math. *Educational Leadership, 60*(4), 44–48.

Hrabowski, F. A., & Maton, K. I. (1995). Enhancing the success of African-American students in the sciences: Freshman year outcomes. *School Science and Mathematics, 95*(1), 19–27.

Hrabowski, F., Maton, K., & Greif, G. (1998). *Beating the odds: Raising academically successful African-American males*. New York: Oxford University Press.

Hrabowski, F., Maton, K., & Greif, G (2002). *Overcoming the odds: Raising academically successful African-American young women*. New York: Oxford University Press.

Hrabowski, F. A., & Pearson, W. (1993). Recruiting and retaining African-American males in college science and engineering. *Journal of College Science Teaching, 22*(4), 234–238.

Jackson, J. F. L., & Moore, J. L. (2006). African American males in education: Endangered or ignored. *Teachers College Record, 2,* 201–205.

Kimbrough, W. M., & Harper, S. R. (2006). African American men at historically Black colleges and universities: Different environments, similar challenges. In M. J. Cuyjet (Ed.), *African American men in college (pp. 189–209)*. San Francisco: Jossey-Bass.

Kim, M. M. (2002). Historically Black vs. White institutions: Academic development among Black students. *Review of Higher Education, 25*(4), 385–407.

Kim, M. M., & Conrad, C.F. (2006). The impact of historically Black colleges and universities on the academic success of African-American students. *Research in Higher Education, 47*(4), 399–427.

Majors, R., & Billson, J. B. (1992). *Cool pose: The dilemmas of Black manhood in America*. New York: Touchstone.

Maton, K. I., Hrabowski, F. A., & Schmitt, C. L. (2000). African American college students excelling in the sciences: College and postcollege outcomes in the Meyerhoff scholars program. *Journal of Research in Science Teaching, 37*(7), 629–654.

Minor, J. T. (2008). *Contemporary HBCUs: Considering institutional capacity and state priorities* (A research report). East Lansing, MI: College of Education, Department of Educational Administration, Michigan State University.

Moore, J. L., Madison-Colmore, O., & Smith, D. M. (2003). To prove-them-wrong syndrome: Voices from unheard African-American males in engineering disciplines. *Journal of Men's Studies, 12*(1), 61–74.

Museus, S. D., & Liverman, D. (2010). High-performing institutions and their implications for studying underrepresented minority students in STEM. In S. R. Harper & C. B. Newman (Eds.), *Students of color in STEM (pp. 17–27)*. San Francisco, CA: Jossey-Bass.

Museus, S. D., Nichols, A. H., & Lambert, A. (2008). Racial differences in the effects of campus racial climate on degree completion: A structural model. *Review of Higher Education, 32*(1), 107–134.

Museus, S. D., Palmer, R. T., Davis, R. J., & Maramba, D. C. (2011, March). *Racial and ethnic minority students' success in STEM education* (ASHE-Higher Education Report Series, 36[6]). Las Vegas, NV: ASHE.

National Action Council for Minorities in Engineering. (2008). *Confronting the "new" American Dilemma: Underrepresented minorities in engineering—A data based look at diversity*. White Plains, NY: Author.

Padilla, R. V., Trevino, J., Gonzalez, K., & Trevino, J. (1997). Developing local models of minority student success in college. *Journal of College Student Development, 38*(2), 125–135.

Palmer, R. T., Davis, R. J., & Hilton, A. A. (2009). Exploring challenges that threaten to impede the academic success of academically under-prepared African American male collegians at an HBCU. *Journal of College Student Development, 50*(4), 429–445.

Palmer, R. T., Davis, R. J., & Maramba, D. C. (2010). Popularizing achievement: The role of an HBCU in supporting academic success for underprepared African American males. *Negro Educational Review, 61*(1–4), 85–106.

Palmer, R. T., & Gasman, M. (2008). "It takes a village": Social capital and academic success at historically Black colleges and universities. *Journal of College Student Development, 49*(1), 1–19.

Palmer, R. T., & Griffin, K. (2009). Desegregation policy and disparities in faculty salary and workload: Maryland's historically Black and predominantly White institutions. *Negro Educational Review, 60*(1–4), 7–21.

Pascarella, E. T., & Terenzini, P. T. (2005). *How college affects students: A third decade of research* (2nd ed., Vol. 2). San Francisco CA: Jossey-Bass.

Pearson, W., & Pearson, L.C. (1985). Baccalaureate origins of Black American scientists: A cohort analysis. *Journal of Negro Education, 54*(1), 24–34.

Perna, L. W. (2002). Retaining African Americans in higher education: Challenging paradigms for retaining students, faculty, and administrators. *Journal of Higher Education, 73*(5), 652–659.

Perna, L. W., Gasman, M., Lundy-Wagner, V. C., & Drezner, N. D. (2010). Identifying strategies for increasing degree attainment in STEM: Lessons from minority-serving institutions. In S. R. Harper & C. B. Newman (Eds.), *Students of color in STEM* (pp. 41–51). San Francisco, CA: Jossey-Bass.

Perna, L. W., Lundy-Wagner, V. C., Drezner, N. D., Gasman, M., Yoon, S., Bose, E., & Gary, S. (2009). The contribution of HBCUs to the preparation of African American women for STEM careers: A case study. *Review of Higher Education, 50*(1), 1–23.

Perna, L. W., & Titus, M. A. (2005). The relationship between parental involvement as social capital and college enrollment: An examination of racial/ethnic group differences. *Journal of Higher Education, 76*(5), 485–518.

Qian, Z., & Blair, S. L. (1999). Racial differences in educational aspirations of high school seniors. *Sociological Perspectives 42*(4), 605–625.

Russell, M. L., & Atwater, M. M. (2005). Traveling the road to success: A discourse on persistence throughout the science pipeline with African American students at a predominantly White institution. *Journal of Research in Science Teaching, 42*(6), 691–715.

Ryu, M. (2010). *Minorities in higher education: Twenty-fourth annual status report, 2010.* Washington, DC: American Council on Education.

Seymour, E., & Hewitt, N. M. (1997). *Talking about leaving: Why undergraduates leave the sciences.* Boulder, CO: Westview Press.

Smedley, B. D., Myers, H. E., & Harrell, S. P. (1993). Minority-status stresses and the college adjustment of ethnic minority freshmen. *Journal of Higher Education 64*(4), 434–452.

Solórzano, D. G. (1995). The doctorate production and baccalaureate origins of African Americans in the sciences and engineering. *Journal of Negro Education, 64*(1), 15–32.

Strayhorn, T. (2008). The role of supportive relationships in supporting African American males' success in college. *NASPA Journal, 45,* 26–48.

Swail, W. S., Redd, K. E., & Perna, L. W. (2003). *Retaining minority students in higher education: A framework for success* (ASHE-ERIC Higher Education Report.*30*[2]). San Francisco, CA: Wiley.

Terenzini, P. T., Cabrera, A. F., Colbeck, C. L., Parente, J. M., & Bjorklund, S. A. (2001). Collaborative learning vs. lecture/discussion: Students' reported learning gains. *Journal of Engineering Education, 90,* 123–130.

Tinto, V. (1993). *Leaving college: Rethinking the causes and curses of student attrition.* Chicago, IL: University of Chicago Press

White, J., & Cones, J. (1999). *Black man emerging: Facing the past and seizing the future in America.* New York: W. H. Freeman.

Whitten, B. L., Foster, S. R., & Duncombe, M. L. (2003). What works for women in undergraduate physics? *Physics Today, 56*(9), 46–51.

7

BICULTURAL EXPERIENCES OF SECOND-GENERATION BLACK AMERICAN MALES

Lorenzo DuBois Baber

In Dreams From My Father, President Barack Obama reflects on his experiences as a Black American male with a father from Kenya and a mother from Kansas. In this personal narrative, he describes the internal and external conflicts that occur as one attempts to blend multiple cultures and contexts. At times, he felt that a connection to Black American identity "meant only the knowledge of your own powerlessness, or your own defeat" (p. 85), while at other times a reflection of "survival, and freedom, and hope" (p. 294). Perhaps more than most Black American males, identity development among second-generation immigrants lies between the agonizing push of White racism and inequality and the invigorating pull of Black American pride and opportunity.

In examining the experiences of Black students in higher education, researchers have increasingly acknowledged the heterogeneity among Blacks, suggesting the need to study within-group differences, including gender. As such, various studies have examined the unique experiences of Black males in postsecondary education (Cuyjet, 2006; Harper & Harris, 2010). As this volume suggests, moving beyond a monolithic perspective is critical for understanding Black male experiences in postsecondary education. The growing cultural heterogeneity among Black Americans has created varied racial experiences based on intersections between race and gender, socioeconomic background, geographic location, and sexuality. As with other institutional types, it is particularly important that researchers, policymakers, and administrators avoid homogenous perspectives of Black students who are attending historically Black colleges and universities (HBCUs). Unfortunately, current research on students attending HBCUs rarely disaggregates outcomes beyond racial/ethnic affiliation. As Patton (2011) noted, Black males enter HBCUs with multiple overlapping, dynamic identities that may influence their interactions and integration in the academic and social environment.

One identity typically overlooked within the Black male identity is second-generation immigrant status. Rumbaut (1995) defined second-generation status as belonging to those individuals who were born in the United States with at least one immigrant parent. Second-generation Black males are uniquely situated between immigrant Blacks, particularly from African and Caribbean cultures, and Black American culture. While they have a connection through their family with a homeland outside of the United States, second-generation Black males are primarily socialized in the United States, facing the same socio-historical stereotypes associated with Black American male identity. As such, second-generation Black males may be either positioned to develop healthy self-perceptions rooted in close ties with their ancestral lineage or face extreme marginalization and discrimination as part of their social context.

This chapter examines the unique challenges faced by second-generation Black male students as they transition from high school to college. More specifically, I consider ways in which family culture and campus environments contribute to the development of racial identity among second-generation Black male students. With this in mind, I sought to answer the following questions: How do students negotiate their multiple identities? How do transitional moments of racial identity influence academic and social connections to the institution? How do students negotiate meanings and identity rooted in African–Caribbean and American backgrounds? While the participants in this study decided to attend predominately White institutions (PWIs), their experiences growing up in the United States exemplify the challenges of second-generation Black American males enrolled at all types of institutions, including HBCUs. At the conclusion of the chapter, I present specific implications and recommendations for HBCUs in serving the unique needs of second-generation Black American males.

Literature Review

Black Immigration Post-1965

Once scarce within the Black American population, Black immigrants and second-generation Black Americans have grown in numbers as a result of changes to the immigration laws (Kent, 2007; Sakamoto, Woo, & Kim, 2010). Prior to 1965 legislation, immigration opportunities were based on the existing ethnic composition of the United States. Since the United States was overwhelmingly European American, immigration laws, policies, and procedures heavily favored European countries, specifically the United Kingdom, Ireland, and Germany (Daniels & Graham, 2001; Hirschman, 2006). The Hart-Cellar Act of 1965 removed restrictions on immigration based on ethnicity, establishing immigration criteria that included family connections, refugee status, and persons with valuable occupational training. While limits were no longer based on ethnic origin, numerical ceilings were developed for each country. However, as Murata (2006) noted, higher caps were established for countries in the Western Hemisphere, including newly independent Caribbean nations. Combined with the highly restrictive immigration laws passed in the United Kingdom during the 1960s, an increasing number of people from the West Indies migrated to the United States.

The Refugee Act of 1980 was the second piece of legislation that was critical to opening opportunities for African–Caribbean immigration to the United States (Arthur, 2008; Yewah & Togunde, 2010). This act established a systematic procedure for dealing with emergencies around the world by annually reviewing and adjusting refugee ceilings based on political and humanitarian concerns (Chacko, 2003; Chisholm, 1982; Kennedy, 1981). Sponsors of this legislation also redefined the term *refugee* from a narrow definition (a person fleeing from a communist country or the Middle East) to a broader definition in line with United Nations protocol (a person who is unable or unwilling to return to their country because of persecution on account of race, religion, nationality, or membership in a particular social or political group). In addition, the Act provided an increase on the annual cap on refugee immigrants from 17,400 to 50,000. Further, it gave the President, in consultation with Congress, the ability to exceed the limit if necessary. These changes stimulated African–Caribbean immigration as a number of counties—including Ethiopia, Sudan, Somalia, Ghana, Liberia, and Haiti—struggled with civil wars and totalitarian regimes between 1980 and the early 2000s.

The Diversity Immigrant Visa Program, established in 1995, also promoted Black immigration, particularly from African countries (Arthur, 2008; Chacko, 2003; Yewah & Togunde, 2010). This congressionally mandated program offers 50,000 visas annually for persons originating from countries with historically low rates of immigration to the United States. To receive a permanent resident visa under this program, individuals are required to have a high school education (or its equivalent) or 2 years of work experience in an occupation requiring at least 2 years of experience or training (U.S. Department of State, 2011). The percentage of visas awarded under this program to individuals from African countries has risen steadily, from 37% in 1995 to 51% in 2009. Among the these nations, Nigeria, Ethiopia, Egypt, and Ghana are typically awarded the most visas, although in recent years there has been a dramatic increase of visas awarded to Kenya and Cameroon.

The immigration reforms since the 1960s provided opportunities for serial migration during the following decades. That is, immigrants and refugees, once obtaining permanent resident status, often sought to sponsor entry of additional family members. The influence of increasing migration patterns from African–Caribbean backgrounds can be observed in the shifts within the

Black population in the United States (Sakamoto et al., 2010). In 1960, immigrants made up less than 1% of the total U.S. Black population. By 2006, the percentage of Black immigrants represented 13.8% of the total Black American population. Additionally, more than a million Black Americans born in 2005 had at least one foreign-born parent (Kent, 2007).

Second-Generation Black Americans and Identity

While social and economic opportunities compel many individuals and families to migrate to the United States, as Bennett and Lutz (2009) pointed out, Black immigrants occupy a unique intersection of race and immigration:

> On the one hand, they are an immigrant group in a country whose identity [has been] profoundly shaped by its immigrant-achievement narrative.... On the other hand, there is an unmistakable Racial hierarchy within the United States, one in which Blacks occupy multiple locations of disadvantage while whites occupy positions [of] power and privilege.
>
> *(p. 72)*

Positioned between the achievement narrative for immigrants and the oppressive racism experienced by Blacks in the United States, Black immigrants face a complex adjustment period. This process can be particularly challenging for the children of Black immigrants. Born and primarily socialized in the United States, second-generation Black Americans are faced with the unique challenge of experiencing lifelong racism and the oppressive forces associated with White privilege while maintaining core social and cultural immigrant connections through their parents' place of birth (Waters, 1994; Zhou, 1997).

Segmented assimilation theory is often used as a framework for examining the process by which second-generation Black Americans incorporate into this system of stratification (Bennett & Lutz, 2009; Jung, 2009; Portes & Zhou, 1993; Zhou, 1997). Neoclassical views on assimilation propose acculturation as a beginning process for upward social and economic mobility. However, this perspective fails to explain the varied assimilation processes among different immigrant populations. Segmented assimilation theory proposes distinct forms of adaptation for Black immigrants and their children. Among the forms of adaptation is selective acculturation, whereby the family members retain cultural values rooted in their ethnicity (e.g., Jamaican, Haitian, Ghanaian) while incorporating selected American cultural practices related to upward mobility. Retaining an ethnic identity rooted in their parents' country of origin promotes participation in strong immigrant social networks while it attempts to isolate children of Black immigrants from the historical stigma and racist stereotypes attached to a Black American identity.

Jung (2009) provided a detailed critique of segmented assimilation theory, noting that while it overcomes limitations of earlier theories, it does not address concerns connected to the assimilation paradigm. First, it fails to challenge connotations associated with the terms *assimilation, acculturation*, and *adaptation*. These words are rooted in the idea of similarity, "to assimilate is to become less different" (p. 381). Jung (2009) argued that while assimilation theories do not wholly ignore inequalities, the terminology prevalent in the literature implicitly suggests that difference, rather than race and White racism, is synonymous with inequality. Second, Jung (2009) suggested that segmented assimilation tends to isolate Black American culture from the positive "mainstream" American values, rendering Black American culture wholly deficient and negative. This reflects a monolithic perception of Black Americans rooted in stereotypical racist perspectives, limiting both the positive strengths and benefits associated with Black American communities and their contribution to "mainstream" values.

Rather than being conflicted over choosing core identities reflective of Black Americans *or* their parents' native culture, second-generation Black Americans may process their identity through bicultural perspectives. The bicultural concept grows from Valentine's (1971) ethnographic study of Black Americans in an urban community during the 1960s. Valentine (1971) concluded that individuals need not abandon their culture of origin in order to succeed in another culture. Instead, a person may develop the ability to operate in two cultures through a bicultural model. Building upon Valentine, de Anda (1984) suggested that the bicultural experience is possible because there is overlap between multiple cultures. The blending of perspectives allows individuals to function effectively and less stressfully. The model of bicultural socialization proposed by de Anda (1984) includes various factors related to bicultural development, including overlap between the two cultures with regard to norms, values, beliefs, and perceptions; availability of cultural mediators and models; feedback provided by each culture regarding attempts to produce normative behaviors; and a degree of bilingualism. While the bicultural concept refers to the merging of mainstream values and ethnic-centered values among second-generation Black Americans, the overlap may be between Black American culture and their parents' native culture.

Bicultural Perspective and Educational Contexts

A bicultural perspective challenges the assumption that distinct cultural systems are mutually exclusive, never intertwined or simultaneously available to individuals. Formations for development of a bicultural perspective are influenced by multiple contexts including family, community, and school environments (Ortiz & Santos, 2009; Phinney & Devich-Navarro, 1997; Wiley & Deaux, 2010). Parents are initial socializing agents who provide feedback for desired behaviors, beliefs, and values among their children. From a segmented assimilationist perspective, Black immigrants are concerned with maximizing beliefs related to the "immigrant achievement" narrative while minimizing internalization of behaviors connected to racial stereotypes and assumptions. The work of the late John Ogbu (Fordham & Ogbu, 1986; Ogbu, 2003) suggested that Black immigrant parents worked to keep children from developing the "oppositional culture" perspective dominant in Black American youth. Oppositional culture refers to the resistant norms cultivated by Black Americans in response to the oppressive White American culture within institutional structures. From this perspective, positive achievement in White-dominant spaces, such as schools, are a violation of expected norms and those who succeed become marginalized among their peers. Thus, Black immigrant parents look to disassociate from majority Black American communities to avoid such contexts.

However a bicultural perspective would argue that this highly conflicted process generates negative consequences for second-generation Black Americans. Similar to segmented assimilation, oppositional culture presents a monolithic, deficit perspective of Black American culture. Indeed, they are aspects of Black American culture that adolescents rely upon for support (Carter, 2006, 2010; Yosso, 2006). These nondominant behaviors are necessary to counteract racial microaggressions (subtle and often unconscious racist communications) which confront students in White-dominant institutions. For example, Yosso (2006) framed "resistant" capital as a positive community norm, providing young people with the knowledge and skills to challenge racism and stereotypes which devalue Black American culture. This behavior is grounded in the history of perseverance through racist social structures including slavery, segregation, and unequal opportunities.

While families and communities serve as the initial influences for identity development, research suggests school environments play a critical role in self-perceptions as children of immigrants advance through the educational system (Craythorne, 2006; Phinney, Horenczyk, Liebkind, & Vedder, 2002; Suarez-Orozco, 2004). Within the school context "youth see and compare themselves in relation to those around them, based on their social similarity or dissimilarity with the references that most directly affect their experiences" (Rumbaut, 1995, p. 754). Positive concepts of racial identity are heightened as social dissimilarity is reduced, whereas when dissimilarity is observed, self-appraisals of identity are negative and youth employ perceptual defenses. Engaged in multiple cultural worlds, second-generation Black Americans are susceptible to dissimilarity within various contexts—the greater the dissonance, the more difficult it becomes to merge a healthy, blended self-concept.

Studies suggest that a bicultural orientation among second-generation Black Americans is conducive to better school performance (Phinney et al., 2007; Rong & Brown, 2001; Wiley & Deaux, 2010). These findings are consistent with the role of healthy psychosocial development in transition to and persistence in postsecondary education for Black American students, particularly at PWIs (Fries-Britt & Turner, 2002; Pillay, 2005; Smedley, Myers, & Harrell,

1993; Wei et al., 2010). For Black American students entering college, unique anxiety related to racial identity development supplements general transition stress. In particular, Black American males, subject to intense stereotypes via mainstream media images (hooks, 2004; Jackson & Moore, 2008) are particularly susceptible to anxiety over perceptions of identity. Among Black American males attending a PWI, Harper (2006) found that peer support from other Black American male students triggered effective development of racial identity, including bicultural development. Less explicit is the exploration of bicultural development among Black American males who are offspring of immigrant parents.

Most research on bicultural development within HBCU contexts examines this concept within the framework of Cross' racial identity model (Awad, 2007). A stage model, Cross' theory suggests that bicultural identities are developed within the final stage, characterized by an internalized multicultural worldview which stresses openness to other cultures. However, in a study of Black students attending an HBCU, Brown (1997) suggested that students develop multiple, overlapping identities within various sociocultural contexts. Rather than developing these healthy identities through a stagelike process, a cyclical form of identity development emerges as students search for a deeper understanding of identity which includes intersection of race with other forms of identity such as gender and immigrant status. For example, the significant differences observed between Black American males and females in regard to racial identity development, specifically the fifth stage of the Cross model (internalized multiculturalist), may be an outcome related to the added complexity of gender. Rather than view identity development through the arrival of various "stages," it may be more valuable to examine individual shifts within and among their multiple forms of identity. With this in mind, this particular study focused on race, gender, and immigrant status.

Bicultural Experiences of Second-Generation Black American Males in College

This chapter is based on a larger, year-long study on transitional experiences of Black American students entering college. Specifically, three Black American males who participated in the larger project were second-generation Black Americans who were born or raised in the United States, but had at least one immigrant parent. While their second-generation status was not a primary inquiry for the study, it was clear during interviews that this aspect of the students' background had a significant influence on their educational experiences. Two of the students, Warren and Elijah, have parents who are from Nigeria, while Charles' parents are from Trinidad. Warren and Elijah come from a two-parent household; Charles is from a single-parent household (with extended family present).

Each student participated in three face-to-face interviews over the course of an academic year. Semistructured questions that encouraged in-depth responses focused on the transitional experiences of students from their high school to the university. The first set of interviews focused on family background and a review of precollege academic and social experiences. The second interviews focused on how renegotiated identities connected to or clashed with family and home community traditions. The last set of interviews reviewed the balance (or lack of balance) between school community and home community. For this chapter, three emerging themes related to bicultural identity development are presented: centrality of parents' home country; contextual influence; and emerging development.

Centrality of Parents' Home Country

Students discussed how parents stressed a strong orientation toward their Nigerian or Trinidadian identity. All three mentioned that they spent extended time in the parental home country. Warren's parents sent him to boarding school in Nigeria during middle school (6th to 8th grade). Both Elijah and Charles spent an occasional summer in the parental home country, visiting grandparents and other relatives. Each student described these experiences as intentionally planned by their parents to maintain roots and experience the culture of the home country. As Elijah stated, "my parents wanted us to be in another culture and actually know where we were from so we can have a sense of being African." By staying firmly grounded in their parents' culture, whether Nigerian or Trinidadian, students had cultural and familial connections that provided various forms of support and encouragement. For these students, the movement between American context and the parents' home country did not cause conflict in their identity development before the students entered college. The goal was not to assimilate to American culture, but rather to ground an identity within the home culture of their parent(s). Consequently, this provided students with a strong sense of identity. At times, this strong identity created conflict with other second-generation Black Americans who, perhaps, did not have extended experiences in their parents' home country. During our initial conversation, Warren described one such conflict during the first weeks of class:

> I asked (a student) where he was from and he told me "I'm from (Mid-Atlantic State)." And I know, I can tell when I see an African person. And I said, "No, what's your country of origin?" And he said, "My parents are Nigerian. I'm from here." I said, "If your parents are Nigerian, that means you're Nigerian too." If somebody asks you that question and you don't say your African or Nigerian, I mean, that doesn't happen to me. If someone asks me where I'm from, I'm from Nigeria. I'm from Africa.

Warren's identity appeared so embedded in his parents' home country that he did not value the potential of a bicultural perspective. Elijah discussed the importance of maintaining a solid connection to his Nigerian background, although it was not rooted as firmly as was Warren's connection. He defined his most influential role models as "Nigerians" because they were known for "being hard workers" and "very focused on education and doing well in education so you can get better things in life." Charles also described his "family that is based in the Caribbean" as instilling a "lot of pride and stuff ... like education and academic achievement." Further, unlike Warren and Elijah, Charles had extended family in the United States. "It was like a big house ... my mother, my grandmother, my aunt, my uncle.... Trinidad was represented in (Mid-Atlantic city)!"

These experiences counter neoclassical views on assimilation, which stress the need and desire for immigrants to merge with mainstream culture (Bennett & Lutz, 2009; Waters, 1994). It also indicates that the process of segmented acculturation is initiated foremost by maintaining the values of the parents' cultural norms. The national origin identity was encouraged and stressed to second-generation Americans by their immigrant parents. For these second-generation Black Americans, memories of the complex formation of identity were centered exclusively on their parents' heritage. The centrality of their national origin identity among these students while growing up is evident as they discussed their upbringing. For the students in this study, initial grounding in culture, via visits to the home country and promotion of family role models, did not come at the expense of moving away from another identity, but rather focused on their pride in their home culture. For Warren, his identity was so strong that he was genuinely surprised how anyone would voluntarily move away from, in this case, a Nigerian identity. The degree to which parents maintained control of contexts experienced by their children also helped heighten particular identities, reducing potential conflicts. However, as experiences in contexts shift, it appeared that identity development became a more complex process.

Contextual Influence on Identity Development

All three young men discussed moving frequently during their youth, as least three times, with Charles recalling five moves since middle school. Each student moved from an urban area to a suburban neighborhood. They discussed proximity to better social institutions—specifically schools, churches, and community centers—as reasons for relocation. Students also noted how the neighborhoods were less "diverse" than previous contexts and this stimulated different experiences. For Elijah, taking Advanced Placement courses placed him in classes that were "really not diverse anymore." He continued:

> Usually I would be the one Black kid or one out of two or something in most of my higher level classes.… I don't think I really paid attention to the isolation in that setting. More of the isolation from my … from our race of Black Americans and so I think that really bothered me.

Elijah's observations on and feelings about the structural influences that shaped this academic context and the low number of Black Americans in advanced courses, sharply contrasted with the positive, family-centered influence on identity. Similarly, Charles discussed this shocking contrast in describing the first time he was affected by racism during a science and math summer camp in a predominately White neighborhood where he perceived being constantly marginalized because of his race. In discussing this encounter he noted:, "That was the first time I ever encountered anybody who was racist…that's the only experience that I had to deal with … I had heard about it and I knew that there were racist people out there … I know that, but I hadn't encountered it full on."

The influence on Black identity development of encountering racism and observing institutional inequalities is well-developed in psychosocial literature (Cross 1995; Cross, Parham, & Helms, 1991; Phinney, 1996; Sellers, Smith, Shelton, Rowley, & Chavous, 1998). These experiences trigger an internal process of identity that heightens racial sensitivity and influences salience and regard for one's racial membership. Typically, adolescents rely on mediators to help them navigate these experiences and the self-reflection they generate. Based on the experiences of students in this study, a stark difference among second-generation Black Americans appears to be that their parents, not having lifelong experiences with racism in the United States, are less able to serve as sources of support. For example, when Elijah discussed dealing with perceptions of racism at school with his parents, he stated:

> I would talk with them every once in awhile when it really bothered me and they would just … I guessed they never experienced it since they have always been in their own Nigerian culture. So, they never really had problems with that so they would tell me to ignore it or whatever … and that it really didn't matter. But they really didn't give me great advice.

The difference in cultural experiences between immigrants and their American born children may serve to encourage second-generation Black Americans away from an exclusive identity rooted in the national origin of their parents and toward acknowledging and valuing an American, specifically Black American, identity. Even for Warren, extended experience in an American context encouraged a process of reflection. "I mean, I know I'm Black American.… Yeah, I would say my (American identity) has grown stronger." As opposed to a separate perspective of identity, these students recognized that while their parents' immigrant background provided valuable connections to another country, they cannot minimize the effects of growing up as a Black person in the United States. As students develop a bicultural identity, one that acknowledges both cultural experiences, they began to seek supportive environments not accessible through their parents. For many, the college context, specifically the Black American subculture, became a valuable source of support for combating the racialized microaggressions experienced in White dominant social structures.

Emerging Development of a Bicultural Perspective

As students reflected on their emerging bicultural development, they also referenced the tensions that developed with their parents. Warren talked about how his parents stressed, as he got older, that they "never want us to try to do what all the Americans do. They don't want us to get cornrows or tattoos. They probably would get really mad if we did something like that." Elijah discussed negative perceptions he felt his parents had for Black American communities, highlighting a conversation with his mother as he discussed potentially attending an HCBU near home, "my mom was saying ... if it's run by Black people it probably won't be as good as other institutions." Elijah would later admit that this perspective by his mother influenced his decision to consider the HBCU. Both Elijah and Warren stated that, as they began to exhibit sociocultural behaviors connected to Black American culture, their parents seemed to resist this development. However, as opposed to countering by highlighting positive aspects of their native heritage, Elijah and Warren described pronouncements of negative views of Black American culture. This became accentuated during breaks, as Warren stated, "(my mother) says I'm too Americanized ... (other) Black Americans are (influencing) me. I was just like, whatever. I don't care." For Elijah, these tensions became particularly stressful during the winter break:

> My mom has actually said some funny things like because I started buying a lot of my own stuff like when I go out on weekends ... umm, that I look more like a hoodlum or whatever when I come home.... I didn't really correct her, I just told her that my style has always been this way I just never really had access to get it myself or whatever.

As Warren and Elijah engaged with other Black Americans, particularly males, they received negative feedback from their parents. However, because of the similarity of experiences with other Black Americans, particularly the gendered stereotypes they perceived were assigned to them by others, they sought to mesh with the styles of Black American culture. This suggests that peer support, particularly among Black American male college students, is critical for combating internalized racism and stereotypes (Fries-Britt & Griffin, 2007; Harper 2006). It is interesting that, while a student organization for Nigerian students was present on this particular campus, neither Warren nor

Elijah discussed interacting with this organization or other Nigerian students (although they discussed informal interactions with other second-generation Black Americans).

In contrast to the experiences of Elijah and Warren, Charles stated that he faced no tension from his mother as he fully embraced his Black American identity while remaining equally proud of his Trinidadian roots.

> I didn't feel like there is any tension and I love being Black American ... I think, to me it's like the best race to be ... that's just because I've lived it ... I feel like we are so much more free than the other races in that we came from you know...from being really low. You know what I'm saying? That's the only thing you can do, there is no more falling now. There's no more resting ... it's just shining now ... from now on into the future so ... to me it's the best place to be, you can't fall anywhere.

Charles stated that he never recalled his mother discouraging him from embracing this aspect of his identity. However, he did recall his mother continuing to take him to Caribbean cultural events in the area, presumably to maintain connection to their roots. This positive relationship with Black American identity was further exemplified by his dismissal of stereotypical portrayals of Black American males. "People look at the average Black guy...(they will say) one out of 10 Black men sell drugs, but they don't tell you nine out of 10 Black men don't sale drugs. They don' promote the better aspects of the Black male." He continued, "To me if you know how they say (President) Barack (Obama) acts like a White person 'cause he talks that way, I don't see that, I see him as a Black man." de Anda (1984) referred to bicultural models as individuals whose behavior "serves as a pattern to emulate in order to develop a behavioral repertoire..." (p. 104). While not in Charles' immediate environment, the visibility of a well-educated Black American male served as a key source for developing positive concepts about various aspects of his identity.

Implications for Practice at HBCUs

While this study examined the bicultural experiences of second-generation Black American males who attended a PWI, general implications for practice can be connected to policy development and administrative practices at HBCUs. Foremost, it is critical that Black males not be lumped into a broad category when developing programs and policies geared toward addressing disparities in access, persistence, and completion. As several studies indicate, immigrant background is an important variable to consider when disaggregating outcome data (Bennett & Lutz, 2009; Massey, Mooney, Torres, & Charles, 2007). However, second-generation status is often overlooked because researchers focus on comparisons between Black immigrant students and native-born Black Americans (i.e., Black American students who have had family roots in the United States for multiple generations). As this study has shown, the unique experiences of second-generation Black American males have potential implications for educational outcomes as these students struggle with identity development within various contexts.

Disaggregation of data is particularly important for research on HBCUs because this may provide administrators with some critical insight regarding gender disparities among students attending these institutions. Unfortunately, national data sets often overlook the diversity among Black students, severely limiting intragroup comparisons. While disaggregation of Black students at PWIs may produce subpopulations too small for statistical comparisons, the large Black student populations enrolled at HBCUs almost require a disaggregation for detailed investigation of student experiences. As we see from this small study, second-generation Black American males will enter HBCUs with past experiences that are very different from those of native-born Black American males. The degree to which these past experiences negatively or positively influence academic and social involvement within the HBCU context is an important question to consider, particularly as immigrant populations increase.

Examining the unique experiences of second-generation Black American males also provides a contradiction in viewing Black immigrants and their children as a "model minority," a popular perspective emanating from comments such as those of Henry Louis Gates who stated "We need to learn what the immigrants' kids have so we can bottle it and sell it, because many members of the Black American community, particularly among the chronically poor, have lost that sense of purpose and values, which produced our generation" (cited in Rimer & Arenson, 2004, para. 30). This serves to paint a broad negative characterization of Black Americans from economically disadvantaged communities and, as we see with the experiences of students in this study, falsely suggests that the children of Black immigrants have modest challenges related to their ethnicity. Even if one were to suggest that second-generation Black Americans are successfully overcoming major challenges and obstacles, characterizing their resilience as something that can be generally "bottled-up and sold" seems simplistic given the other variables which influence successful educational outcomes among this group (i.e., why and when parents immigrated to the United States; socioeconomic position of parents; proximity of family to mainstream institutional anchors, to name a few).

For HBCUs, avoiding this type of monolithic treatment of Black immigrants and second-generation Black Americans is important given the influence of institutional environments on identity development. If the unique challenges for these populations are not acknowledged and addressed in meaningful ways, students may feel marginalized by the dominant culture within the HBCU. Further, because second-generation Black American status may be a "hidden" form of identity, students may feel the need to reduce this dimension of difference to fit within the cultural norms; for example, by Americanizing their names. For the student, bicultural development may be stunted as students feel they have to choose their "American" identity over their "African–Caribbean" identity. From an institutional perspective, this reductionism limits the opportunity to honor and celebrate the diversity within the Black Diaspora. As Black America becomes diversified based on socioeconomic background, sexuality, and immigrant status, HBCUs must maintain a position of inclusiveness rather than exclusiveness.

It is understood that internalized racial and gendered stereotypes influence the identity development of all young Black males, so particular attention should be paid to the institutional and social structures that support such stereotypes. While schools have little control over the portrayal of Black males in popular culture and media that reinforce longstanding labels, they are able to pay attention to sociocultural influences within the institution that reinforce such labels. The Harper and Harris (2010) volume provided a comprehensive portrait of how notions of hegemonic masculinity influence educational aspirations for Black males. Among the ways to counterbalance traditional notions of gender are role models that provide contrary evidence and alternative notions of masculinity. This is particularly valuable for second-generation Black American males who may not have immediate access to Black American male role models. While male immigrant family members are a source of support, findings from the students in this study suggest that advice from their family is limited when addressing experiences related to their race and gender within the American context. Certainly, to *be* a Black male in the United States provides some perspective, but immigrant family members did not *grow up* as Black males, and that, it appears, is a unique experience that is difficult to understand.

Given that HBCU campuses tend to include a critical mass of Black male faculty, administrators, and staff, this environment may be particularly supportive to second-generation Black American males. For students coming from White-dominant high schools, the HBCU may be their first extended experience within a majority Black American context. As observed in this study, some second-generation Black American males may arrive with particular stereotypes of Black American culture developed through structural observations or mainstream media propaganda. This is especially evident for Black American male stereotypes which stress hypermasculinity through promotion of competition and domination. It is important that programs and policies emphasize mentorship opportunities—peer mentoring as well as faculty–student mentoring—to combat these larger structural influences. In particular, second-generation Black American males may benefit from connection with other children of Black immigrants to support the process of bicultural development rather than general mentoring programs that focus just on gender and do not incorporate other forms of identity.

Conclusion and Recommendations for Future Studies

For Black Americans coming out of the shadow of slavery, the beginning of the 20th century would present the struggle between self-conception as a person of African descent and American birth, "One ever feels his two-ness,—an American, a Negro; two souls, two thoughts, two unreconciled strivings; two warring ideals in one dark body, whose dogged strength alone keeps it from being torn asunder" (DuBois, 1905, p. 194). Over 100 years later, while DuBois' notion of a double-consciousness for Black Americans remains relevant, one may argue that rather than being "torn asunder" there is opportunity for cultural congruency. The experiences of second-generation Black Americans, who were born in the United States and the offspring of immigrant parents, reveal the complexity of the bicultural development process. For second-generation Black American males, the path toward healthy self-concepts of racial identity is further complicated by the specific gendered stereotypes present in the persistent racism in the United States. One may look no further than to the ways in which racist movements attempt to negatively cast the most visible second-generation Black American male, President Barack Obama as being too "Black," not being "Black enough," or not being a legitimate citizen.

For the Black American males interviewed in this study, while the roots of identity development were firmly planted in the native country of their parents—via frequent trips to Nigeria or Trinidad—experiences in American contexts sent signals to these students that their experiences would not be similar to those of their parents. They sought cultural role models outside their family to combat racist, and stereotyping experiences. In the case of two students, their immigrant parents attempted to counter this development. Perhaps this was out of fear of their children rejecting the parents' native culture or concern about the consequences of a Black American male status in a society that ignores the evidence of systematic inequality for this population. Eventually, the male students in this study found support via peers and cultural role models with similar backgrounds, stimulating a healthy bicultural perspective.

Of course this study is limited because it reflects the experiences of students who made it to postsecondary education. There are many second-generation Black males who, damaged by unequal opportunities or lack of access to cultural mediators and role models, do not persist through the educational pipeline. This is reflective of gender disparities among all generations of Blacks in the United States—immigrants, second-generation, and multigenerational (Massey et al., 2007). As future research continues to address this issue, scholars and practitioners must continue to pay attention to multiple aspects of Black male characteristics, including generation status. Additionally, this chapter reviewed the experiences of second-generation Black American males whose parents migrated from two countries—Ghana and Trinidad. Even within these three experiences, there was evidence of differentiated experiences. Future research should consider comparing experiences of children whose parents are from other countries. Finally, closer attention should be paid to the influence of institutional type, most notably HBCUs.

This study used experiences of students who attended PWIs to discuss bicultural development and suggested potential implications for HBCUs, but future studies should be developed to capture the experiences of second-generation Black American male students attending HBCUs. While researchers often consider the diversity that exists among Black students attending PWIs, the heterogeneity of Black students attending HBCUs is rarely considered. This examination is especially critical as we consider the decline of Black male students in higher education. The degree to which researchers can investigate, in-depth, the experiences of Black males from multiple backgrounds has severe implications for proactively addressing this important issue.

References

Arthur, J. A. (2008). *The African diaspora in the United States and Europe: The Ghanaian experience.* Burlington, VT.: Ashgate

Awad G. H. (2007). The role of racial identity, academic self-concept, and self-esteem in the prediction of academic outcomes for African American students. *Journal of Black Psychology, 33,* 188–207.

Bennett, P. R., & Lutz, A. (2009). How African American is the net Black advantage? Differences in college attendance among immigrant Blacks, native Blacks, and Whites. *Sociology of Education, 82,* 70–100.

Brown, M. C. (1997). Revising nigrescence theory: Racial identity development among students attending historically Black institutions. *Journal of the Pennsylvania Black Conference on Higher Education.* Retrieved from http://eric.ed.gov/ERICDocs/data/ericdocs2sql/content_storage_01/0000019b/80 15/8a/2 c.pdf

Carter, P. L. (2006). Straddling boundaries: Identity, culture, and school. *Sociology of Education, 79,* 304–328.

Carter, P. L. (2010). Race and cultural flexibility among students in different multiracial schools. *Teachers College Record, 112*(6), 1529–1574

Chacko, E. (2003). Identity and assimilation among young Ethiopian immigrants in metropolitan Washington. *Geographical Review, 93*(4), 491–506.

Chisholm, S. (1982). U.S. Policy and Black refugees. *Issue: A Journal of Opinion, 12*(1), 22–24.

Craythorne, J. (2006). *Assimilating to Black America: How the identity choices of Haitian immigrant and Haitian-American students are impacted by racial and economic segregation* (Unpublished doctoral dissertation). University of Florida.

Cross, W. (1995). The psychology of nigrescence: Revisiting the Cross model. In J. Pontero, J. Casas. L. Suzuki, & C. Alexander (Eds.), *Handbook of multicultural counseling* (pp. 93–122). Thousand Oaks, CA: Sage.

Cross, W. E., Parham, T., & Helms, J. (1991). The stages of Black identity development: Nigrescence models. In R. Jones (Ed.), *Black psychology* (pp. 319–338). Berkeley, CA: Cobb & Henry.

Cuyjet, M. (Ed.). (2006). *African American men in college.* San Francisco, CA: Jossey-Bass.

Daniels, R., & Graham, O. L. (2001), *Debating American immigration 1882–present.* Lanham, MD: Rowman & Littlefield.

de Anda (1984). Bicultural socialization: Factors affecting the minority experience. *Social Work, 29*(2) 101—107.

Dubois W. E. B. (1905). *The souls of Black folks.* Chicago, IL: McClurg.

Fordham, S., & Ogbu, J. (1986). Black students' school success: Coping with the burden of "acting white." *The Urban Review, 18*(3), 176–206

Fries-Britt, S. L., & Griffin, K. A. (2007). The Black box: How high-achieving Blacks resist stereotypes about Black Americans. *Journal of College Student Development, 48*(5), 509–524.

Fries-Britt, S., & Turner, B. (2002). Uneven stories: Successful Black collegians at a Black and a White campus. *Review of Higher Education, 25*(3), 315–330.

Harper, S. R. (2006). Peer support for African American male college achievement: Beyond internalized racism and the burden of "acting white." *Journal of Men's Studies, 14*(3), 337–358.

Harper, S. R., & Harris, F. (Eds.). (2010). *College men and masculinities: Theory, research and implications for practice.* San Francisco, CA: Jossey-Bass.

Hirschman, C. (2006). *The impact of immigration on American society: Looking backward to the future.* New York: Social Science Research Council.

hooks, B. (2004). *The will to change: Men, masculinity, and love.* New York: Atria Books.

Jackson, J. J., & Moore, J. (2008). Introduction: The African American male crisis in education: A popular media infatuation or needed public policy response. *American Behavioral Scientist, 51,* 847–853.

Jung, M-K. (2009). The racial unconscious of assimilation theory. *DuBois Review, 6*(2), 375–395.

Kennedy, E. M. (1981). Refugee Act of 1980. *International Migration Review, 15*(1), 141–156.

Kent, M. M. (2007). Immigration and America's black population. *Population Bulletin, 62*(4), 1–16.

Massey, D. S., Mooney, M., Torres, K. C., & Charles, C. Z. (2007). Black immigrants and Black natives attending selective colleges and universities in the United States. *American Journal of Education, 113,* 243–271.

Murata, K. (2006). Searching for a framework for a synthetic understanding of post-1965 immigration from the Western Hemisphere. *Transforming Anthropology, 14*(1), 95–101.

Obama, B. (2004). *Dreams from my father.* New York: Three Rivers Press.

Ogbu, J. U. (2003). *Black American students in an affluent suburb: A study of academic disengagement.* Mahwah, NJ: Erlbaum.

Ortiz, A. M., & Santos, S. J. (2009). *Ethnicity in college: Advancing theory and improving diversity practices on campus.* Sterling, VA: Stylus.

Patton, L.D. (2011). Perspectives on identity, disclosure, and the campus environment among African American gay and bisexual men at one historically Black college. *Journal of College Student Development, 52*(1), 77–100.

Phinney, J. S. (1996). Understanding ethnic diversity: The role of ethnic identity. *American Behavioral Scientist, 40,* 143–152.

Phinney, J. S., & Devich-Navarro, M. (1997). Variations in bicultural identification among African American and Mexican American adolescents. *Journal of Research on Adolescence, 7,* 3–32.

Phinney J. S, Horenczyk, G., Liebkind K., & Vedder P. (2001). Ethnic identity, immigration, and well-being: An interactional perspective. *Journal of Social Issues, 57,* 493–510

Pillay, Y. (2005). Racial identity as a predictor of the psychological health of African American students at a predominantly White university. *Journal of Black Psychology, 31*(1), 46–66.

Portes, A., & Zhou, M. (1993). The new second generation: Segmented assimilation and its variants. *Annals of the American Academy of Political and Social Science, 530,* 74–96.

Rimer, S., & Arenson, K.W. (2004, June 24). Top colleges take more Blacks, but which ones? *New York Times.* Retrieved from http://www.nytimes.com/2004/06/24/us/top-colleges-take-more-blacks-but-which-ones.html

Rong, X., & Brown, F. (2007). Educational attainment of immigrant and non-immigrant young Blacks. In X. Rong & F. Brown (Eds.), *Narrowing the achievement gap* (pp. 97–107). New York: Springer.

Rumbaut, R. G. (1995). The crucible within: Ethnic identity, self-esteem, and segmented assimilation among children of immigrants. *International Migration Review, 28,* 748–794.

Sakamoto, A. Woo, H., & Kim, C. (2010). Does an immigrant background ameliorate racial disadvantage? The socioeconomic attainments of second-generation African Americans. *Sociological Forum, 25,* 123–146.

Sellers, R. M., Smith, M. A., Shelton, J. N., Rowley, S. A. J., & Chavous, T. M. (1998). Multidimensional model of racial identity: A reconceptualization of African American racial identity. *Personality and Social Psychology Review, 2*, 18–39.

Smedley, B. D., Myers, H. F., & Harrell, S. P. (1993). Minority-status stresses and the college adjustment of ethnic minority freshmen. *Journal of Higher Education, 64*, 434–452.

Suarez-Orozco, C. (2004). Formulating identity in a globalized world. In M. M. Suirez-Orozco & D. B. Qin-Hilliard (Eds.), *Globalization: Culture and education in the new millennium* (pp. 173–202). Berkeley: University of California Press.

U.S. Department of State. (2011). *Immigrant number use for visa issuances and adjustments of status in the diversity immigrant category fiscal years 1995–2010.* Retrieved from http://travel.state.gov/pdf/MultiYearTableVII.pdf

Valentine, C. (1971). Deficit, difference and bicultural models. *Harvard Educational Review, 41*(2), 137–157.

Waters, M. C. (1994). The new second generation. *International Migration Review, 28*(4), 795–820.

Wei, M., Liao, K. Y-H., Chao, R. C., Mallinckrodt, B., Tsai, P.-C., & Botello-Zamarron, R. (2010). Minority stress, perceived bicultural competence, and depressive symptoms among ethnic minority college students. *Journal of Counseling Psychology, 57*(4), 411–422.

Wiley, S., & Deaux, K. (2010. The bicultural identity performance of immigrants. In A. E. Azzi, X. Chryssochoou, B. Klandermans, & B. Simmon (Eds.), *Identity and participation in culturally diverse societies* (pp. 49–68). Hoboken, NJ: Wiley-Blackwell.

Yewah, E., & Togunde, D. (2010). *Across the Atlantic: African immigrants in the United States.* Champaign, IL: Common Ground Press.

Yosso, T. J. (2006). Whose culture has capital? A critical race theory discussion of community cultural wealth. *Race, Ethnicity and Education, 8*(1), 69–91.

Zhou, M. (1997). Segmented assimilation: Issues, controversies, and recent research on the new second generation. *International Migration Review, 31*(4), 975–1008.

8

STANDING AT THE INTERSECTION

Black Male Millennial College Students

Fred A. Bonner, II

> The images of Black males as presented by the media, popular culture, and social science omit three vitally important considerations: the role of ordinary Black men, the continuing impact of racism, and a clear explanation of the steps involved for a Black male to become successful in American society.
>
> *(White & Cones, 1999, p. 79)*

Introduction

The above quote speaks to the ongoing challenges that Black males have endured related to the multiple and competing images society has assigned to them. Just recently, I sat in the audience at the American Association for Blacks in Higher Education (AABHE) annual meeting and listened to the acceptance speech given by the AABHE Lifetime Achievement Award recipient Norman Francis, President of Xavier University of Louisiana. Francis' clarion call extolled what he said should be one of the most critically important goals of the organization; namely, the development and dissemination of transformative research that would contribute to the status of Black participation in postsecondary education. Perhaps one of the best points of departure on the journey to address Francis's call is to focus on a population that all too often finds itself the staccato rhythm in an otherwise placid tune—the Black male.

It is at the intersection of numerous vectors that the Black male collegian attempts to work out his identity development (Bonner & Bailey, 2006; Bridges, 2010; Spurgeon, 2009; Spurgeon & Myers, 2010; Warde, 2008). This chapter theorizes how race, gender, and education attainment are influenced by generational status; namely, how the moniker *Millennial* is applied and misapplied to this particular cohort in historically Black college and university (HBCU) contexts. Ultimately, this chapter seeks to underscore how HBCUs can better meet the needs of Black male Millennials. An overview of the impact that the P-16 context has on Black males is followed by a review of Millennial culture in general and Black male Millennial culture in particular. To conclude, recommendations are offered for future research and practice.

Navigating the P-16 Terrain

A focus on the Black male, particularly as a subject of scholarly investigation parallels the title of Paula Gidding's book *When and Where I Enter*. The complexities associated with the experiences of this cohort constitute a congeries of intersections and vectors, parallel lines and sharp angles that all meld into the assigned label—Black male experience. Contextualizing the experience in education gives way to discussion across the educational continuum. Contemporary language speaks to the need of creating a more seamless experience across elementary, secondary, and postsecondary settings (Farmer-Hinton & Adams, 2006; Muhammad, Smith, & Duncan, 2008; Smith & Zhang, 2009). In 2006, Bonner and Bailey stated, "Like its K-12 predecessor, higher education too has presented a major stumbling block for many [Black] males" (p. 25). Hence, the language du jour around these issues includes rhetoric that embraces a P-16 view of how education should function.

For Black males, schooling experiences early in their academic careers do not significantly differ from later-life engagements. Said differently, the maladies experienced in P-12 quite often parallel what happens in academe—albeit codified differently. For example, the lack of support regarding these students' participation in advanced courses in high school mirrors the lack of mentoring and guidance they receive when seeking to participate in challenging majors (e.g., science, technology, engineering, and mathematics [STEM]; Babco, 2001; Chubin, 2002; Chubin & Babco, 2003; Green & Glasson, 2009; Hrabowski & Maton, 2009). Also, being the lone voice in secondary school courses or the sole representative in collegiate contexts too presents formidable challenges. Numerous other challenges are worthy of articulation, some of the most critical are cited in the following sections.

P-12 Challenges Impacting Success

Data on the number of Black males who graduate from our nation's secondary schools is sobering. *Yes We Can: The Schott 50 State Report on Public Education and Black Males* (2010) reports that less than 47% of Black males graduate from high school. Additionally, although data reveal that there had been a significant increase in the numbers of Blacks taking the Advanced Placement (AP) examination—they had the lowest mean scores among all racial groups (National

Center for Education Statistics [NCES], 2010). A host of factors have been advanced as contributing to the lack of success this cohort has experienced in P-12 contexts (Bonner & Hughes, 2007; Bonner, Jennings, Marbley, & Brown, 2008; Kunjufu, 2005a, 2005b; Noguera, 2003). A few of these factors include *cool pose, disidentification,* and *stereotype threat.* Each of these terms conveys a profound meaning when contextualizing the schooling experiences of Black males. Cool pose, according to White and Cones (1999),

> is a form of self-presentation designed to show others that the person is on top of things, that everything is under control. It is an assertion of masculinity that enhances pride, dignity, and a sense of personal power in a society that offers African American males a limited range of options.
>
> *(p. 91)*

What cool pose offers Black males in the P-12 setting is a set of actions, behaviors, identities, and strategies that set them apart as Black males. In essence, these young men are able to establish some sense of agency by using cultural expressions that are unique to their own sense of style and are fashioned within their own communities. A key aspect in understanding cool pose is that as a "coping mechanism, cool pose can be adaptive or maladaptive" (White & Cones, 1999, p. 93). Thus, in P-12, cool pose can be used to positively enhance self-esteem and pride among these students who often suffer the travails of interfacing with institutions that are at best lukewarm and at worst cold in their treatment of them. However, cool pose can take a negative turn if it is used to reinforce counterproductive Black male subcultures—particularly those emphasizing anti-intellectualism and crime (Hall & Pizarro, 2010; hooks, 2004; White & Cones, 1999).

Another challenge many Black males experience in elementary and secondary school is disidentification—referred to by Steele (1997, 1999) as academic disidentification. According to Griffin (2002),

> Academic *disidentification* occurs when students attempt to devalue the perceived importance of academic performance in an effort to protect their perceptions of self. In essence, this means that once academics is discounted as a relevant domain, then performance in academic endeavors will have little bearing on formation and maintenance of self-perceptions.
>
> *(para. 4)*

By embracing this notion of disidentification, Black males opt out of educational pursuits that would ultimately lead to their academic achievement. Many have been found to sabotage their own chances for success (Bonner, 2000; Ford, 2003, 2004). Fortunately, this process of disidentification has not gone unnoticed and is being addressed by ongoing and recent scholarship. One model in particular, the scholar identity model, posed by Whiting (2006, 2009) sheds light and offers great promise in redirecting efforts toward engaging these students in P-12 schools. Whiting's (2006) nine characteristics frame what he identifies as the scholar identity; namely, self-efficacy, future orientation, willingness to make sacrifices, internal locus of control, self-awareness, need for achievement (versus need for affiliation), academic self-confidence, racial identity, and masculinity. What this model and related discussions concerning disidentification must hold as central is the continued push to include rather than exclude Black males from conversations involving academic success.

It is the third challenge, stereotype threat, that has been cited for more than a decade as a significant piece of the education achievement puzzle. The work of Steele has perhaps been best known in the debate about the application of stereotype threat to educative situations involving Black males (Steele, 1992, 1997; Steele & Aronson, 1995). Stereotype threat is defined as being at risk of validating negative stereotypes about the group(s) to which one belongs (Steele & Aronson, 1995). Additionally, Aronson, Fried, and Good (2002) report that,

> Stereotype threat appears to undermine academic achievement primarily in two ways. First in the short run, it can impair performance by inducing anxiety.... The second way stereotype threat appears to undermine achievement is through "disidentification," the psychological disengagement from achievement hypothesized to help students cope with stereotype threat and underperformance in a given domain.

(p.114)

To combat the nefarious implications of stereotype threat among Black males in schools, it is critical that these enclaves examine "the possibility that the academic performance of Black males can be improved by devising strategies that counter effects of harmful environmental and cultural forces" (Noguera, 2008, p. 19). Environmental settings and cultural mores and traditions that are embedded within school settings that depict and reinforce stereotypical notions about this group should be jettisoned. Safe and inclusive spaces must be created where these males can engage with schools that do not view their academic potential and racial identities as being at odds.

Postsecondary Issues Impacting Success

Black students and their experiences in academe have been long chronicled in the higher education literature. In her landmark work *Blacks in College* (1984), published almost three decades ago, Jacqueline Fleming provided an empirical investigation of this population's experiences in both predominantly Black and traditionally White postsecondary contexts. In more contemporary research, several authors too have taken on the mantle of providing insight as to what it means to be Black and collegian in these two contexts (Allen, Epps, & Hanniff, 1991; Bonner, 2001; Brower & Ketterhagen, 2004; Fleming, 1984; Griffin, Jayakumar, Jones, & Allen, 2010; Negga, Applewhite, & Livingstone, 2007;

Palmer & Gasman, 2008; Spurgeon, 2009). Similar to their P–12 predecessors, Black males in higher education encounter a number of factors that potentially serve to thwart their achievement and success. Taking a slightly different approach, it is the absence of key factors (i.e., mentoring, peer support, inclusive environments) in the postsecondary experience as opposed to the presence of key factors listed above in the elementary and secondary context that impede the academic development of Black males.

At all points across the education continuum mentors serve in important capacities for Black males. It is as crucial to engender expectations about success for the middle school student as it is for the collegiate freshman. However, it is in the higher education context that mentoring becomes increasingly tied not only to academic progression but also to future career behavior strategies (Brittian, Sy, & Stokes, 2009; Hughes & Howard-Hamilton, 2003). Mentoring is viewed as a complex relationship that supports career advancement, personal support, role modeling, and advocacy (Tillman, 2001). According to Bonner and Bailey (2006), who mainly speak of the role that faculty mentors play in the lives of Black college students, "it is the relationship that students develop with faculty that so often serves as the primary factor in their retention and success" (p. 39). Additionally, Sutton (2006) goes on to report that mentoring, specifically through mentoring programs, must include dimensions that extend beyond the classroom. Instructional programs alone will not suffice in combating the serious developmental challenges that loom on college and university campuses (Brittian et al., 2009; Fries-Britt, 1997, 2000; Grant & Simmons, 2008; LaVant, Anderson, & Tiggs, 1997; Patton, 2009; Strayhorn & Saddler, 2009). What is needed is mentoring that focuses on all facets of development—cognitive, social, and psychosocial, even physical.

Not to be underestimated in the postsecondary milieu of factors that contribute to the success of Black males is the role of the peer group. It was Astin (1993) who posited, "The single most powerful source of influence on the undergraduate student's academic and personal development is the peer group … the amount of interaction among peers has far-reaching effects on nearly all areas of student learning and development" (p. 8). What the peer group provides to these males is a "safe space" in which they can assume a sense of comfort in knowing that their very identities are not being called into question. Bonner (2001), in speaking to the experiences of academically gifted Black males in postsecondary contexts, reported that these groups expose students to valuable achievement and socially oriented circles of like-minded peers that reify their future aspirations and goals.

Another factor that constitutes a challenge for many students is the campus environment (Strange & Banning, 2001). For the Black male on the predominantly White campus, negotiating varying campus contexts can be exhausting. Phillips's (2005) study that compared the perceptions of Black and White students participating in an equal opportunity program on a predominantly

White campus, revealed that the Black students reported the institutional environment to be *marginalizing*. In addition, Bonner and Bailey (2006) report that "[Black] students often struggle to develop coping strategies to fit in and succeed in PWIs, due to the lack of successful matching between their background experiences and the collegiate context" (p. 37). Thus, for collegiate environments to be growth producing, they must be attentive and willing to meet the unique academic and social integration needs of these students. However, this process cannot be accomplished without a qualitative investigation in which the students' "authentic" voices can be heard and speak into existence the necessary and sufficient conditions that would lead to an optimal postsecondary environment.

Engaging the Historically Black College and University (HBCU) Context

The Black experience in higher education would be incomplete without reviewing these experiences in HBCUs. Approximately 103 of these institutions enroll approximately 14% of the Black students in U.S. higher education—this despite their representation of a mere 3% of the total pool of postsecondary institutions in the country. These enclaves, which were birthed in an American context that treated the education of Blacks, particularly at the postsecondary level, as anything but "separate and equal," continue to produce vast numbers of African American degree holders.

Although initially established in the North, most HBCUs today are located in the South. According to Hirt (2006), HBCUs represent an institutional type that emerged subsequent to the Civil War and offered to the millions of emancipated slaves some form of education that had heretofore been prohibited. Jennings, Bonner, Lewis, and Nave (2007) report:

> [Black] participation in higher education has been characterized as one of both struggle and triumph. From the earliest days of the HBCU, to the unique and complex institutions we see today, the Black college has left an indelible mark on the higher education landscape. In keeping with the goal of educating young [Black] collegians—many that would not otherwise be afforded the opportunity to obtain a higher education—the HBCU continues to make monumental strides.
>
> *(p. 87)*

Despite the monumental strides that HBCUs have made in providing education to the Black masses, they have not been immune to naysayers. Additionally, given the current climate of accountability in American higher education, the naysayers are often backed by those who too seek verisimilitude in claims regarding educational attainment. For example, LeMelle (2002) stated, "the dilemma surrounding the HBCU has traditionally been posed around three major questions: Should the HBCU even exist? What kind of education should it provide.... How should the HBCU relate to the dominant political, economic, and social environment that prevails in society?" (p. 190).

Regardless of the current debates regarding the relevance of HBCUs, these institutions continue to register impressive gains and play an important role among Black populations. Key is the statement made by Stewart, Wright, Perry, and Rankin (2008), who advance that students who attend HBCUs profit from their ability to not only connect with African American peers, but also with African American faculty. What will be key for these institutions as they attempt to maintain balance in an unbalanced economic and political national environment is to heed that suggestion advanced by Minor (2005), who asserted that the continued survival of the HBCU will be heavily dependent on a rejuvenated institutional commitment and newfound vision.

Millennials and Diversity in Academe

A majority of the college students occupying space in academe can be identified as Millennials. This moniker is a generational label that has been popularized in the book *Millennials Rising* completed by Neil Howe and William Strauss (2000). According to Howe and Strauss (2000), Millennials are individuals who were born after 1982—with an age cohort cap in and around the year 2002. What these generation researchers and other researchers (Bonner & Hughes, 2007; Bonner, Marbley, & Howard-Hamilton, 2011; Coomes & Debard, 2004; Debard, 2004; Howe & Strauss, 2000; Pew, 2010) of the same ilk have found is that those who fit within the parameters defining this generation share a number of key characteristics. Perhaps the most noted framework used to conceptualize the machinations of this group has been advanced by Howe and Strauss (2000); namely, they report that Millennials are:

1. Special—Because they have been told all their lives by their Baby Boomer parents that they are special, they tend to feel a sense of importance.
2. Sheltered—As the "Baby on Board" generation, they have grown up under the intense and watchful gaze of doting and often overly protective parents.
3. Confident—Highly optimistic, this generation has been rewarded for its behavior. Millennials have also been told consistently that they are extremely capable of achieving any goal they set their minds to.
4. Conventional—Accepting of social rules and order promoted by members of the Baby Boomer generation, they tend to be more conservative than many people realize.
5. Team-Oriented—The axiom, "We rise and fall together" is an apt description of this group's attitude toward collaboration and working together.
6. Achieving—Since they are no strangers to accountability standards and high-stakes testing, they tend to be very achievement-oriented and driven.

7. Pressured—Because they are achievement-oriented and their intellectual prowess has been affirmed consistently, they tend to feel pressured to perform at optimal levels at all times.

These seven characteristics advanced by Howe and Strauss (2000) have not gone unchallenged. Several scholars have contested the rigid adherence to these labels given the lack of diversity found in the norm reference group from which these labels emerged. Coomes and Debard (2004) noted that "the big picture seldom contains images of marginalized groups" (p.14). Additionally, Bonner and Hughes (2007), in the special edition of the *National Association of Student Affairs Professionals (NASAP) Journal,* lament the fact that recent higher education literature underscoring the experiences of Millennials has lacked a focus on issues such as culture, ethnicity, and race (Bonner, 2010). Finally Bonner, Marbley, and Howard–Hamilton's edited volume, *Diverse Millennials in College: Implications for Faculty and Student Affairs* (2011) will provide a more holistic picture of Millennials from backgrounds and cultural communities that have been undertheorized in discussions relating to this cohort.

Millennial Black Males in HBCUs

A number of parallel variables have to be held in steady state to fully understand the experience of the Black Millennial male. Using the seven characteristics above as a framework, each has to be problematized and treated individually as a totem of the Millennial experience in the HBCU context. Addressing these three variables concomitantly requires:

1. A focus on the Black male experience in P-16 education.
2. A focus on the alignment or misalignment of the Black male experience with the Howe and Strauss framework.
3. A focus on how both numbers 1 and 2 are embedded in the HBCU context.

Thus, the first characteristic, *Special,* adheres to the very mission of HBCUs. According to Stevenson (2007) and Abelman and Delessandro (2009), HBCUs were created to provide educational opportunities for Blacks, a unique and special population. However, a focus on the experiences of Black males in P-16 settings reveals that the majority of their engagements have made them feel anything but special (Bonner, 2001; Graves, 2010; Majors & Dewar, 2002; Milner, 2007; Monroe, 2005; Payne & Brown, 2010; Thomas, Coard, Stevenson, Bentley, & Zemel, 2009; Tucker, Dixon, & Griddine, 2010). Thus, this Millennial moniker in the HBCU environment becomes particularly important as these institutions seek to mend the broken pieces and cater to the holistic development of these young men.

The second characteristic, *Sheltered,* also serves as a source of contention when applied as a cynosure to depict the Millennial Black male experience.

According to Dilworth and Carter (as cited in Bonner & Hughes, 2007), Black males have not grown up in economically stable conditions nor did they feel sheltered from the harsh realities of life. So, the HBCUs for many of these students will provide them with their very first experiences of feeling protected and sheltered from looming crises. It will be imperative for the HBCUs to attend to these students' most basic needs. Using Bloom's taxonomy as a model, it is apparent that the need for safety must be addressed before high order needs can be experienced.

The third characteristic, *Confident,* is intimately connected to the Millennial Black males' self-esteem and self-perception. HBCUs are ideally situated to develop and foster the confidence of these men who have been made to feel less that confident in their engagements across the P-16 continuum. LeMelle (2002) posited, "The HBCU has now come full circle in fulfilling its mission—the production of highly competent black students who have no ambivalence about who they are and how they should use their skills and talents to maximize their own and their community's interests" (p. 20).

Conventional, the fourth characteristic identified in the framework, is represented by the responses uncovered in the studies conducted by the Pew Forum on Religion and Public Life, which reported that Black Millennials between the ages of 18 and 29 when asked about their belief in God and their belief in heaven responded affirmatively at 88% and 94% respectively. Additionally, older Black Millennials—those age 30 and above—responded affirmatively at 91% when asked about their belief in God. For the HBCUs, many of which are denominational institutions, capitalizing on the religious zeal exhibited by this cohort may serve as another way to engage them. Careful attention must be paid to those students who embrace more of a spiritual and less of a religious fervor—but in any case, intentional programming that speaks to these sensibilities is encouraged.

Characteristic five, *Team-oriented,* should not be a foreign concept to the Millennial Black male who is transitioning from the P-12 setting. Many of the activities that are structured in the elementary and secondary classroom are geared toward student-centered learning and collaboration. Although these experiences were provided in the earlier grades, it is important to assess how effectively they were utilized by these males. Were these collaborative and team-oriented opportunities designed to place them in groups that empowered and challenged their thought processes as well as encouraged critical thinking? Much as Spurgeon and Myers (2010) report, there is "the need for college campuses to develop effective programs that promote positive relationship development for [Black] males" (p. 539).

The sixth characteristic, *Achieving,* is not the typical descriptive term used to identify Black males. Noguera (as cited in Fashola, 2005) stated, "For [Black] males, who are more likely than any other group to be subjected to negative forms of treatment in school, the message is clear: Individuals of their race and gender may excel in sports, not in math or history" (p. 63). Thus, renarrating the experience of the Millennial Black male will be imperative. HBCUs are noted for their development of the potential of Black students; they can serve as a crucible that allows the Millennial Black male to test out multiple identities, with an academic and scholarly identity being one of the most critical.

The final characteristic, *Pressured*, speaks to the high-stakes testing environments and competing school forces that require the P-12 student to strive for success. Added pressures for the Millennial Black male come from forces that challenge both his gender and racial identity. Additionally, these males often find themselves in educational settings that do not support their academic success. Davis (2003) reported

> [Black] males need to be cared for and nurtured in responsive schools; that these schools and teachers need to be supported in meeting the needs of Black males; and that a critical component of support includes increasing the ability of school to contribute to Black males' social, cognitive, gender, and academic development.
>
> *(pp. 516–517)*

HBCUs with their mission of concern for the holistic development of the Millennial Black male are ideally situated to provide these individuals with viable ways to handle life pressures (Bonner, 2010).

Conclusion and Recommendations

This chapter underscores how race, gender, and education attainment are influenced by generational status. An active discussion of how the moniker *Millennial* is applied and misapplied to Black males in HBCUs serves as the organizing center for much of the discussion. Millennial Black males function at the intersection of a multitude of overlapping and competing forces that make their experiences both within and outside of the P-16 pipeline at times challenging. For higher education contexts, particularly HBCUs, a number of recommendations are offered to meet the learning, growth, and developmental needs of this generational cohort.

1. *Create opportunities for mentoring relationships to develop.* Although the HBCU environment offers a greater likelihood of exposure to Black administrators, faculty, and staff members, it is critically important to create opportunities for the Black Millennial male to interface with these individuals in meaningful engagements. Adopting a "because we are here ... they (students) will come" philosophy when it comes to these students seeking out mentoring relationships is at best problematic and at worst incorrect. Whether it is through planned programming initiatives at the department or college level, creating opportunities for these males to come into con–

tact with individuals who can facilitate their journey through the academy is important.

2. *Create opportunities for peer groups to develop and support each other.* Given what is said about the Millennial population and its affinity for its peer communities, it will become ever more important to connect with these cohorts in getting valuable information to them. This suggestion is not given to circumvent the important role that is played by mentors and those who serve as guides to these student groups; however, it is a reality that the majority of information that is being passed among these student enclaves is being done internally, so our role should include injecting the correct information into these circles.

3. *Create opportunities for learning communities to develop and flourish.* A spate of literature speaks to the benefit accrued by students who engage in learning communities. Bringing together a group of like-minded peers in a forum that promotes critical thinking and synergistic dialogue about matters of academic importance are some of the many highlights of these enclaves. What will be key in the HBCU environment is to bring these males together to not only discuss academic issues but matters of social and psychosocial importance as well.

4. *Create opportunities for the family to be involved.* Discussions about Millennials typically include attendant discussions about the close relationships this generational cohort maintains with family. HBCUs capitalize on being inclusive of family in the college-going experience; thus, creating programming that involves family with their Black Millennial male student will support them in their academic journey. Family should be involved in both academic and student affairs related experiences on campus.

5. *Create opportunities to train administrators, faculty, and staff on college student development theory.* The use of theory in understanding how college students learn, grow, and develop is too often overlooked. Creating programs and workshops that would provide key academic and student affairs administrators as well as faculty and staff with information on the student populations they serve would enhance the institutional context in immeasurable ways. The faculty member who understands the learning motivations or the staff member who is positioned to provide counsel to the Black male Millennial in crisis will only add in positive ways to the functioning of the institution.

References

Abelman, R., & Dalessandro, A. (2009). The institutional vision of historically Black colleges and universities. *Journal of Black Studies, 40*(2), 105–134.

Allen, W. R., Epps, E. G., & Haniff, N. Z. (Eds.). (1991). *College in Black and White: African American students in predominantly White and in historically Black public universities.* Albany, NY: SUNY Press.

Aronson, J., Fried, C., & Good, C. (2002). Reducing the effects of stereotype threat on African American college students by shaping theories of intelligence. *Journal of Experimental Social Psychology. 38,* 113–125.

Astin, A. W. (1993). What matters in college? *Liberal Education, 79*(4), 4–15.

Babco, E. L. (2001). *Under-represented minorities in engineering: A progress report.* Washington, DC: American Association for the Advancement of Science.

Bonner, F. A. (2000). African American giftedness. *Journal of Black Studies, 30*(5), 643–664.

Bonner, F. A. (2001). *Gifted African American male college students: A phenomenological study* (The National Research Center for the Gifted and Talented, RM01148). Storrs, CT: University of Connecticut.

Bonner, F. A. (2010). *Academically gifted African American males in college.* Santa Barbara, CA: ABC-CLIO.

Bonner, F. A., & Bailey, K. (2006). Assessing the academic climate for African American men. In M. Cuyjet (Ed.), *African American Men in College* (pp. 24–46). San Francisco, CA: Jossey-Bass.

Bonner, F. A., & Hughes, R. L. (Eds.). (2007). African American millennial college students [Special issue]. *National Association of Student Affairs Professionals Journal, 10*(1).

Bonner, F. A., Jennings, M. E., Marbley, A. F., & Brown, L. (2008). Capitalizing on leadership capacity: Gifted African American males in high school. *Roeper Review, 30*(2), 93–103.

Bonner, F. A., Marbley, A. F., & Howard-Hamilton, M. (2011). *Diverse millennials in college: Implications for faculty and student affairs.* Sterling, VA: Stylus.

Bridges, E. (2010). Racial identity development and psychological coping strategies of African American males at a predominantly White university. *Annals of the American Psychotherapy Association, 13*(1), 14–26.

Brittian, A. S., Sy, S. R., & Stokes, J. E. (2009). Mentoring: Implications for African American college students. *Western Journal of Black Studies, 33*(2), 87–97.

Brower, A. M., & Ketterhagen, A. (2004). Is there an inherent mismatch between how Black and White students expect to succeed in college and what their colleges expect from them? *Journal of Social Issues, 60*(1), 95–116.

Chubin, D. E. (2002). The competition for talent [letter]. *Science, 295,* 972–973.

Chubin, D. E., & Babco, E. L. (2003). *"Walking the talk" in retention-to-graduation: Institutional production of minority engineers—A NACME Analysis.* White Plains, NY: NACME.

Coomes, M.D., & DeBard, R. (2004). A generational approach to understanding students. In M. D. Coomes & R. DeBard (Eds.), *Serving the millennial generation* (New Directions in Student Services, No. 106, pp. 5–16). San Francisco, CA: Jossey-Bass.

Davis, J. E. (2003). Early schooling and the achievement of African American males. *Urban Education, 38,* 515–537.

DeBard, R. (2004). Millennials characteristics coming to college. In M. D. DeBard & R. DeBard (Eds.), *Serving the millennial generation* (New Directions in Student Services, No. 106, pp. 33–45). San Francisco, CA: Jossey-Bass.

Farmer-Hinton, R. L., & Adams, T. L. (2006). Social capital and college preparation: Exploring the role of counselors in a college prep school for Black students. *Negro Educational Review, 57*(1/2), 101–116.

Fashola, O. S. (2005). *Educating African American males: Voices from the field.* Thousand Oaks, CA: Corwin.

Fleming, J. (1984). *Blacks in college* (Higher Education series). San Francisco, CA: Jossey-Bass.

Ford, D. Y. (2003). Two other wrongs don't make a right: Sacrificing the needs of diverse students does not solve gifted education's unresolved problems. *Journal for the Education of the Gifted, 26,* 283–291.

Ford, D. Y. (2004) A challenge for culturally diverse families of gifted children: Forced choices between affiliation or achievement. *Gifted Child Today, 27,* 26–29.

Fries-Britt, S. L. (1997). Identifying and supporting gifted African American men. In M. J. Cuyjet Associates (Ed.), *Helping African American men succeed in college* (New Directions for Student Services, No. 80, pp. 65–78). San Francisco, CA: Jossey-Bass.

Fries-Britt, S. L. (2000). Identity development of high-ability Black collegians. In M. B. Baxter Magolda (Ed.), *Teaching to promote intellectual and personal maturity: Incorporating students' worldviews and identities into the learning process* (New Directions for Teaching and Learning, No. 82, pp. 55–65). San Francisco, CA: Jossey-Bass.

Grant, C. M., & Simmons, J. (2008). Narratives on experiences of African-American women in the academy: Conceptualizing effective mentoring relationships of doctoral student and faculty. *International Journal of Qualitative Studies in Education (QSE)*, *21*(5), 501–517.

Graves, S. (2010). Are we neglecting African American males: Parental involvement differences Between African American males and females during elementary school? *Journal of African American Studies*, *14*(2), 263–276.

Green, A., & Glasson, G. (2009). African Americans majoring in science at predominantly White universities (A review of the literature). *College Student Journal*, *43*(2), 366–374.

Griffin, B. W. (2002). Academic disidentification, race, and fight school dropouts. *High School Journal*, *85*(4), 71–81.

Griffin, K. A., Jayakumar, U. M., Jones, M. M., & Allen, W. R. (2010). Ebony in the Ivory Tower: Examining trends in the socioeconomic status, achievement, and self-concept of Black, male freshmen. *Equity & Excellence in Education*, *43*(2), 232–248.

Hall, R. E., & Pizarro, J. M. (2010). Unemployment as conduit of Black self-hate: Pathogenic rates of Black male homicide via legacy of the Antebellum. *Journal of Black Studies*, *40*(4), 653–665.

Hirt, J. B. (2006). *Where you work matters: Student affairs administration at different types of institutions.* Washington, DC: American College Personnel Association.

hooks, b. (2004). *We real cool: Black men and masculinity.* New York, NY: Routledge.

Howe, N., & Strauss, W. (2000). *Millennials rising: The next great generation.* New York: Random House.

Hrabowski, F. A., & Maton, K. I. (2009). Change institutional culture, and you change who goes into science. *Academe*, *95*(3), 11–15.

Hughes, R. L., & Howard-Hamilton, M. F. (2003). Insights: Emphasizing issues that affect African American women. In M. F. Howard-Hamilton (Ed.), *Meeting the needs of African American women* (New Directions for Student Services, No. 104, pp. 95–104). San Francisco, CA: Jossey-Bass.

Jennings, M., Bonner, F. A., Lewis, C. W., & Nave, F. M. (2007). The historically Black colleges and university: A question of relevance for the African American millennial college student. *National Association of Student Affairs Professionals Journal*, *10*(1), 85–96.

Kunjufu, J. (2005a). *Hip hop street curriculum.* Chicago, IL: African American Images.

Kunjufu, J. (2005b). *Keeping Black boys out of special education.* Chicago, IL: African American Images.

Lavant, B. D., Anderson, J., & Tiggs, J. W. (1997). Retaining African American men through mentoring initiatives. In M. J., Cuyjet (Ed.), *Helping African American men succeed in college* (New Directions for Student Services, No. 80, pp. 43–52). San Francisco, CA: Jossey-Bass.

LeMelle, T. J. (2002). The HBCU: Yesterday, today, and tomorrow. *Education*, *123*(1), 190–196.

Majors, R., & Dewar, S. (2002). Mantra rites of passage: Teaching and nurturing our boys to be men in the 21st century. *Education Review*, *16*(1), 80–85.

Milner, H., IV. (2007). African American males in urban schools: No excuses—Teach and empower. *Theory into Practice*, *46*(3), 239–246.

Minor, J. T. (2005). Discerning facts about faculty governance at HBCUs. *Academe*, *91*, 34–38.

Monroe, C. R. (2005). Why are "bad boys" always Black? *Clearing House*, *79*(1), 45–50.

Muhammad, C., Smith, M. J., & Duncan, G. (2008). College choice and college experiences: Intersections of race and gender along the secondary to post-secondary education continuum. *Negro Educational Review*, *59*(3/4), 141–146.

National Center for Education Statistics (NCES). (2010). *Status and trends in the education of racial and ethnic minorities.* Washington, DC: Author.

Negga, F., Applewhite, S., & Livingston, I. (2007). African American college students and stress:

School racial composition, self-esteem and social support. *College Student Journal, 41*(4), 823–830.

Noguera, P. (2003). *City schools and the American dream: Reclaiming the promise of public education.* New York, NY: Teachers College.

Noguera, P. A. (2008). *The trouble with Black boys and other reflections on race, equity and the future of public Education.* San Francisco, CA: Jossey-Bass.

Palmer, R. T., & Gasman, M. (2008). "It takes a village to raise a child": The role of social capital in promoting academic success of African American men at a Black college. *Journal of College Student Development, 49*(1), 52–70.

Patton, L. D. (2009). My sister's keeper: A qualitative examination of mentoring experiences among African American women in graduate and professional schools. *Journal of Higher Education, 80*(5), 510–537.

Payne, Y., & Brown, T. M. (2010). The educational experiences of street-life-oriented Black boys: How Black boys use street life as a site of resilience in high school. *Journal of Contemporary Criminal Justice, 26*(3), 316–338.

Pew Research Center. (2010). Confident. Connected. Open to change. Retrieved from http://pewsocialtrends.org/2010/02/24/millennials-confident-connected-open-to-change/

Phillips, C. D. (2005). A comparison between African American and White students enrolling in an equal opportunity program on predominantly White college campus: Perceptions of the campus environment. *College Student Journal, 39*(2), 298–306.

Schott Foundation for Public Education. (2010). *Yes we can: The Schott 50 state report on public education and Black males.* Cambridge, MA: Author. Retrieved from: http://blackboysreport.org/bbreport.pdf

Smith, W. L., & Zhang, P. (2009). Students' perceptions and experiences with key factors during the transition from high school to college. *College Student Journal, 43*(2), 643–657.

Spurgeon, S. L. (2009). Wellness and college type in African American male college students: An examination of differences. *Journal of College Counseling, 12*(1), 33–43.

Spurgeon, S. L., & Myers, J. E. (2010). African American males: Relationships among racial identity, college Type, and wellness. *Journal of Black Studies, 40*(4), 527–543.

Steele, C. M. (1992, April). Race and the schooling of Black Americans. *The Atlantic Monthly, 269,* 68–78.

Steele, C. M. (1997). A threat in the air. *American Psychologist, 52*(6), 613.

Steele, C. M. (1999). Thin ice. *Atlantic Monthly, 284*(2), 44–54.

Steele, C. M., & Aronson, J. (1995). Stereotype threat and the intellectual test performance of African-Americans. *Journal of Personality and Social Psychology, 69*(5), 797–811.

Stevenson, J. (2007). From founding purpose to future positioning: Why historically Black colleges and universities must maintain but modify mission. *Jackson State University Researcher, 21*(3), 99–102.

Stewart, G., Wright, D., Perry, T., & Rankin, C. (2008). Historically Black colleges and universities: Caretakers of precious treasure. *Journal of College Admission, 201,* 24–29.

Strange, C. C., & Banning, J. H. (2001). *Educating by design: Creating campus learning environments that work.* San Francisco, CA: Jossey-Bass.

Strayhorn, T., & Saddler, T. (2009). Gender differences in the influence of faculty–Student mentoring relationships on satisfaction with college among African Americans. *Journal of African American Studies, 13*(4), 476–493.

Sutton, E. (2006). Developmental mentoring of African American college men. In M. Cuyjet (Ed.), *African American men in college* (pp. 95–111). San Francisco, CA: Jossey-Bass.

Thomas, D. E., Coard, S. I., Stevenson, H. C., Bentley, K., & Zamel, P. (2009). Racial and emotional factors predicting teachers' perceptions of classroom behavioral maladjustment for urban African American male youth. *Psychology in the Schools, 46*(2), 184–196.

Tillman, L. C. (2001). Mentoring African American faculty in predominantly White institutions. *Research in Higher Education, 42*(3), 295–325.

Tucker, C., Dixon, A., & Griddine, K. (2010). Academically successful African American male urban high school students' experiences of mattering to others at school. *Professional School Counseling, 14*(2), 135–145.

Warde, B. (2008). Staying the course: Narratives of African American males who have completed a baccalaureate degree. *Journal of African American Studies, 12*(1), 59–72.

White, J. L., & Cones, J. H. (1999). *Black man emerging: Facing the past and seizing a future in America.* New York: W. H. Freeman.

Whiting, G. W. (2006). The scholar identity institute: Guiding Darnel and other Black males. *Gifted Child Today, 32*(4), 53–56.

Whiting, G. W. (2009). Gifted Black males: Understanding and decreasing barriers to achievement and identity. *The Roeper Review, 31*, 224-233. doi: 10.1080/02783190903177598

9

BLACK FATHERS IN COLLEGE

Multiple Identities, Persistence, and Contextual Differences

T. Elon Dancy, II and Gralon A. Johnson

Introduction

In one of his saddest rap songs, "Shed So Many Tears," slain rapper Tupac Shakur describes a distinctly Black male cognitive dissonance not unlike the sentiments of other Black males across organizations. In the lyrics, the desire to produce children symbolizes a fresh beginning for a Black man who has coped with the social ills of his world in ways he regrets. Yet, the maze in which he is trapped is not one entirely of his choosing as he must exist in a world marked by oppression and in an America in which Black males are arguably in crisis. Notwithstanding, the desire to produce children as embedded in these lyrics bespeaks a hopeful act in which one Black male may potentially avow or reclaim an identity as a good man. Ironically, Black males in college may also know of what Shakur speaks.

Higher education research traditionally studies parental involvement in college student lives. For instance, a well-established body of research and scholarship investigates the role parents play in the collegiate choices of students (Ceja, 2006; Freeman, 2005; Hossler, Schmit, & Vesper, 1997; McDonough, 1997). However, the experiences of college students who are also parents are largely missing from the literature. Even less obvious is how student groups in various college contexts negotiate college participation and parenting. Black males, one of the most elusive student groups in higher education, are an intriguing site for investigation because multiple identities among Black male students are scant topics in the research.

In general, the experiences of Black males in college constitute a large research and scholarly literature (Allen, 1984, 1985, 1988; Allen, Epps, & Haniff, 1991; Astin, 1982, 1993; Cuyjet, 2006; Dancy & Brown, 2007; Davis,

1994; Fleming, 1984; Flowers & Pascarella, 1999; Harper, 2006; Jackson & Moore, 2006; Nettles, 1988; Palmer & Dancy, 2009; Palmer & Gasman, 2008; Strayhorn; 2008a, 2008b, 2010; Willie & McCord, 1972). Because little is known about Black fathers in college, investigation about how this group negotiates multiple identities is valuable knowledge in the quest of colleges and universities to comprehensively serve them. Such study additionally disrupts the assumption that Black males are a monolithic group (Dancy, in press).

Fatherhood is largely defined as the state in which a male parents an offspring (McAdoo, 1981). Thus, fatherhood assumes a father–child relationship. However, this relationship is not always a biological one, as men who exercise paternal care over others also define a fathering relationship (National Center for Education Statistics [NCES], 2006). Using qualitative approaches, this chapter meditates on the identity construction of Black males who are both fathers and college students. The data which ground this chapter are drawn from a larger study of 24 Black men enrolled across 12 colleges located in the southern and border states of America (Dancy, 2011). The purpose for this study is to illustrate how Black males negotiate multiple identities and college experiences, particularly in historically Black colleges and universities (HBCUs). After a discussion of the study of Black male fatherhood in society, the chapter describes the study, reports participant reflections, and concludes with thoughts for higher education and society.

Social, Familial, and Economic Contexts: Vistas on Black Fatherhood

Within the past 2 decades, the experiences of fathers in society have received increased attention in the research literature (Benokraitis, 1985; Canfield, 2005; Madhubuti, 1990; Miller, 2010; Pitts, 1999; Pruitt, 2008; Wesemann, 2002). However, most of the literature on fathers' experiences concern White, middle-class, educated, and intact families (Pitts, 2006). Narrowly found in the literature are the experiences of fathers among other racial groups, familial structures, and socioeconomic statuses; for example, Black fathers. Although limited, studies of the paternal experiences among Black men are organized around the following key subjects in the literature: (a) social stereotypes, (b) persistence and determination among Black sons, (c) and economic conditions.

Social Stereotypes

Much of the previous literature on Black fathers underscores society's common construction of Black men as absent or noncustodial, as the insignia for the failure of fathers, for abusive behavior, and a general inability to fully accept the responsibilities of paternity (Black, Dubowitz, & Starr, 1999; Bowman & Sanders, 1988; Cochran, 1997; Madhubuti, 1990; McAdoo, 1988, 1993). It is a perspective that casts Black men as missing and often ignores their capacity to properly define and conceptualize fatherhood. Further, the implicit trajectory is that Black boys without a father become Black men who abandon their own children (Coles, 2003).

Some of this work attributes such typecasting to cultural pathology, racial oppression, Black elitism, structural barriers (i.e., marriage as the heavily favored family strategy of welfare policy and government programs), Black men's struggles with manhood and gender roles, and Black males having few healthy models of masculinity and fatherhood from which to learn and emulate (via factors such as hip hop music; Carbado, 1999; Davis & Hunter, 1994; Frazier, 1997; Majors, & Gordon, 1994; McAdoo, 1981; Neal, 2005; Pitts, 1999; Silver, 2008). Consequently, the literature asserts that because little has been done to dispute the existing depiction of Black fathers, it is likely that society and lamentably a number of Black men themselves espouse these constructions (Silver, 2008).

Additional and more recent work presents critiques of the various ways in which society constructs Black fathers as negligent and absentee parents, non-dedicated to their wives and children, and not playing an important role in childrearing (Best, Chu, Krohn, & Smith, 2005; Pitts, 1999; Taylor, 2003). In an attempt to remedy this situation, studies began to focus on cohabiting or married Black fathers (Allen, 1981), but have been overshadowed by the amount of studies which focus on nonresident fathers, especially teenage fathers, who have come to typify our understanding of "Black fathers" or more customarily, "absent fathers" (Black et al., 1999; Bowman & Sanders, 1988; Cochran, 1997; Miller, 1994; Rivara, Sweeney, & Henderson, 1985).

Even so, this does not imply that the picture of Black fathers as largely absent is entirely a result of perpetuated societal belief. Blacks have contributed to this picture as well via high teen and nonmarital births, cohabitation, and divorce rates. Nevertheless, findings from several studies on nonresidential Black fathers show that lack of cohabiting or marriage to the mother is not necessarily indicative of paternal noninvolvement, as may be inferred from the *absent* postulation (Coles, 2003; Danziger & Radin, 1990; Pruitt, 2008; Seltzer, 1991; Wattenberg, 1993). Indeed, Allen (1981) and McAdoo's (1981) studies both found Black fathers from various family structures and classes to be very involved and nurturing.

Moreover, research finds that black nonresident fathers are more likely to visit their children and participate in primary care responsibilities than nonresident White and Hispanic fathers (Best, Chu, Krohn, & Smith, 2005). For example, Best et al. (2005) investigated the extent and indicators of involvement by young fathers. The study protocol used data from the Rochester Youth Development Study, which tracks a representative sample of urban adolescents from the seventh or eighth grade. Specifically, the researchers sought to determine the percentage of the young men in the sample who were fathers by

age 22, 67% of whom were Black. Results suggest that there is not a significant difference between Black fathers and other young fathers in terms of the
amount of contact with and support provided to their children. Black fathers
related active participation in their children's lives with successful transition
into adulthood.

In an earlier and similar study, Seltzer (1991) used data from the National
Survey of Families and Households to explain the paternal involvement among
nonresident fathers. Like Best et al. (2005), Seltzer found that Black fathers
had higher probabilities than Whites of visiting and participating in decisions
about their children. Participation included economic involvement, childrearing activities, and social contact.

Persistence and Determination among Black Sons

In the context of the family, the relationship between Black fathers and their
sons have been more closely studied in the literature (Barnes 2007; Dobson
2001; James & Thomas, 2009; Johnson, 2006). More specifically, a major portion of the literature on Black fathers explores the implications of father absence
on the ways in which Black sons ultimately make meaning of fatherhood (Clayton, Mincy, & Blackenhorn, 2006; Coles & Green, 2009; Coley & Medeiros,
2007; Connor & White, 2006; Pitts, 1999). Many studies find that Black men
who have been wounded and abandoned by their own fathers make respectable
fathers of themselves through persistence and determination (Best et al., 2005;
Hamer & Marchioro, 2002; Pitts, 1999; Ross, 2005; Taylor, 2003).

For example, Pitts (1999) conducted a qualitative study investigating how
fatherlessness impacts Black men over time. Using a sequence of cross-section
interviews, he examined the ways in which a troubled father history impacted
Black men's ability to father their own children. Pitts (1999) found that for men
who come from households where the father was absent or abusive, the desire
to overturn the cycle of their ill-experienced upbringing augmented the potential for parental involvement.

In a more contemporary analysis, Hunter et al. (2006) also investigated
young Black men's reflections on adulthood and father absence. In a study of 20
participants, the researchers used a series of focus groups to explore the intricate
ways young men coped with the absence of their father. Findings suggest that
when young Black men are given a place of refuge to express their accounts of
pain and loss, they are less likely (than young Black men who do not have this
resource) to construct their future selves as "deadbeat daddies" and are more
likely to have a constructive sense of the man that they would like to become.
The qualitative data of this study appear to confirm the aforementioned studies.

Reporting similar results, Coles (2003) joined quantitative and qualitative
data to investigate the motivating and enabling factors to take full custody of
children among single Black fathers. The sample size included 10 adult-age and

college-educated men. Findings indicate a difference between motivating and enabling factors. While the primary enabling factor to take full custody was employment, like Pitts (1999) and Hunter et al. (2006), Coles found that the desire to personify the kind of father that they themselves did not have was a major motivating factor to parent.

Economic Conditions

Research finds that the availability of fiscal resources is an important factor in the extent of father participation in childrearing among Black men (Ben-okraitis, 1985; Black et al., 1999; Nelson, 2004). More specifically, in families where the mother and father are cohabiting, the income level of the mother plays a key role in the father's contribution to household labor. For example, Coverman's (1985) quantitative study explored how mothers' employment impacted the father's involvement in domestic tasks. Coverman's study evaluated three hypotheses concerning this trend: (a) the more the husband's earnings exceeded the wife's, the less household tasks the husband will carry out; (b) the more conventional the husband's sex-role philosophy, the less likely he is to do housework; and (c) the more that the household workload is on the husband, the greater his contributions will be. Findings revealed that fathers begin to increase their family work when their wives are working.

Like Coverman (1985), Hamer and Marchioro (2002) explored the role of income in improving or impairing the parenting among low-income Black fathers. Twenty-four men from a low-income, urban Midwestern area participated in the study. The hypotheses in this study largely replicated hypotheses in the Coverman (1985) study. More specifically, a parallel theme of traditional sex-role ideologies influencing paternal involvement was revealed. However, the study found an important new distinction. Some fathers accepted responsibility for the child only when a safety net was identified. The safety net included social, emotional, and monetary support from extended kin. Adjustment to father roles appeared to be improved by fathers who made use of support networks.

Socioeconomic experiences in childhood have also influenced how Black men subsequently make meaning of fatherhood. Some studies suggests that Black men from low-income environments may be more favorably inclined than middle-class Black men to parent because they are exposed to a culture (defined as the modeling influence of family structure or a set of general beliefs) that encourages it. For example, in a study of approximately 91 Black males aged 16 through 22 from urban backgrounds, Gohel, Diamond, and Chambers (1997) found that nonfathers in the sample were more likely than the fathers in the sample to have a solid 5-year plan, to have a satisfactory father figure vis-à-vis the fathers, to feel that their family and friends would criticize early parenting, and to believe that fatherhood would hinder their future. Nonfathers were also more likely to be sons of mothers who gave birth during their teens (Gohel et al., 2007). Similar work found parallel outcomes (Nelson, 2004). Another similar study compared 100 Black nonfathers to 100 fathers (both groups being teenaged) and found that nonfathers were more likely to view pregnancy as very disruptive to their academic matriculation and success (Rivara et al., 1985).

In conclusion, the paternal experiences of Black men in society have been studied through both quantitative and qualitative frames. This literature review indicates that social stereotypes, past-lived experiences with one's father, and economic conditions are important influences on how Black men make meaning of fatherhood. Because the fatherhood experiences (across classes and family structures) among Black men is so scarce in the literature, coupled with an implicit trend that *parenting* and *Black man* are oxymoronic terms, all of the abovementioned studies emphasize a critical need for further investigation. Researchers and practitioners are urged to take into account the context of environmental factors that might influence the decision to parent, and the multitude of social, institutional, and cultural barriers which might impede Black fathers from being actively involved in child care. While growing up without a father has been the reality for a significant percentage of Black children in the past few decades, the literature raises two critical points: (a) father absence is a reality in the larger American society and is only mirrored in some Black communities, and (b) in many cases, common labeling among Black fathers as absent and negligent is a myth (Best et al., 2005; Hamer & Marchioro, 2002; Ross, 2005; Taylor, 2003).

Theorizing Multiple and Intersecting Identities

Reviews of the literature support notions that the fathering self is a part of holistic identity development among Black fathers. Accordingly, theories in this study consider the meaning of identity and the ways in which identities intersect. Theorizing identity, Erikson (1968) wrote that individuals enter eight stages of development. Each stage of development, he argued, is anchored in a personal sense of sameness or continued understanding of oneself.

Building on Erikson's work, Chickering and Reisser (2011), envision identity construction in college students as vectors, or major pathways toward a sense of individuality. Thus, processes of identity occur across an individual's race, class, gender, sexual orientation, spiritual, other social categories, and other identities or selves (i.e., college students, daughters, sons, employees).

To reproduce children is theorized as being a critical component of Black manhood. For instance, Hunter and Davis (1992) argue that providing for children is critical to the meanings Black men make of themselves as men. Even more, fathering identity meshes with other identities to comprise manhood among Black fathers (Hunter & Davis, 1992).

Intersectionality theory is a way of understanding the intersecting identities of Black men's lives in American society (Mutua, 2006). At the core of this theory is the assumption that Black men are privileged in society by their gender (male) and underprivileged by their race. However, additional interpretations stress the importance of context in understanding intersectionality in Black men. For instance, Black men are unjustly privileged in Black communities but publicly subordinated beyond these communities (Mutua, 2006). Both environments, however, contribute to overpolicing and stress in Black men. Intersectionality theory requires researchers to study context as a way of determining which identifies intersections actually privilege or oppress Black men.

Banks (1997) writes, "My life stories influence my perspective, a perspective unable to function within a single paradigm because I am too many things at one time" (p. 99). In this vein, multidimensionality theory argues that individuals embody physical, biological, and social differences all at once (Crenshaw, 1991). Multidimensional models of identity rest on a similar assumption (Jones & McEwen, 2000; Reynolds & Pope, 1991). At the center of multiple dimensions of identity is a core sense of self, which is understood as one's innermost identity, which is possibly unidentified by others. Outside identities (e.g., race, gender, class, culture), or those presented to the world that are often easily named by others, represent significant dimensions and contextual influences. A revisiting of this model argues that individuals' meaning-making helps them understand contextual influences, self-perceptions of identity dimensions, and the individual perceptions of the relationship between social identities (i.e., race, class, and gender) and innermost core identity (Abes, Jones, & McEwen, 2007).

The Brother Code: A Study of Amalgamated Identities in Black Males

The Brother Code: Manhood and Masculinity among African American Men in College (Dancy, in press), details a larger qualitative study from which the knowledge in this chapter is drawn. The study investigated Black manhood in college and the institutional role in shaping these constructions. Grounded theory, phenomenological, and case study approaches complemented micro- and macrolevels of data analysis. More specifically, grounded theory guided participant selection and initial coding of data while phenomenological and case study methods guided categorical and contextual analyses respectively.

The men selected for this study attended 12 4-year colleges situated across southern and border states of America. Arguably, these states continued to operate dual systems of higher education despite Title VI of the Civil Rights Act of 1964 barring legalized segregation (Brown, 1999). The 12 institutional sites for this study were selected according to their Carnegie Commission classification.

The most recent classifications were used and doctorate-granting institutions, master's institutions, and baccalaureate institutions were selected. Within these classifications, institutions were disaggregated according to their historical and predominant student population (HBCUs and PWIs) and institutional funding (public, private). This matrix resulted in four colleges per Carnegie classification. Given this site selection design, tribal colleges and special focus institutions were ineligible.

Twenty-four men enrolled in 4-year colleges and universities were selected to participate in the study. Respondents were Black, traditional college-aged (18–24), and upperclassmen (sophomores, juniors, and seniors). The participants in this study were majoring across a breadth of disciplines, maintained at least a 2.5 grade point average (GPA), and were involved or engaged students in college. This study draws its understanding of engagement from Chickering and Gamson's (1987) seven principles (i.e., student–faculty contact, cooperation among students) of student activities that reflect "good institutional practice." Therefore, activities reflecting good institutional practice may include using an institution's human resources, curricular and extracurricular programs or organizations, and other opportunities for learning and development.

Data were gathered in face-to-face interviews. Average interview length was over 2 hours long. Interviews were reviewed for accuracy and then compared against the author's journals. In general, the interview instrument prompts and protocols were modified as appropriate to inform research questions. Specifically, the interview instrument to gather this data partially included questions from Terenzini and colleagues' (1992) *The Transition to College Project* interview instrument, which assessed participant precollege, in-class, and out-of-class experiences in college. Questions from this instrument included: "What is it like for you as a Black man getting used to life as a student at (institution)?" and "Are Black men valued here? If no, who is valued? In what ways? If yes, in what ways?" Other questions included, "What identities have been significant for you as [you] grew up?" and "Tell me what went into your decisions to go to college?" Additional questions were informed by theory and research around Black male behavior, identity, and manhood development.

Grounded theory guided participant selection and initial coding of data. A rigorous coding technique described by Charmaz (2006) was used to keep codes close to data and provide responses to how and why participant experiences were as they described. In addition, phenomenological methods were used to add rigor to the analysis of the interviews. After an initial coding, statements were compared to the research questions to discover "horizons" of spirituality and their interconnections across collegiate spaces (Moustakas, 1994). Last, case study methodologies were elected to draw contextual understandings (HBCUs and PWIs) with the author drawing heavily on the process of correspondence (Stake, 1995). Stake defines correspondence as the search for patterns or consistency that emerges when data are aggregated.

Patterns were grouped across respondents, collegiate classification (i.e., Carnegie classification), collegiate funding type (public vs. private), and collegiate context (i.e., historically Black vs. predominantly White) to display themes that are consistent across these categories. After conducting analysis on each interview, textural–structural descriptions of spiritual identity constructions and collegiate experiences were compiled for each participant. Textural–structural descriptions entail the "whats" and "hows" of experiences (Moustakas, 1994). These descriptions, which captured the themes of each participant's interview, were e-mailed to participants to serve as vehicles for member checking.

Six study participants were parents of at least one child at the time of study. Five were enrolled in an HBCU and one was enrolled in a PWI. At the discovery of this information, two research questions emerged, "How do these men make meaning of themselves as college students and fathers? How do these meanings influence their college persistence?" All participants who were fathers responded to additional identity construction questions around fatherhood, manhood, and college experience. More specifically, questions interrogated participants' attitudes toward parenting while a college student and the role participants play in their children's lives. The following section entails researcher reflections on the knowledge shared by the participants.

Men and Fathers: College Lessons at the Intersections

The study deliberately centered on the gendered constructions of Black men to remind colleges and universities that Black male college students are men as well as Black and college students. Accordingly, manhood is defined in the data as ideas and ideals about what it means to be a man, a finding shared in the literature (Hunter & Davis, 1992). One domain of manhood emergent in the study is a sense of relationships and responsibilities to family, particularly assuming roles as providers to women and children (the other two domains of manhood are self-expectations and worldviews). Thus, the six fathers in this study not only saw college as necessary for fulfilling career goals, advancing the Black community, and developing global citizenship, but also as a training ground to assume roles as provider and patriarch. More specifically, three themes of identity construction among Black fathers emerged.

Tensions between Fatherhood and Studenthood. Codes like "man points" or "respect as men" emerged from analysis as all six participants referred to social rewards associated with additional responsibilities as fathers while enrolled in college. In fact, participants felt entitled to additional masculine credit and social value as men because they produced progeny. Surprisingly, participant statements also suggested that they needed to prove manhood through fatherhood as soon as possible despite the financial and emotional challenges that they feel fatherhood responsibility poses for college completion. Thus, participants valued the ability to produce children as teen fathers. The result is teen fathers who willingly shoulder responsibilities that college enrollment demands but also feel compelled to demonstrate an ability to reproduce and provide for others as the patriarchal system demands.

hooks (2004a) defines patriarchy as a political–social system in which men inherently dominate, are superior to everything and everyone deemed weak, especially women, and endowed with the right to dominate the weak and to maintain that dominance through various forms of psychological terrorism and violence. Thus, a patriarchal system, which is "imperialist white-supremacist capitalist" in scope continues to shape and inform Black men's constructions of manhood and masculinity (hooks, 2004a, p. 18). The participants in this study freely display patriarchal masculinity, or in other words, behave in ways that honor a "natural" position of providing for others without liberating themselves from the historical process in which Whites inculcated notions of weakness, docility, and ignorance in the minds of Black males.

All participants also asserted or suggested that producing children is evidence of virility, a necessary characteristic of manhood embedded in their self-expectations. Accordingly, to participants, a "real" man is one who is innately and monolithically heterosexual and the production of children serves as evidence of this. This finding supports the presence of compulsory heterosexuality, a term referring to the ways in which sexual identity is used to foster hegemony, or social domination in America. Compulsory heterosexuality is the assumption that women and men are innately attracted to each other emotionally and sexually and that heterosexuality in America leads to an institutionalized inequality of power, not only between heterosexuals and lesbian, gay, bisexual, and transgender (LGBT) persons, but also between men and women, with far-reaching consequences (Rich, 1994). The study participants used producing children as evidence of virility and to garner social respect, but it was also used to correct past mistakes by participants' fathers or as a means to continue their own role as fathers in children's lives.

Promoting Fatherhood.   Five of the six men shared an experience of having absent fathers in their family background. Participants without fathers were desperate to remain in their children's lives, particularly for boys. This affinity for boys was primarily rooted in the assumption that only men can teach boys how to be men. According to participant suggestions, efforts to remain in their children's lives directly confronted stereotypical explanations of trends describing father absence in the Black home. Such stereotypes of Black fathers as lazy and negligent often exclude proper contextualization of the intersections of race and class discrimination and how this discrimination has systemically denied access and opportunity to Black men. Thus, this discrimination potentially collides with Black men's patriarchal feelings of entitlement and may result in crisis. Participants, however, envision college as a space to foster access and opportunity to what they feel their Black manhood denies.

For all six participants, colleges were spaces of transformation that promised to develop participants into the role model fathers they desired to become. A role model fatherhood, as framed by the participants, brings to mind the idea of benevolent patriarchy discussed in the historical literature (hooks, 2004b). Implicit in the idea of benevolent patriarchy is the assumption that Black men would approach family life in similar ways to White men in their homes. Benevolent patriarchs are those who provide for and protect women without the use force. In the community, benevolent patriarchy refers to men who see themselves as civically engaged or liberators of the indigent (Summers, 2004). While participants chose to attend college to bring them closer to the goal of benevolent patriarchy, specific colleges were chosen that allowed for an easy commute from campus to the homes where participants' children lived.

Contextual Differences.   Collegiate contexts, HBCUs and PWIs, reinforce certain constructs of manhood already shaped in American society. For example, all men in this study thought about the Black community in collectivist ways, emphasizing a need to strengthen a racialized "we" and "us." This worldview is one that the collegiate fathers in the study are planning to teach their children. However, this worldview is more intensely reinforced in historically Black contexts which largely abound with Black people and culture.

Relevantly, study participants either declared or suggested that other Black students at the HBCUs they attended endorsed Black males who fathered as being more masculine and thus more socially desirable and valuable. However, this message conflicted with the advice of some mentoring personnel who were attempting to encourage participants to think more critically about how they shape their lives. Unfortunately, some participants asserted that many collegiate personnel understand at best or endorse at worst the desire to prove manhood despite the fact that the participants were boys and not men when they fathered children.

Discussion and Concluding Thoughts

Because colleges were viewed by the participants as gateways to society, colleges were also in a position to inform participant thinking about who Black men are as well as what they can be, become, and do. College fathers in this study, most of whom attended HBCUs, expressed ways in which they felt college personnel and students endorse a construction of Black men that is patriarchal, hypermasculine, and hypersexual. Colleges must bring together appropriate stakeholders (e.g., administrators, faculty, staff, students, parents) in critical dialogues that expand the meanings that Black male students make of themselves as Black men. These conversations work to weed cultural tensions and foster inclusive and equitable climates for women and various groups of men (e.g., gay men). Stereotypes that attempt to locate Black male collegians' cultural authenticity have no place in college and only fuel the divisiveness that the arbiters of the patriarchal system in America intended.

Study participants' words pointed to the need for cultural awareness workshops on all campuses, including HBCUs, to discuss strategies for fostering climates of equity, tolerance, and inclusion. In HBCUs, workshop dialogues must consider the intersections of race, gender, sexual orientation, spirituality, skin-color, and other states of consciousness. These cultural workshops should be required by institutional policy and held both routinely and as needed with diverse faculty, staff, and student representatives. Thinking about these additional consciousnesses may inform deeper and more diversified strategies aimed at serving many and varied groups of Black males. These workshops and open dialogues must be at the center of institutional conversations about recruitment, enrollment, retention, and persistence strategies. These conversations should occur often to ensure institutional accountability for and commitment to serving the needs of ever-changing institutional student populations, particularly males who enroll and graduate from college at dire rates. Colleges, including HBCUs, are cautioned against engaging with Black males as though they were members of a monolithic group. As this study demonstrates, some college-going Black males are also persisting in college as fathers.

Analysis of participant identities additionally offers critical fodder for how we theorize about student persistence in higher education. Tinto's (1994) work suggests that how students perceive the college experience relates to the degree they engage in the social and academic communities of college. Subsequently, negative perceptions of the college experience become predictors of attrition. In other words, students who perceive incongruence between themselves and the institution experience difficulty becoming integrated and are therefore less likely to persist. Tinto details a process in which students navigate through stages of separation, transition, and incorporation. More specifically, students leave the norms of past, precollege communities (i.e., family and friends), become exposed to unfamiliar norms, and are incorporated when (and if) they adapt to institutional norms. Once incorporated, according to Tinto (1994), students who experience academic or social difficulties face a certain propensity to abandon collegiate persistence despite the odds.

However, participants did not exactly operate in their college persistence in the ways Tinto outlines. The assertions of the college fathers in this study suggest that their decisions to remain in college and persist are more complex. Study participants' understandings of themselves as men also represent a place from which they persist. Thus, it is possible to remain in college through development of an oppositional identity, one that compels men to persist despite incongruence because that is what men do in general and what Black men do in particular. Their persistence reflects a unique masculine struggle to claim or reclaim positions as benevolent and community patriarchs and to escape the stereotypical strongholds of American society. In other words, these men described how they located and experienced, yet ignored perceived misdeeds of their institutions and used college as a means to incorporate themselves into the broader American society, not the institution. Thus, in this study it is difficult to assert that participants were more likely to leave their institutions due to perceived incongruencies between self and context.

While colleges do not represent society in its wholeness, colleges play an important role in the identity development and socialization of Black fathers upon enrollment. Thus, colleges are spaces in which men, both with and without children, learn to reorganize or reproduce their understandings about who they are. Colleges are reminded that their missions not only articulate commitment to teaching and learning for academic outcomes but also to shaping students into civically responsible and global citizens. This involves developing individuals who can think critically about their own development as well as teach and inspire others in similar ways. The Black fathers in this study are doing this with members of the next generation—their children—and colleges can play an important role in reconstructing ideas about race, gender, and fatherhood.

References

Abes, E., Jones, S., & McEwen, M. (2007). Reconceptualizing the model of multiple dimensions of identity: The role of meaning-making capacity in the construction of multiple identities. *Journal of College Student Development, 48*(1), 1–22.

Allen, W. (1981). Mom, dads, and boys: Race and sex differences in the socialization of male children. In L. Gary (Ed.), *Black men* (pp. 99–114). Beverly Hills, CA: Sage.

Allen, W. R. (1984). Race consciousness and collective commitment among Black students on White campuses. *Western Journal of Black Studies, 8*(3), 156–166.

Allen, W. R. (1985). Black student, White campus: Structural, interpersonal, and psychological correlates of success. *Journal of Negro Education, 52*(2), 134–147.

Allen, W. R. (1988). The education of Black students on White college campuses: What quality the experiences? In M. Nettles (Ed.), *Toward Black undergraduate student equality in American higher education* (pp. 57–86). Albany, NY: SUNY Press.

Allen, W. R., Epps, E. G., & Haniff, N. Z. (Eds.). (1991). *Colleges in Black and White: African American students in predominantly White and in historically Black public universities.* Albany, NY: SUNY Press.

Astin, A. W. (1982). *Minorities in higher education: Recent trends, current prospects, and recommendations.* San Francisco, CA: Jossey-Bass.

Astin, A. W. (1993). What matters in college? Four critical years revisited. San Francisco, CA: Jossey-Bass.

Banks, T. L. (1997). Two life stories: Reflections of one Black woman law professor. In A. Wing (Ed.), *Critical race feminism* (pp. 96–100). New York: New York University Press.

Barnes, K. D. (2007). *Successfully raising young Black men.* Joshua, TX: Torch Legacy.

Benokraitis, N. (1985). The father in two-earner families. In S. M. Hanson & F. W. Bozett (Eds.), *Dimensions of Fatherhood* (pp. 243–265). London: Sage.

Best, O., Chu, R., Krohn, M., & Smith, C. (2005). African American fathers: Myths and realities about their involvement with their firstborn children. *Journal of Family Issues, 26*(7), 975–1001.

Black, M., Dubowitz, H., & Starr, R. H. (1999). African American fathers in low income, urban families: Development, behavior, and home environment of their three-year-old children. *Child Development, 70*(4), 967–978.

Bowman, P. J., & Sanders, R. (Eds.). (1988). *Black fathers across the life cycle: Provider role strain and psychological well-being.* Proceedings of the Empirical Conference on Black Psychology, Ann Arbor, MI.

Brown, M. C. (1999). *The quest to define collegiate desegregation: Black colleges, Title VI compliance, and post-Adams litigation.* Westport, CT: Bergin & Garvey.

Canfield, K. (2005). *They call me dad: The practical art of effective fathering.* New York: Howard Books.

Carbado, D. (1999). *Black men on race, gender, and sexuality: A critical reader.* New York: New York University Press.

Ceja, M. (2006). Understanding the role of parents and siblings as information sources in the college choice process of Chicana students. *Journal of College Student Development, 47*(1), 87–104.

Charmaz, K. (2006). *Constructing grounded theory: A practical guide through qualitative analysis.* London: Sage.

Chickering, A. W., & Gamson, Z. F. (1987). Seven principles for good practice in undergraduate education. *American Association for Health Education Bulletin, 39*(7), 3–7.

Chickering, A. W., & Reisser, L. (2011). The seven vectors. In M. Wilson (Eds.), *ASHE reader on college student development theory* (2nd ed.) (pp. 139-148). Boston, MA: Pearson.

Clayton, O., Mincy, R., & Blackenhorn, D. (2006). *Black fathers in contemporary American society: Strengths, weaknesses, and strategies for change.* New York: Russell Sage Foundation.

Cochran, D. L. (1997). African American fathers: A decade review of the literature. *Journal of Contemporary Human Services 78*(4), 340–350.

Colbert, S., & Harrison, V. (2006). *Color him father: Stories of love and rediscovery of Black men.* Portland, OR: Kinship Press.

Coles, R. (2003). Black single custodial fathers: Factors influencing the decision to parent. *Families in Society, 84*(2), 247–258.

Coles, R., & Green, C. (2009). *The myth of the missing Black father.* New York: Columbia University Press.

Coley, R. L., & Medeiros, B. L. (2007). Reciprocal longitudinal relations between nonresident father involvement and adolescent delinquency. *Child Development, 78*(1), 132–147.

Connor, M. E., & White, J. (2006). *Black fathers: An invisible presence in America.* Mahwah, NJ: Erlbaum.

Coverman, S. (1985). Explaining husbands' participation in domestic labor. *The Sociological Quarterly, 26*(1), 81–97.

Crenshaw, K. (1991). Mapping the margins: Intersectionality, identity politics, and violence against women of color. *Stanford Law Review, 43*(6), 1241–1299.

Cuyjet, M. (Ed.). (2006). *African American men in college.* San Francisco, CA: Jossey-Bass.

Dancy, T. E. (in press). Colleges in the making of manhood and masculinity: Gendered perspectives on African American males. *Gender and Education.*

Dancy, T. E. (2011). *The brother code: Manhood and masculinity among African American men in college.* Charlotte, NC: Information Age.

Dancy, T. E., & Brown, M. C. (2007). Unintended consequences: African American male educational attainment and collegiate perceptions after *Brown v. Board of Education. American Behavioral Scientist, 51*(7), 984–1003.

Danziger, S., & Radin, N. (1990). Absent does not equal uninvolved: Predictors of fathering in teen mother families. *Journal of Marriage and the Family, 52*(3), 636–642.

Davis, J. E. (1994). College in Black and White: The academic experiences of African American males. *Journal of Negro Education, 63*(4), 620–633.

Davis, J. E., & Hunter, A. G. (1994). Hidden voices of Black men: The meaning, structure, and complexity of manhood. *Journal of Black Studies, 25*(1), 20–40.

Dobson, J. C. (2001). *Bringing up boys.* Carol Stream, IL: Tyndale House.

Erikson, E. (1968). *Identity: Youth and Crisis,* New York: Norton.

Fleming, J. (1984). *Blacks in college: A comparative study of students' success in Black and in White institutions.* San Francisco, CA: Jossey-Bass.

Flowers, L., & Pascarella, E. (1999). Does racial composition influence the openness to diversity of African American students? *Journal of College Student Development, 40*(4), 377–389.

Frazier, E. F. (1997). *Black bourgeoisie: The book that brought the shock of self-revelation to middle-class Blacks in America.* New York: Free Press.

Freeman, K. (2005). *African Americans and college choice: The influence of family and school.* Albany, NY: SUNY Press.

Gohel, M., Diamond, J. J., & Chambers, C. V. (1997). Attitudes toward sexual responsibility and parenting: An exploratory study of young, urban males. *Family Planning Perspectives, 29*(6), 280–283.

Hamer, J., & Marchioro, K. (2002). Becoming custodial dads: Exploring parenting among low-income and working-class African American fathers. *Journal of Marriage and Family, 64*(1), 116–129.

Harper. S. R. (2006). Peer support for African American male college achievement: Beyond internalized racism and the burden of "acting White." *Journal of Men's Studies, 14*(3), 337–358.

hooks, b. (2004a). *The will to change: Men, masculinity, and love.* New York: Atria Books.

hooks, b. (2004b). *We real cool: Black men and masculinity.* New York: Routledge.

Hossler, D., Schmit, J., & Vesper, N. (1997). *Going to college: How social, economic, and educational factors influence the decisions students make.* Baltimore, MD: Johns Hopkins University Press.

Hunter, A. G., & Davis, J. E. (1992). Constructing gender: An exploration of Afro-American men's conceptualization of manhood. *Gender & Society, 6,* 464–479.

Hunter, A. G., Friend, C. A., Murphy, S. Y., Rollins, A., Williams-Wheeler, M., & Laughinghouse, J. (2006). Loss, survival, and redemption: African American male youths' reflections on life without fathers, manhood, and coming of Age. *Youth & Society, 37*(4), 423–452.

Jackson, J. F. L., & Moore, J. L. (2006). African American males in education: Endangered or ignored. *Teachers College Record, 2,* 201–205.

James, S., & Thomas, D. (2009). *Wild things: The art of nurturing boys.* Carol Stream, IL: Tyndale House.

Johnson, R. (2006). *Better dads, Stronger sons: How fathers can guide boys to become men of character.* Ada, MI: Revell.

Jones, S. R., & McEwen, M. K. (2000). A conceptual model of multiple dimensions of identity. *Journal of College Student Development, 41*(4), 405–414.

Madhubuti, H. (1990). *Black men: Obsolete, single, dangerous? Afrikan American families in transition: Essays in discovery, solution, and hope.* Chicago, IL: Third World.

Majors, R., & Gordon, J. (1994). *The American Black male: His present status and his future.* Chicago, IL: Burnham.

McAdoo, J. (1981). Involvement of fathers in the socialization of Black children. In H. P. McAdoo (Ed.), *Black families* (pp. 225–337). Newbury Park, CA: Sage.

McAdoo, J. (1988). Changing perspectives on the role of the Black father. In P. Bronstein & C. Cowan (Eds.), *Fatherhood today: Men's changing role in the family* (pp. 79–92). New York: Wiley.

McAdoo, J. L. (1993). The roles of African American fathers: An ecological perspective. *Families in Society: Journal of Contemporary Human Services, 74*(1) 28–35.

McDonough, P. (1997). *How social class and schools structure opportunity.* Albany, NY: SUNY Press:

Miller, D. (1994). Influences on parental involvement of African American adolescent fathers. *Child and Adolescent Social Work Journal, 11*(5), 363–379.

Miller, D. (2010). *Father fiction: Chapters for a fatherless generation.* New York: Howard Books.

Moustakas, C. (1994). *Phenomenological research methods.* Thousand Oaks, CA: Sage.

Mutua, A. (2006). Theorizing progressive Black masculinities. In A. Mutua (Ed.), *Progressive Black masculinities.* (pp. 235–252). New York: Routledge.

National Center for Education Statistics (NCES) (2001). *Measuring father involvement in young children's lives: Recommendations for a fatherhood module for the ECLS-B* (Working Paper No. 2001-02). Washington, DC: Author.

Neal, M. A. (2005). *New Black man.* London: Routledge.

Nelson, T. (2004). Low-income fathers. *Annual Review of Sociology, 30*(1), 427–451.

Nettles, M. (Ed.). (1988). *Toward Black undergraduate student equality in American higher education.* New York: Greenwood.

Palmer, R. T., & Dancy, T. E. (2009). Shaping success among Black men in an HBCU: A study of barriers and benefits. *Georgia Journal of Student Affairs.* Retrieved from http://www.kennesaw. edu/student_life/gcpajournal/2008/Black%20Males.pdf

Palmer, R. T., & Gasman, M. (2008). "It takes a village to raise a child": The role of social capital in promoting academic success for African American men at a Black college. *Journal of College Student Development, 49(1),* 52–70.

Pitts, L. (1999). *Becoming dad: Black men and the journey to fatherhood.* Athens, GA: Longstreet Press.

Pruitt, B. (2008). *The power of dad: The influence of today's fathers and the destiny of their children.* Longwood, FL: Xulon Press.

Reynolds, A. L., & Pope, R. (1991). The complexities of diversity: Exploring multiple oppressions. *Journal of Counseling and Development, 70,* 174–180.

Rich, A. (1994). *Blood, bread, and poetry.* New York: Norton.

Rivara, F. P., Sweeney, P. J., & Henderson, B. F. (1985). A study of low socioeconomic status, Black teenage fathers and their non-father peers. *Pediatrics, 75*(4), 648–656.

Ross, D. (2005). *Black fatherhood: Reconnecting with our legacy.* Philadelphia, PA: Pure Quality.

Seltzer, J. A. (1991). Relationships between fathers and children who live apart: The father's role after separation. *Journal of Marriage and the Family, 53*(1), 79–101.

Silver, A. (2008). *Be a father to your child: Real talk from Black men on family, love, and fatherhood.* New York: Soft Skull Press.

Stake, R. E. (1995). *The art of case study research.* Thousand Oaks, CA: Sage.

Strayhorn, T. (2008a). The role of supportive relationships in facilitating African American males' success in college. *NASPA Journal, 45*(1), 26–48.

Strayhorn, T. (2008b). Examining the relationship between collaborative learning and perceived intellectual development among African-American males in college. *Journal of Excellence in College Teaching, 19*(2&3), 31–50.

Strayhorn, T. (2010). When race and gender collide: Social and cultural capital's influence on the academic achievement of African American and Latino males. *Review of Higher Education, 33*(3), 307–332.

Summers, M. (2004). *Manliness and its discontents: The Black middle class and the transformation of masculinity, 1900–1930.* Chapel Hill: University of North Carolina.

Taylor, K. C. (2003). *Black fathers: A call for healing.* New York: Doubleday.

Terenzini, P. T., Allison, K. W., Millar, S. B., Rendon, L. I., Upcraft, M. L., & Gregg, P.(1992) *The transition to college project: Final report.* University Park, PA: National Center on Postsecondary Teaching, Learning, and Assessment, Pennsylvania State University. (Code of Federal Domestic Assistance No.: CFDA 84.117G)

Tinto, V. (1994). *Leaving college: Rethinking the causes and cures of student attrition* (2nd. ed.). Chicago, IL: University of Chicago Press.

Wattenberg, E. (1993). Paternity actions and young fathers. In R. Lerman & T. Ooms (Eds.), *Young unwed fathers: Changing roles and emerging policies* (pp. 213–234). Philadelphia, PA: Temple University Press.

Wesemann, T. (2002). *Being a good dad: When you didn't have one.* Kansas City: Beacon Hill.

Willie, C. V., & McCord, A. (Eds.). (1972). *Black students at White colleges.* New York: Praeger.

10

BLACK MEN, FRATERNITIES, AND HISTORICALLY BLACK COLLEGES AND UNIVERSITIES

Dorian L. McCoy

This chapter focuses on Black Greek-letter fraternities (BGLFs) and their presence at historically Black colleges and universities (HBCUs). In this chapter, a historical overview is provided for the five National Pan-Hellenic Council (NPHC) fraternities, the roles and contributions of BGLFs in the Black community, their commitment and responsibility to social activism-justice, and the benefits of collegiate membership. In addition, several prominent challenges that confront the fraternities are discussed (hazing, membership, identity development, image-public perception, and advising). Although the chapter focuses on BGLFs at HBCUs, much of the discussion is relevant to collegiate chapters at predominantly White institutions (PWIs).

In the Beginning

Since the founding of Phi Beta Kappa at the College of William and Mary in 1776, Greek-letter fraternal organizations have been an integral component of collegiate undergraduate life. Established as an honorary society, Phi Beta Kappa was a predecessor to contemporary social Greek-letter fraternities. In 1825, the first "social" fraternity, Kappa Alpha was established at Union College. However, it would not be until the beginning of the 20th century that a historically Black collegiate fraternal organization would be established.

Alpha Kappa Nu Greek Society was founded at Indiana University in 1903 and is recognized as the first Black Greek-letter organization: Described as a "precursor" (Kimbrough, 2003, p. 22) to contemporary BGLFs, Alpha Kappa Nu's existence was short-lived. Historical records fail to provide accurate data about the organization's demise; however, within 2 years, Pi Gamma Omicron at Ohio State University and Gamma Phi at Wilberforce University (Ohio) were established. Much like Alpha Kappa Nu, these organizations' existence was short-lived.

In 1906, at Cornell University (Ithaca, NY) the first continuous Black Greek-letter collegiate fraternity, Alpha Phi Alpha, was established as a study and support society for Black males. Alpha Phi Alpha and Kappa Alpha Psi's (founded at Indiana University in 1911) emerged, in part, as cultural and social opposition to the segregated White Greek-letter organizations of the early 20th century. Whaley (2009) surmised, "the site of their emergence had a direct bearing upon their organizational structure and the ensuing cultural, social and political consciousness" (p. 55) of each organization.

Despite opposition from administrators at Howard University, in November 1911, Omega Psi Phi became the first Black Greek-letter social fraternity established at an HBCU. Phi Beta Sigma organized shortly thereafter, becoming the second BGLF founded at Howard University, often referred to as the "cradle of Black Greek civilization" (Kimbrough, 2003, p. 32). The youngest NPHC fraternity, Iota Phi Theta, was founded at Morgan State University in 1963 by 12 nontraditional students. Unlike the four other NPHC fraternities, Iota Phi Theta was founded during the height of the Civil Rights Movement, the same year as the March on Washington and W. E. B. DuBois's death.

The 1920s and 1930s were a period of rapid expansion and growth for BGLFs. Expansion on the historically Black campuses provided opportunities for leadership and involvement in campus organizations, resulting in the fraternities being at the center of campus life. In 1930, Kappa Alpha Psi and Omega Psi Phi joined with three Black Greek-letter sororities (Alpha Kappa Alpha, Delta Sigma Theta, and Zeta Phi Beta) to establish the National Pan-Hellenic Council, a collaborative organization to promote interaction among the organizations and the exchange of information. By the end of the decade, Alpha Phi Alpha and Phi Beta Sigma had joined the NPHC. Iota Phi Theta was not admitted until 1996. This was significant, given the organization's

TABLE 10.1 Black Greek-Letter Fraternities with National Pan-Hellenic Council Membership

Fraternity	Date Founded	Location	Motto
Alpha Phi Alpha	December 4, 1906	Cornell University	*First of All, Servants of All, We Shall Transcend All*
Kappa Alpha Psi	January 5, 1911	Indiana University	*Achievement in Every Field of Human Endeavor*
Omega Psi Phi	November 17, 1911	Howard University	*Friendship is Essential to the Soul*
Phi Beta Sigma	January 9, 1914	Howard University	*Culture for Service, Service for Humanity*
Iota Phi Theta	September 19, 1963	Morgan State University	*Building a Tradition, Not Resting Upon One!*

brief existence. Iota Phi Theta was the first organization granted membership to the NPHC since the 1930s, providing the fraternity with recognition as a national organization and credibility. Despite World War II, BGLFs continued to experience significant growth during the 1940s. By the 1950s, expansion had waned and it would be the 1970s before BGLFs would once again experience significant growth. However, expansion during this period primarily occurred at PWIs in the South.

Social Action

Alpha Phi Alpha's founders initially struggled with how best to confront the sociopolitical challenges of the early 20th century, eventually leading to the development of programming and initiatives designed to aid students' transition from high school to college (Go-to-High School, Go-to-College), promote positive masculine development among boys (Project Alpha), and increase voter participation (A Voteless People Is a Hopeless People). Similarly, other BGLFs developed commitments to racial uplift, education, community service, and humanitarian initiatives which also became paramount to their missions and purposes. Washington and Nuñez (2005) acknowledged, "They [BGLFs] are rooted in the history of the Black journey toward recognition and respect through the portal of higher education" (p. 139). This became evident through the roles of BGLFs and HBCUs during the Civil Rights Movement.

BGLFs were at the forefront of the Civil Rights Movement, organizing and participating in boycotts and marches, protesting social injustices, campaigning for civil rights, and promoting education as a means for racial uplift in the Black community. The Civil Rights Movement provided opportunities for fraternity members to assume leadership positions on campus and in local communities. HBCUs were at the epicenter of the Civil Rights Movement, with BGLF members providing critical leadership. BGLF members were involved in organizations such as the Student Non-Violent Coordinating Committee (SNCC), established on the Shaw University campus. They sought to engage students in civil disobedience campaigns (participating in sit-ins, marches, and the Freedom Rides) in their efforts to dismantle the South's segregationist laws, Jim Crowism, and in securing Black voting rights.

BGLFs remain involved in the racial uplift of the Black community and are engaged in philanthropic and civic endeavors. Educational and health initiatives are central to BGLFs efforts to support, involve, and mentor involved Blacks. Alpha Phi Alpha's Educational Foundation provides scholarships for undergraduate education, as well as training and development for its members. Phi Beta Sigma's partnership with the March of Dimes seeks to prevent premature births and build strong fathers and male role models in the Black community by sponsoring seminars; Iota Phi Theta's Afya Njema Program educates the public on health-related matters. Kappa Alpha Psi's Kamp Kappa and Phi Beta Sigma's Sigma Beta Club offer mentoring and role models for young Black men.

Campus Involvement and Leadership Development

BGLFs afford their members friendship/brotherhood, a sense of belonging, and opportunities for involvement in campus life and activities. Black students at historically Black institutions are more engaged than nonmembers in student life and campus activities, particularly in leadership roles such as student government (e.g., Kimbrough & Harper, 2006; Palmer & Young, 2009). BGLFs offer opportunities for Black men to become involved in other campus organizations (e.g., student government) and for leadership development. BGLFs include collegiate members in the national organizations' structure, providing additional opportunities for involvement and nurturing the development of future national leaders. The relationship between collegiate chapters, alumni chapters, and the national organization is enhanced by including collegiate members on governing boards.

Racial Identity Development and Masculinity

Membership in BGLFs contributes to Black men's multiple identity development. The intersectionality of race, ethnicity, class, gender, and sexual orientation often defines a member's Greek-letter experience. BGLFs promote positive racial identity development Afrocentric perspectives, and significantly contributing to how Black men construct and define masculinity.

Masculinity in BGLFs is often defined by members engaging in ritualistic aggressive behaviors with neophytes and aspiring members. The "crossing of the burning sands" and other rituals contribute to BGLF members' individual and collective identities. Dancy (2011) argues that Black men's adherence to "a rigid model of masculinity [is grounded in] the histories of social exclusion and racism" (p. 102) in the United States. Black men in BGLFs must learn to express their masculinity in positive and productive ways that promote their personal, academic, and social development and not conform to the socially constructed and accepted definitions of masculinity.

21st Century Challenges

BGLFs at HBCUs are confronted with several noteworthy challenges. Prominent among these are pledging and hazing, membership, contemporary Black-Greek letter organizations, creating a more inclusive organization, image/public perception, and advising members. These challenges are systemic, some of which threaten BGLFs' existence as recognized student organizations, and others that must be addressed if more inclusive and effective organizations are to be to created. The remainder of this chapter focuses on these issues.

Pledging/Hazing

Since the early 1990s, the most contentious issue confronting BGLFs has been the pledging and hazing of new members. Pledging has been described as a defining characteristic of the Black Greek experience, is engrained in the fraternities' cultures, and is often viewed as a rite of passage to "manhood." For numerous members, enduring the "pledge process" is perceived as a means of elevating their status on campus. The idea that pledging is required to prove your "manhood" and worthiness of membership is grounded in how masculinity historically and socially has been constructed within BGLFs.

Pledging was recognized as early as 1919, when Kappa Alpha Psi's chapter at Ohio State University organized a Scrollers Club. By the 1950s, pledging and hazing had become an acceptable practice on historically Black campuses and was often depicted in college yearbooks. During the next 30 years, pledging developed a life of its own. Initiates wore similar clothing, walked in single-file formation (typically from shortest to tallest), and were permitted to speak only to fraternity members when not in engaged in academic endeavors. During the 1970s, pledge classes (or lines) became known by their collective name (e.g., the Omnipotent 7), with each pledge class member having a line name or identity (e.g., Insane). As the pledge process became more elaborate, hazing by fraternity members increased. The most common forms of hazing included endurance tests, strenuous exercise, sleep deprivation, paddlings, and physical beatings. Injuries and death were not uncommon with numerous injuries unreported for fear of retaliation or isolation by members. By the end of the 1980s the national organizations were compelled to take action.

In 1990, the eight existing NPHC fraternities and sororities convened to mandate an end to pledging as a recognized practice in their respective organizations. The decision to end pledging met significant resistance from collegiate brothers and young alumni who most often identified more with their chapter of initiation than with the national organization. Concerns were immediately expressed by collegiate chapters and the limited input from collegiate members in the decision to officially end pledging as a membership intake process led to "underground pledging," a continuation of the presummit pledge practices.

Despite the ban on pledging, the practice continues in the NPHC fraternities. Initiates are confronted with an ethical dilemma—do they report hazing and risk membership or do they remain loyal and risk both physical and emotional harm. Nuwer (1999) called for Black Greek leaders to "create some sort of ritual with which to replace pledging in order to satisfy undergraduates' need for socialization" (p. 193).

The legislation to end pledging, moratoriums on initiating new members, and the reluctance of collegiate members to initiate "paper" brothers (new members who participated in a membership intake process instead of pledging) has perpetuated the pledging and hazing culture within the fraternities. The failures of the membership intake process are highlighted by the 2009 hazing-related death of a Phi Beta Sigma initiate after being subjected to an "instant, systematic, and continuous hazing incident" (Horswell, 2009).

It is critical to acknowledge that the membership intake process has not succeeded. Greater emphasis has to be placed on educational initiatives; with collegiate members and chapters being held accountable for their actions. The prospect of civil and legal consequences, however, has not reduced hazing among the collegiate chapters. Kimbrough (2005) questioned whether or not collegiate chapters should be abolished given their "brazen defiance" (p. 27) of the national organizations' bans on pledging. Until the pledging and hazing issues are resolved at the collegiate level, BGLFs are at risk for imminent demise.

Diverse Memberships

Much like their White counterparts' exclusionary behavior toward Blacks, BGLFs excluded students who were not of Black descent. It was not until the mid-20th century that non-Blacks joined BGLFs. Despite the lack of a critical mass, the number of non-Blacks in BGLFs has increased since the racial turbulence of the 1960s. Non-Blacks often seek membership in BGLFs because of the greater emphasis on service and social action. It is doubtful that the inclusion of members who do not identify as Black will cause BGLFs to lose focus on issues affecting Blacks; however, the limited number of non-Black members contributes to the tokenization of White, Latino, and Asian members. A more pressing issue is how these organizations create more inclusive environments for members who identify as gay/queer.

Homophobia is rampant in BGLFs and the inclusion of gay members fundamentally challenges traditional concepts of brotherhood and masculinity. An openly gay/queer Black male has a minimal chance of gaining admission to a BGLF. De Santis and Coleman (2008) stated "the rationales for homophobia are collectively shared and crafted within these very isolated and insulated fraternal groups" (p. 308). The presence of gay/queer members leads to cultural tensions in both BGLFs and the Black community. These cultural tensions manifest in part because of how the Black community has historically and socially constructed masculinity and Christianity has prominently influenced Black males' moral development and ethical beliefs.

Postmodern/Contemporary Greek Organizations

Postmodern concepts of Blackness and the hegemonic traditions and cultures that exist in the NPHC fraternities have given rise to other fraternal and Greek-letter organizations. These organizations are not necessarily "threats" to the NPHC fraternities' existence, but their increased presence contributes to declining membership in the NPHC organizations. Prominent examples include Groove Phi Groove and Delta Phi Upsilon. Groove Phi Groove was founded in 1962 at Morgan State University to bring "cultural national-ism to the college campus" (Shelton, 2008, p. 221). The founders of Groove Phi Groove sought to decenter the organization from Western beliefs and to embrace Afrocentricity. During the late 20th century, Delta Phi Upsilon was established in Tallahassee, Florida as the first Black international fraternity for gay men. Delta Phi Upsilon strives to serve the immediate community and ultimately the larger region and nation because "The well-educated gay man of color, [is] unable to find any outlets for his potential for leadership and ser-vice, and [is] denied affiliation with the kinds of groups open to heterosexuals" (www.dphiu.org).

In addition to fraternal organizations with Afrocentric ideologies and those that serve members with specific identities, the number of multicultural Greek-letter organizations has increased since the mid- to late 1980s. Multicultural fraternities assert their multiracial memberships but the groups are primarily Black or Latino.

Masculinity

BGLFs construction of masculinity and manhood is in many aspects counter-productive and perpetuates a socially unjust and oppressive perception. Mas-culinity in BGLFs is grounded on practices which perpetuate gender roles, intolerance of homosexuality, and patriarchy (Jenkins, 2011). Unfortunately, alumni members and advisors contribute to the perpetuation of hegemonic traditions and values. Chapter members, faculty advisors, alumni members, and university administrators must engage in developmentally appropriate educa-tional programs that will dismantle fraternities' hegemonic cultures and values. A critical step in this process is adherence to De Santis' (2007) assertion that chapters become an "unsafe environment for racism, sexism, and homophobia."

It is appropriate to evaluate fraternity values and cultures, but examining institutional policies is also warranted. Many institutional policies were and are established without critically examining how they contribute to an organi-zational climate that is not inclusive. Administrators should ask: "How do our institutional policies contribute to or promote fraternity cultures and values that are inconsistent with stated institutional values and fail to promote socially just values?" The challenges of creating a more inclusive and socially just fra-ternity are daunting. Doing so does not solely involve BGLFs, but requires the involvement of the entire campus community. Regrettably, organizational change and cultural shifts in higher education are often slow and methodical; to expect BGLFs to be different is unrealistic. Programs and initiatives that educate members of fraternal organizations and the university community are essential; however, mandatory educational programs alone will not create more inclusive and socially just organizations. To create more inclusive and socially just fraternities, all constituents involved (governing boards, alumni members, chapter advisors, collegiate members, and university administrators/educators) must critically examine their role in perpetuating a culture that is continuously scrutinized by individuals both affiliated and unaffiliated with BGLFs.

Image/Public Perception

The socially constructed and accepted definitions of racism and masculinity may contribute to how BGLFs are publicly perceived. BGLF members have been characterized as violent, aggressive, and predatory; they have been referred to as "educated gangs" (Hughey, 2008, p. 385). In many ways, BGLF members conform to the negative stereotypes associated with membership, through their engagement in sexist, homophobic, and misogynistic behaviors. Members must ask themselves if they are upholding the high ideals of brotherhood, scholarship, and service to the organization, the Black community, and most importantly, to themselves.

Elitism has plagued BGLFs since their inception during the early 20th century. A delicate balancing act is required between promoting brotherhood, scholarship, and service and being perceived as elitist. Jones (2004) emphasizes that the historically Black fraternities have always had a "proclivity for exclusivity" (p. 26). The perception of elitism further limits the historical and cultural significance of BGLFs and hinders recognition of the positive aspects of membership. To challenge the media's and the public's perception of BGLFs and to dismantle negative stereotypes, collegiate members, faculty and alumni advisors, and university administrators must be relentless in promoting BGLFs positive contributions to HBCUs, the Black community, and the global community.

Advising

Hughey and Parks (2007) argue that a culturally competent and engaged advisor is critical for the continued success of collegiate chapters. Unlike at PWIs, where the absence of a critical mass of active alumni members employed by the institution may necessitate the advisor not identifying as Black or as a fraternity member, advisors for collegiate chapters at HBCUs are typically fraternity members active in the local alumni chapter. Unfortunately, many advisors are disconnected from the collegiate chapters' day-to-day operations and are most present during crisis management. This ineffective mode of advising limits collegiate chapters' potential for success. Developing an understanding and familiarity with student development theories (such as racial identity development theories, Astin's theory of involvement), an awareness of the issues and challenges confronting collegiate chapters, and engaging in effective advising practices, will assist chapter advisors in maximizing collegiate chapters' potential. Johnson, Bradley, Bryant, Morton, and Sawyer (2008) present compelling reasons for incorporating a student development approach for BGLOs' advisors. Specifically, they noted that employing a student development approach promotes racial identity, moral and leadership development, and encourages involvement in campus programs and activities for collegiate members.

Chapter advisors can assist in overcoming the perceptions of elitism and classism prevalent in BGLFs. Hughey and Parks (2007) contend that "advisors must be aware of the dynamic of an entrenched BGLO classism." Finally, chapter advisors must recognize and embrace their role as mentors and understand that an engaged presence will promote not only chapter success but the success of individual collegiate members.

Conclusion

Since the founding of Omega Psi Phi at Howard University, BGLFs have had prominent roles on historically Black campuses. Despite the challenges confronting BGLFs, they offer Black men at HBCUs opportunities for campus involvement, leadership development, professional and social networking, and civic engagement. The challenges confronting collegiate chapters are not insurmountable; however, they are persistent. With increased emphasis on educational initiatives at the collegiate level, more proactive engagement and advising by chapter advisors, alumni chapters, governing boards, and university administrations, these challenges can be overcome.

References

Dancy, T. E. (2011). Becoming men in burning sands: Student identity, masculinity, and image construction in Black Greek-letter collegiate fraternities. In M. W. Hughey & G. S. Parks (Eds.), *Black-Greek letter organizations 2.0: New directions in the study of African American fraternities and sororities* (pp. 95–111). Jackson: University of Mississippi Press.

De Santis, A. D. (2007). *Inside Greek u.: Fraternities, sororities, and the pursuit of pleasure, power, and prestige.* Lexington: University of Kentucky Press.

De Santis, A. D., & Coleman, M. (2008). Not on my line: Attitudes about homosexuality in Black fraternities. In G. S. Parks (Ed.), *Black Greek-letter organizations in the 21st century: Our fight has just begun* (pp. 291–312). Lexington: University of Kentucky Press.

Horswell, C. (2009, November 3). Parents sue over Prairie View student's death. *The Houston Chronicle.* Retrieved from http://www.chron.com/disp/story.mpl/metropolitan/6701675.html

Hughey, M. W. (2008). Brotherhood or brothers in the "hood"? Debunking the "educated gang" thesis as Black fraternity and sorority slander. *Race Ethnicity and Education, 11*(4), 443–463.

Hughey, M. W., & Parks, G. S. (2007, October). Measuring up: Twelve steps closer to a solution for BGLO hazing. Retrieved from www.fraternityadvisors.org

Jenkins, A. D. (2010). *On-line: The pledging experiences of members of Black greek-lettered organizations from 1970 to 1990.* Unpublished Doctoral Dissertation, the University of Memphis, TN.

Johnson, R., Bradley, D., Bryant, L. Morton, D. M., & Sawyer, D. C., III. (2008). Advising Black Greek-letter organizations: A student development approach. In G. S. Parks (Ed.), *Black*

Greek-letter organizations in the 21st century: Our fight has just begun (pp. 437–458). Lexington: University of Kentucky Press.

Jones, R. L. (2004). *Black haze: Violence, sacrifice, and manhood in Black Greek-letter fraternities.* Albany, NY: SUNY Press.

Kimbrough, W. M. (2003). *Black Greek 101: The culture, customs, and challenges of Black fraternities and sororities.* Cranbury, NJ: Rosemont.

Kimbrough, W. M. (2005). Should Black fraternities and sororities abolish undergraduate chapters? Yes, unless…. *About Campus, 27,* 27–29.

Kimbrough, W. M., & Harper, S. R. (2006). African American men at historically Black colleges and universities: Different environments, similar challenges. In M. J. Cuyjet & Associates (Ed.), *African American men in college (pp. 189–209).* San Francisco, CA: Jossey-Bass.

Palmer, R. T., & Young E. M. (2009). Determined to succeed: Salient factors that foster academic success for academically unprepared Black males at a Black college. *Journal of College Student Retention, 10*(4), 465–482.

Shelton, C. L. (2008). Strategic essentialism and Black Greek identity in the postmodern era. In G. S. Parks (Ed.), *Black Greek-letter organizations in the 21st century: Our fight has just begun* (pp. 213–231). Lexington: University of Kentucky Press.

Washington, M. H., & Nunez, C. L. (2005). Education, racial uplift, and the rise of the Greek-letter tradition: The African American quest for status in the early twentieth century. In T. L. Brown, G. S. Parks, & C. M. Phillips (Eds.), *African American fraternities and sororities: The legacy and the vision* (pp. 137–179). Lexington: University of Kentucky Press.

Whaley, D. E. (2009). Links, legacies, and letters: A cultural history or Black Greek-letter organizations. In C. L. Torbenson, & G. S. Parks (Eds.), *Brothers and sisters: Diversity in college fraternities and sororities* (pp. 46–82). Madison, NJ: Fairleigh Dickinson University Press.

11

"MAN-TO-MAN"

An Exploratory Study of Coaches' Impact on Black Male Student-Athlete Success at Historically Black Colleges and Universities

David Horton Jr.

This chapter discusses Black male student-athletes and their academic success in historically Black colleges and universities (HBCUs). Over the past five decades extensive research has been conducted on college athletics and Black male student-athletes; yet minimal attention has been given to exploring these topics within the context of HBCUs (e.g., Blackman, 2008; Jackson, Lyons, & Gooden, 2001; Quarterman, 1992). To date, an overwhelming majority of the scholarly literature has been inclusive regarding the study of institutions and athletic programs that compete in major athletic conferences (Martin, Harrison, Stone, & Lawrence, 2010); those with large revenue-generating athletics programs (Meggyesy, 2000; Sperber, 2000; Tucker, 1992, 2004); and at predominantly White institutions (PWIs; Harrison, Sailes, Rotich, & Bimper, 2011; Singer, 2008). Using these institutional settings as the backdrop, scholars have explored a diverse set of issues and problems with respect to these institutional settings, athletics, and student-athletes. For example, scholars have explored the positive and negative impacts of athletic participation on academic success and degree attainment (Dawkins, Braddock, & Celaya, 2008; Harrison et al., 2011); student-athletes' academic, psychosocial, and identity development (Clopton, 2011; Howard-Hamilton & Sina, 2001; Spigner, 2003); as well as revenue-generating sports (e.g., football, basketball) and athletes that participate in them (Hawkins, 2010; Rhoden, 2006; Sellers, 1992).

This focus on "big-time" athletics programs and student-athletes at PWIs has naturally omitted athletics and student-athletes at HBCUs. This omission has resulted in rather large gaps in the scholarly and practitioner-based literature. Accordingly, the purpose of this study is to (a) add to the current literature by discussing issues that facilitate academic success among Black male student-athletes at HBCUs; (b) suggest cost-effective and pragmatic ways in which athletic coaches at these institutions can better assist and support Black male student-athletes in succeeding; and (c) to provide recommendations for future research to enhance knowledge and understanding of issues that are pertinent to student-athletes' success and well-being.

To accomplish the objectives of this exploratory analysis, this study uses coaches as the primary unit of analysis. In particular, this study places emphasis on what coaches do to enhance the quality of experiences and outcomes for Black male student-athletes. By using coaches as the primary unit of analysis, rather than student-athletes themselves, the aim of this chapter is to use their experiences to develop and provide examples of ways in which coaches can empower, encourage, and support Black male student-athletes to meet or surpass their own academic expectations, and the expectations of their institutions. Due to the exploratory nature of this study, it relies on literature and empirical studies on athletics and student-athletes, in general, to provide the framework for this chapter. Additionally, Academic Performance Program (APP) data from the National Collegiate Athletic Association (NCAA) and a single, semistructured interview with a former coach were collected, analyzed, and incorporated into this discussion.

As discussed, this study will draw upon extant literature to provide a context for Black male student-athletes in higher education. To this end, the subsequent section of this study will review literature on the following: the exploitation of Black male college athletes in nationally recognized athletics programs (Hawkins, 2010; Meggyesy, 2000; Rhoden, 2006); the role of athletics in social mobility (Dawkins et al, 2008); Black males' academic success and degree attainment rates (Martin et al., 2010); and their experiences with and ability to overcome negative stereotypes (Comeaux, 2008, 2010). Issues surrounding these debates will be discussed herein to provide a background for some of the general issues related to Black males and sport.

Exploitation of Black Male Athletes

The exploitation of Black male athletes has been hotly debated. These debates have increased recently as institutions, athletic governing boards, and coaches have reaped large benefits from corporate partnerships; all the while, graduation rates for Black male student-athletes that participate in many of these revenue-generating sports have seen minimal to no improvement (Meggyesy, 2000; Steinbach, 2010). Scholars such as Rhoden (2006) and Hawkins (2010) have fueled these debates by likening college sports to a plantation system in which Black males are the labor source and the NCAA and PWIs are the sole beneficiaries of the blood and sweat of these men. Although difficult to measure beyond anecdotal comparisons, discussions regarding the exploitation of Black student-athletes have required individuals (e.g., coaches, alumni, administrators) on both sides of the debate to critically and thoughtfully consider if there is truly an equitable distribution of costs and benefits between those that govern and those that participate.

Many have argued that the benefit Black male student-athletes receive from their participation in college athletics is the ability to attend and earn a degree from a quality institution and the opportunity to showcase their athletic skills on a nationally televised stage. Were it not for their athletic ability, many contend, opportunities to attend college would not have been extended to many Black male student-athletes (Benjamin, 2004; Messer, 2006). While Messer (2006) would agree, he argued that there are hazards and consequences associated with athletic participation, including the negative impact of athletic commitments on a student's schedule, which can serve to lower the amount of time students can spend studying, interacting with classmates, and other factors relevant to being successful in the college. As a researcher who specializes in retention and persistence among Black male student-athletes, I would contend that the long-term benefits of participating in college athletics are only realized if students are able to earn a quality education and acquire the skills to be competitive in the workforce.

Role of Athletics in Social Mobility

But what happens to student-athletes that do not make it professionally (e.g., NBA, NFL) or who fail to earn a college degree? Weatherspoon (2007) suggested that when dreams of going pro are not realized, former Black male athletes are "left lost, without hope and without the ability to function as everyday citizens" (p. 31). Some of the most vocal concerns about such circumstances have their origin within and outside the Black community. Concerns and frustrations have been voiced regarding the continued athletic socialization of Black males via family members', coaches', and the media's subtle messages that professional sports is the only lucrative path to success and wealth (Beamon, 2010; Messer, 2006). For decades, Black males have been lured into believing that one must learn how to dribble, catch, hit, or throw a ball well in order to live the American Dream (James, 2003; Lawson, 1979). While a focus on making it as a "pro" has proved lucrative for a select few, this single-mindedness has been detrimental to the larger group (Weatherspoon, 2007). Unfortunately, due to media portrayals of Black males that emphasize their contribution to athletics, many student-athletes have an inflated perception of the likelihood of becoming professional athletes. The reality is that only a small percentage of high school seniors will be given the opportunity to compete in athletics at the college leve, very few of whom will ever compete in their sport professionally (NCAA, 2010b).

Regardless of the dismal odds, many Black males still continue to view professional athletics as a more viable option for individual and generational success than education (Harrison, et al., 2011). Edwards (1973) cautions that one major consequence of Black males' past athletic success is that "young Black males are encouraged toward attempts at 'making it' through athletic participation, rather than through pursuit of other occupations that hold greater potential for meeting the real political and material needs of both themselves and their people" (cited in Lawson, 1979, p. 187).

Overcoming Stereotypes

Regardless of whether Black male student-athletes are interested in college athletics as a means to finance their education or as a stepping stone to pro sports, they must continually battle and overcome stereotypes concerning their focus on sport over academics (Comeaux, 2010; Spigner, 1993). Comeaux (2010) found that Black athletes are often perceived on college campuses as being less prepared for their academic studies than their peers and lacking the intelligence of White student-athletes. Harper (2009a) poignantly described the stereotypes and images associated with Black male student-athletes at PWIs as "Niggers with balls who enroll to advance their sports careers and generate considerable revenue for the institution without learning much or seriously endeavoring to earn their college degrees" (p. 701). These negative perceptions, combined with administrators and coaches' low expectations of Black student-athletes' academic performance and development of nonathletically related goals have a profound impact on their collegiate experiences, social engagement with their nonathlete peers, and ability to be academically successful (Beilock & McConnell 2004).

These competing and diverse viewpoints regarding the role and importance of athletics for Black males has provided a conundrum for student-athletes and institutions that sponsor athletic teams and programs (Messer, 2006). Can institutions truly support students' aspirations to reach their full potential in athletics while also enhancing and supporting their ability to compete and be *actively* engaged in their studies? What impact or role do coaches have within this process? These questions are addressed through discussions on HBCUs' athletic conference affiliations and structures, mentoring relationships, and the impact that mentoring relationships between coaches and students have on the personal and academic development of Black male student-athletes. These conversations are critical because they provide a richer context for this study, which examines the role of coaches in helping to facilitate academic success among Black male athletes at HBCUs.

HBCUs' Athletic Conference Affiliations and Structures

HBCUs that sponsor intercollegiate athletic teams are members of a national (i.e., NCAA, National Association of Intercollegiate Athletics [NAIA]) or a regional athletic governing body which oversees, administers, and governs athletic competitions between member institutions. Beyond membership in a governing organization, most institutions are also members of at least one athletic conference—a group of institutions that compete against each other athletically on an annual basis in certain sports. There are currently 38 HBCUs that are members of the NCAA. These institutions compete in one of three divisions (Division I, II, and III) and within five different local or regional athletic conferences: Southwestern Athletic Conference (SWAC), Mid-Eastern Athletic Conference (MEAC), Southern Intercollegiate Athletic Conference (SAIC), Central Intercollegiate Athletic Association (CIAA), and the Ohio Valley Conference (OVC). The CIAA was established in 1912, making it one of the oldest African American athletic conferences in the nation ("History of CIAA", 2011). The MEAC and SAIC are two of the largest conferences in which 4-year HBCUs compete—each currently has 13 member institutions. According to the Equity in Athletics Disclosure Act (EADA; 1994) data obtained for all Black colleges that are affiliate members of the NCAA, more than 6,300 men competed in seven different men's sports at these institutions during the 2009-2010 academic year.

Thirty-one historically Black institutions are represented within the NAIA, another national athletic governing body for 4-year institutions. The NAIA governs athletic programs and competitions throughout the United States and Canada. In addition to these national athletic governing bodies, HBCUs can be found within the membership of the U.S. Collegiate Athletic Association (USCAA) (five HBCUs are members) and the National Junior College Athletic Association (NJCAA) (seven HBCUs are members), which is one of the largest governing bodies in the United States for athletics at community colleges.

Student Success Measures

Regardless of athletic affiliation or institutional characteristics, all institutions of higher education that sponsor athletics are engaged in the collection of academic, financial, gender equity, and student-athlete wellness reporting (Horton, 2010). However, NCAA member institutions are subject to more stringent reporting than institutions that are members of other governing bodies (e.g., NAIA, NJCAA). This section provides information on student-athlete success for NCAA Division I affiliated institutions because these data are required, collected, and reported annually by the NCAA.

In addition to the diminishing student role and time constraints that are a result of sport participation, academic integrity issues among Division I student-athletes have become a major concern in college athletics over the past decades (Blackman, 2008; Comeaux, 2010). Since 2003, the NCAA has increased its focus on academic success and graduation rates for student-athletes and put into place policies that have implications for future funding for student-athletes through athletic related scholarships and HBCUs' ability to sponsor Division

I sports (Blackman, 2008). This comprehensive academic reform package, known as the Academic Performance Program (APP), is designed to improve the academic success and graduation of all student-athletes.

Specifically, in August 2003, the NCAA launched its academic program initiative, which created new initial eligibility standards for prospective student-athletes; continuing eligibility standards for student-athletes in their third, fourth, and fifth year; and created the academic progress rate (APR), which measures students' and teams' annual academic progress (Blackman, 2008; NCAA, 2010a). A single APR score (maximum score is 1,000) is calculated for each athlete and team based on each student-athlete's athletic eligibility standing, retention, and graduation each academic term. Institutions and teams that earn high APR scores are recognized by NCAA, while those that earn low scores are often subject to penalties that include scholarship reductions and the loss of eligibility to compete in championships (NCAA, 2010a).

Teams that historically struggle to meet minimum APR standards are subject to loss of scholarships or being prohibited from participating in postseason competitions (NCAA, 2010a). Since the APR standards were initiated, HBCUs have struggled to meet minimum success standards outlined by the NCAA (Jack, 2006; Sander, 2009). More specifically, Sander reported in 2009, of the 18 teams penalized for underperformance, 11 were from HBCUs. According to Sander, among the 18 institutions in 2009 with the highest number of teams failing to reach the cut score of 925 (equivalent to a 50% graduation rate), eight were HBCUs. As a result, eight received penalties and five lost scholarships; consequently, this indicates that several HBCUs that compete at the Division I level are struggling to graduate at least 50% of their student-athletes.

Blackman (2008) and athletic directors and coaches at HBCUs (Hosick, 2011) have argued that the APP and APR disproportionately discriminate against HBCUs, Black male athletes, and institutions with smaller athletic budgets. However, whether right, wrong, or discriminatory, institutions that are interested in maintaining their membership within the NCAA must meet standards that have been outlined in the organization's most recent legislation. One must remember that membership of the NCAA is voluntary. Therefore, institutions can freely withdraw from the NCAA if they do not feel that they have the human or financial resources to provide the necessary resources for their student-athletes. However, those institutions that desire to remain active members must take appropriate steps to comply with the NCAA's academic standards. I suggest in this study that coaches serve a vital role within this process and have the ability to greatly influence the success of their student-athletes.

Coach as Mentor

Boyd (2007) estimated that "more than half of the 5.6 million Black boys [in the U.S.] live in fatherless households" (p. 2). Athletic coaches usually take on several different roles, regularly assuming a fatherly role. Coaches, especially Black male coaches, have recognized their influence on many young Black males, often being one of the few positive role models these students know or have intimately interacted with prior to enrolling in college. This stems from the reality that many Black males grow up in homes where the father is not present. The personal and professional development of Black male student-athletes can be enhanced greatly through these mentoring relations, especially if past relationships have not provided positive examples. Sutton (2006) suggested that mentors should play four distinct developmental roles as mentors: teacher, guide, gatekeeper, and consultant. As such, it is vital for coaches to be willing to accept their role as mentors if they are truly interested in helping young adult Black student-athletes develop into successful adults.

Examples of the ways in which the mentor–mentee relationship evolves vary substantially. We often hear positive stories from former players at Grambling University about the life lessons they learned from legendary coach Robinson. One former player noted that, "I don't know if I would be where I am today if there had been no Eddie Robinson. He put that spark into everyone, that will to be more, to be the best" (Associated Press, 2007). Mentorship focused on student development can have a significant impact on both mentor and mentee. Sutton (2006) suggests that for Black men, these relationships can be instrumental in young men mastering such developmental tasks as "establishing positive self-esteem, control of emotions, positive interpersonal relationships with women, appreciation for academic success, and basic interaction skills" (p. 98).

Within the literature, it has been suggested that the most influential factors in predicting success are the presence of a father or positive male role model, a positive relationship with family members, mature decision making processes, high self-esteem, race-consciousness, and strong spiritual beliefs and values (Horne, 2007). As the number of incarcerated Black males increase, and those in college classrooms decline, this line of inquiry has dire implications for higher education and the future of Black males in higher education and in society as a whole. How will society view Black males and Black male student-athletes in the years to come? Harper (2009b) suggests that Black men are continually reminded of their distress and subordination. Stevenson (2002) noted that "the negative images of Black males have left a hole so deep in the consciousness of the American society that rarely do Americans accept evidence to the contrary" (p. 357). It arouses concern as to how wide and deep this hole has become since the time Stevenson (2002) wrote those words. What is even more disconcerting is when one considers the negative images that surround Black college athletes; then, the proverbial hole becomes an abyss that has erased the pride, respect, and power that Black men in America once held (Rhoden, 2006).

Methodology

The present study employs an exploratory research design in order to better understand Black male student-athletes' academic success and coaches' perceived impact on this success at HBCUs. Exploratory research designs are often employed to gain insight and familiarity with issues and problems for which little past research exists (Creswell, 2003). Exploratory designs can serve as building blocks for future research on underresearched phenomena.

A secondary data file was created and analyzed using information from the NCAA's Student-Athlete Experiences Data Archive. These data are collected by the NCAA and made publicly available for the public, researchers, and higher education administrators to answer prevailing questions concerning student-athletes and athletics at NCAA member institutions (Hosick, 2010). These data include both individual and institutional level data on current and former student athletes (NCAA, 2009). The data file analyzed in this study was limited to men's sports at HBCUs.

Interview participants were limited to current and former coaches at HBCUs that have worked or currently work with Black male student-athletes. Selection of interview participants was based on a purposeful informant selection process (Morse, 1994). Morse suggests that "a good informant is one who has the knowledge and experience the researcher requires, has the ability to reflect, is articulate, has the time to be interviewed, and is willing to participate in the study" (cited in James, 2003, p. 125). Two former coaches were invited to participate, only one of whom completed the study in its entirety. The interview was semistructured in nature. Semistructured interviews allow for researchers to use a set of predetermined questions to guide the discussion but allow for additional lines of questioning to emerge based upon the dialogue (DiCicco-Bloom & Crabtree, 2006).

The sole informant or participant for this study, Eric (pseudonym) has worked as a head coach and assistant coach at a public, 4-year HBCU for more than 7 years. Eric is between 35 and 44 years of age and identified himself as a Black man. In addition to his years as a coach, he was a former two-sport student-athlete at an HBCU. As discussed, in 2009 the NCAA began a new initiative to collect and release to the public APR scores for Division I head coaches. In 2010, Eric earned one of the highest APR ratings in the conference for his sport—his average rating over a 4-year period between the 2006-2007 and 2009-2010 academic years was 955. Given his commitment to the academic success of his student-athletes, his interview provided valuable data for this chapter.

Findings and Discussion

The fact that HBCUs struggle to meet the NCAA's APR minimum standards cannot be denied. Between the 2005-2006 and 2008-2009 academic years, only seven NCAA Division I men's teams (cross-country [2], tennis [5]) received recognition from the NCAA for earning multiyear APRs in the top 10% of all teams in their given sport. However, during the same time period, 29 teams were penalized because they earned an APR of 900 or less during one or more consecutive years (baseball—2, basketball—11, football—10, indoor track—3, outdoor track—2, and wrestling—1).

Many attribute this problem to a lack of resources—compared to many big-time athletics programs, HBCUs do not have the fiscal or human resources to support their athletes (Hosick, 2011; Jack, 2006). Given that HBCUs lack resource parity with their PWI counterparts, they must be proactive in finding ways to increase the performance of their student-athletes. In the section that follows, this chapter presents a discussion of pragmatic ways to better assist student-athletes, specifically Black male student-athletes.

"Focus! That Is It in a Nutshell"

To begin, parents and coaches must understand that success in athletics is one among many avenues for young Black males to be successful in life. Recent statistics suggests that .03% of high school basketball players will compete professionally in the NBA. This percentage only increases slightly for those hoping to make this transition from college (1.2%). For college athletes that aspire to make the NFL, only 1.7% will reach this goal (NCAA, 2010b). Therefore, the likelihood that high school or collegiate athletes will have the opportunity to compete professionally is relatively small. Eric noted that many student-athletes have a desire to compete in professional sport. He attributed this desire to a poor focus on academic matters, as students were distracted from their academic goals. When asked why his student-athletes were more successful than athletes on other teams at his institution, he responded:

> a lot of other teams are just not as focused on it [academic success]. They got that going to the NFL, going to the NBA mentality and that's what they feed [them]. They feed the dollar signs; they see this, they see that, but it [academic success] is not pushed to them as much as it is being pushed to [our players].

One of the strategies Eric used to confront this "pro or bust" mentality was to invite "positive role models" to campus, such as former players who have graduated, to speak to his players about the importance of earning a degree. He also invited professors on campus to speak with his team members about their future goals and steps they needed to take to accomplish them. These meetings also served as a way to get students and faculty members to interact outside of class.

During data analysis, one theme that emerged from my conversation with Eric is what I labeled as "consistent and repetitive positive messages." This is illustrated in Eric's response when asked to discuss his methods for conveying to his athletes the importance of being successful in the classroom. He stated:

> Our main mission is to get these kids graduated…. And we put it in their heads, put it their head, put it in their head, even those kids that don't come to school thinking that they are going to graduate, we put it in their head so much that they know that once they complete everything they are suppose to complete, they will graduate, they will walk across that stage.

Clearly, the consistent and repetitive positive messages conveyed by Eric underscored the importance of contemplating a life after college which was not dependent upon an athletic career. As this statement makes evident, these messages were able to prepare student–athletes, even those who were not initially focused on graduating from college, about the importance of academic success.

Dress the Part

Earlier, this chapter discussed some of the stereotypes that Black student-athletes are confronted with on college campuses and how these negative perceptions can impact their academic performance. While much of the literature on this issue has been based on studies conducted at PWIs, I asked Eric to discuss how student-athletes, particularly his athletes, were perceived on his campus. I also asked Eric to share with me the strategies he used to convey to his athletes the importance of being "academically attentive" in class. His explained that he believed his student-athletes are viewed "with the utmost respect." He continued:

> I tell them don't wear your hat towards the back, don't allow sagging; you dressed when you go to class. You don't wear pajamas, you don't wear flip-flops nor do you wear tanks, white beaters. None of that is accepted and you pretty much have to wear your shirt tucked in … my student-athletes sat in the front of the class, and like I said, they are respectful— yes ma'am, no ma'am, yes sir, no sir and if that don't happen they suffer the consequences.

As noted by his comments, Eric provided clear directions to his students on how to counter stereotypes, by specifying classroom behaviors, seating location, and even the clothing that should be worn. In particular, his focus on proper attire underscored the professionalism that he expected from his athletes, on and off of the field.

Living by Example

Coaches of intercollegiate sports for men at HBCUs have an opportunity to transform young Black men as well as impact later generations. Although preliminary, initial findings from this study suggest that coaches serve as powerful agents in facilitating the success of Black male student-athletes. When asked about the role of coaches in student-athletes' success, Eric stated, "I think it should be the biggest influence." He continued, "Besides their parent or guardian, I think the coaches are the number one person." As noted earlier, many Black male athletes (and athletes in general) see their coaches as important figures in their lives.

As role models, coaches shape student-athletes' perceptions, values, and behaviors on and off the field. An important aspect of a coach's ability to shape athletes' behaviors is the power they wield over rewards and punishments. Coaches have control over what positions students play, how much practice time they receive, minutes of "game time" play, interactions with other athletes, and physical activities during practice (e.g., running extra laps, water breaks). Eric also acknowledged that he does understand that he is often seen as a role model, and it is a role that he gladly takes: "oh, yea, I consider myself to be a role model to them.... I try to live right. Try to do everything that I ask them to do." By modeling the behavior he expects from his athletes, Eric reinforces his verbal messages through his interactions.

"They're Grown Men"

When asked about the characteristics a coach must have to get students to be successful, especially Black male student-athletes, Eric suggested, "You have to have patience, that's the key." He subsequently stated that it is important to treat athletes with respect, like men. Eric mentioned that dictatorships don't work, "They're grown men as well and if you think you're the dictator and you try to tell them what to do, when to do it, how to do it, then it's not going to work." According to Eric, open and honest communication with his student-athletes is important. He stated:

> You have to be able to open up and let them communicate as a man at some point. There's a point in time where we'll have those conversations, man-to-man, and I'll let that be known at the beginning of the conversation. You come into this office you talk to me man-to-man and we'll talk man-to-man. But once we leave that office its back to coach-player.

These remarks illustrate Eric's understanding of the need for open dialogue where student-athletes can have frank conversations with their coach. He perceived these office-only exchanges as a necessity for manly relationships, even in cases where one person held greater power than the other (e.g., coach vs. student).

Recommendations for Practical Application

Although the data from this study are admittedly limited, they provide some compelling information that could be used to help enhance the retention and persistence of Black male student-athletes. To this end, this chapter will provide some practical recommendations that might be beneficial to coaches or others working directly with Black male student-athletes:

1. Given the data presented in this study, coaches should earnestly help student-athletes remember that while competing athletically may be a priority, doing well academically is equally as important. As the data presented in this chapter revealed, only a very small number of student-athletes will succeed in transitioning to professional competition, thus, student-athletes need to have a strong academic background in case they do not make it professionally. As illustrated by Eric, this goal can be accomplished through discussions focused on careers that are not reliant upon direct athletic competition. Possibly, coaches can provide discussions of athletic related careers (e.g., coaching, athletic directing) that allow students to continue working in areas related to their passion.
2. It is important that coaches or those working closely with student-athletes encourage them to present themselves in a studious manner when they attend class or interact with their professors. Indeed, this is important for all students. Nevertheless, it is especially important for student-athletes because some professors may be less inclined to view them as serious about their academic performance. Thus, presenting themselves in a manner that is conducive to learning may help to challenge this perception. However, this does not remove the responsibility from faculty members in being cognizant of negative stereotypes which exist about athletes. Campus administration should establish policies which lead to the hiring of faculty that demonstrate diversity competence through a positive work history with multicultural communities.
3. Coaches should realize their status as role models to many student-athletes. As this chapter indicated, many Black male student-athletes have a dearth of positive role models in their lives. Given this, coaches can use their status as a role model to help student-athletes succeed academically. Coaches can do this through self-disclosure, giving students a "reality check," or assuming a stance as a parental figure. As discussed by Eric, being a role model does not only consist of what is said to student-athletes, but the actions and behaviors of coaches as well. Thus, just as student-athletes are expected to present themselves as professionals, so too, should coaches. Further, being a role model is an important responsibility that coaches should not take lightly. In assuming a pseudo-parental role, coaches must realize the immense power that they have in shaping both positive and negative behaviors, dispositions, and actions.
4. While this chapter discusses a coach's impact on helping his student-athletes succeed academically, the onus for helping students achieve academic success should not be the sole responsibility of coaches. Rather as

the African proverb says, "It takes a village to raise a child." Consequently, the institutional community (e.g., administrators, student affairs practitioners, and faculty) are responsible for helping student-athletes to reach their full academic potential. Thus, all institutional agents should work arduously to create a positive and affirming campus environment designed to facilitate the success of all students, including student-athletes.

Recommendations for Future Research

It has been suggested that one of the best ways scholars can influence the experiences of Black males is to provide scholarly analysis of the issues and challenges that confront Black men (Phillips, 1996). Based on some of the findings from this study, the following recommendations for future research are offered. First, additional research is needed to understand how institutions with limited financial resources can be equally as effective as institutions with a wealth of resources in supporting Black male student-athletes' collegiate success. In addition, research is necessary to gain a better understanding of the purpose and mission of athletics at HBCUs. More specifically, since many athletic programs at HBCUs are not huge revenue-generators, what other purposes do they serve? Are athletic programs used to build alumni support or do they serve as bases for recruitment? Moreover, a noticeable limitation of this study is that it only used interview data from one participant and NCAA data for Division I institutions. Thus, future research should encompass a larger interview sample in order to explore the experiences of coaches at various levels and diverse institutions (i.e., community colleges, private institutions, and others). The specific intent and purpose of this chapter was to begin a conversation on Black male student-athletes and their academic success in HBCUs. It is my hope that these conversations will continue and that these discussions and considerations for future research will provide best practices for supporting Black student-athletes as they pursue their studies at institutions of all types, settings, and sizes.

References

Associated Press. (2007, April). Quotes on the death of Eddie Robinson. Retrieved from http://sports.espn.go.com/ncf/news/story?id=2825754

Beamon, K. K. (2010). Are sports overemphasized in the socialization process of African American males? A qualitative analysis of former collegiate athletes' perception of sport socialization. *Journal of Black Studies, 41*(2), 281–300.

Beilock, S. L., & McConnell, A. R. (2004). Stereotype threat and sport: Can athletic performance be threatened? *Journal of Sport and Exercise Psychology, 26,* 597–609.

Benjamin, A. B. (2004). College athletics: Reconnecting academic values in college athletics. *Phi Kappa Phi Forum, 84*(4), 9–10.

Blackman, P. C. (2008). The NCAA's academic performance program: Academic reform or academic racism? *UCLA Entertainment Law Review, 15*(2), 225–289.

Boyd, H. (2007). It's hard out here for a Black man! *Black Scholar, 37*(3), 2–9.

Central Intercollegiate Athletic Association (CIAA). (2011). The history of the CIAA. Retrieved from http://www.theciaa.com/information/about_ciaa/index

Clopton, A. W. (2011). Using identities to explore social capital differences among White and African American student athletes. *Journal of African American Studies, 15*(1), 58–73.

Comeaux, E. (2008). Black males in the classroom: A quantitative analysis of student–faculty interactions. *Challenge 14*(1), 1–13.

Comeaux, E. (2010). Racial differences in faculty perceptions of collegiate student-athletes' academic and post-undergraduate achievements. *Sociology of Sport Journal, 27,* 390–412.

Creswell, J. W. (2003). *Research design: Qualitative, quantitative, and mixed methods approaches* (2nd ed.). Thousand Oaks, CA: Sage.

Dawkins, M. P., Braddock, J. H., & Celaya, A. (2008). Academic engagement among African American males who hold aspirations for athletic careers in professional sports. *Challenge, 14*(2), 51–65.

DiCicco-Bloom, B., & Crabtree, B. F. (2006). The qualitative research interview. *Medical Education, 40*(4), 314–321.

Harper, S. R. (2009a). Nigger no more: A critical race counternarrative on Black male student achievement at predominantly White colleges and universities. *International Journal of Qualitative Studies in Education, 22*(6), 697–712

Harper, S. R. (2009b). Race, interest convergence, and transfer outcomes for Black male student athletes. In L. S. Hagedorn & D. Horton, Jr. (Eds.), *Student athletes and athletics* (New Directions for Community Colleges, No. 147, pp. 29–37). San Francisco, CA: Jossey-Bass.

Harrison, L., Jr., Sailes, G., Rotich, W. K., & Bimber, A. Y., Jr. (2011). Living the dream or awakening from the nightmare: Race and athletic identity. *Race, Ethnicity and Education, 14*(1), 91–103.

Hawkins, B. C. (2010). *The new plantation: Black athletes, college sports, and predominantly white NCAA institutions.* New York: Palgrave Macmillan.

Horton, D., Jr. (2010). *Community college athletes: Tracking progress to gauge success* (Monograph No. CHEWP.3.2010). Athens, OH: Ohio University Center for Higher Education. Retrieved from http://www.cehs.ohio.edu/centerspartnerships/centers/c4he/CHEWP_3_2010_DHorton.pdf

Horne, O., Jr. (2007). *Voices of the talented tenth: Values of young Black males in higher education.* Lanham, MD: University Press of America.

Hosick, M. B. (2011). NCAA working with HBCUs to clear APR barriers. *National Collegiate Athletic Association (NCAA).* Retrieved from http://www.ncaa.org/wps/wcm/connect/public/NCAA/Resources/Latest+News/2011/May/NCAA+working+with+HBCUs+to+clear+APR+barriers

Howard-Hamilton, M. F., & Sina, J. A. (2001). *Student Services for Student Athletes* [Special issue]. How college affects student athletes. In M. F. Howard-Hamilton & S. K. Watt (Eds.), (New Directions for Student Services, No. 93, pp. 35–45). San Francisco, CA: Jossey-Bass.

Jack, C. (2006). MEAC schools hit hard for poor performance. *USA Today.* Retrieved from EBSCOhost. J0E180804553506. http://web.ebscohost.com/ehost/detail?vid=6&hid=125&sid=e004dec2-ceaa-4d0f-9e55a4b2ac671387%40sessionmgr113&bdata=JnNpdGU9ZWhvc3QtbGl2ZQ%3d%3d#db=a9h&AN=J0E180804553506

Jackson, E. N., Lyons, R., & Gooden, S. (2001). The marketing of Black college sports. *Sports Marketing Quarterly, 10*(3), 138–147.

James, C. E. (2003). Schooling, basketball and US scholarship aspirations of Canadian student athletes. *Race Ethnicity and Education, 6*(2), 123–144.

Lawson, H. A. (1979). Physical education and sport in the black community: The hidden perspective. *The Journal of Negro Education, 48*(2), 187–195.

Martin, B. E., Harrison, C. K., Stone, J., & Lawrence, S. M. (2010). Athletic voices and academic victories: African American male student-athlete experience in the Pac-Ten. *Journal of Sport & Social Issue, 34*(2), 131–153.

Meggyesy, D. (2000). Athletes in big-time college sport. *Society, 37*(3), 24–28.

Messer, K. L. (2006). African American male college athletes. In M. J. Cuyjet & Associates (Eds.), *African American men in college* (pp. 154–173). San Francisco, CA: Jossey-Bass.

Morse, J. M. (1994) Designing funded qualitative research. In N. K. Denzin & Y. S. Lincoln (Eds.), *Handbook of qualitative research* (pp. 220–235). Thousand Oaks, CA: Sage.

National Collegiate Athletic Association (NCAA). (2009). NCAA student-athlete experiences data archive. In *About the project*. Retrieved from http://www.icpsr.umich.edu/icpsrweb/NCAA/

National Collegiate Athletic Association (NCAA). (2010a). Behind the blue disk: Division I academic reform. Retrieved from http://www.ncaa.org/wps/wcm/connect/public/NCAA/Resources/Behind+the+Blue+Disk/Behind+the+Blue+Disk+-+Division+I+Academic+Reform

National Collegiate Athletic Association (NCAA). (2010b). Probability of going pro: Estimated probability of competing in athletics beyond the high school interscholastic level. Retrieved from http://www.ncaa.org/wps/wcm/connect/public/NCAA/Resources/Basketball+Resources/ Basketball+Resource+Probability+of+Going+Pro

Phillips, M. C. (1996). Painting a varied picture. *Black Issues in Higher Education, 13*(16), n.p.

Quarterman, J. (1992). Characteristics of athletic directors of historically Black colleges and universities. *Journal of Sport Management, 6*(1), 52–63.

Rhoden, W. C. (2006). *$40 million slaves: The rise, fall, and redemption of the Black athlete.* New York: Crown.

Sander, L. (2009, May 15). After years of scrutiny, hundreds of teams still fail to make the NCAA's grade. *Chronicle of Higher Education.* Retrieved from http://chronicle.com/article/After-Years-of-Scrutiny-Hu/44342/

Sellers, R. M. (1992). Racial differences in the predictors of academic achievement of student-athletes in Division I revenue producing sports. *Sociology of Sport Journal, 9*(1), 48–59.

Singer, J. N. (2008). Benefits and detriments of African American male athletes' participation in a big-time college football program. *International Review for the Sociology of Sport, 43*(4), 399–408.

Sperber, M. (2000). *Beer and circus: How big-time college sports is crippling undergraduate education.* New York: Henry Holt.

Spigner, C. (2003). African American student-athletes: Academic support or institutionalized racism? *Education, 114*(1), 144–150.

Steinbach, P. (2010). Academics confront the exploitation of African American male athletes. *Athletic Business,* n.p. Retrieved from http://athleticbusiness.com/articles/article.aspx?articleid=3555&zoneid=8

Stevenson., H. C., Jr. (2002). Wrestling with destiny: The cultural socialization of anger and healing in African American males. *Journal of Psychology & Christianity, 21*(4), 357–364.

Sutton, E. M. (2006). Developmental mentoring of African American Men. In M. J. Cuyjet & Associates (Eds.), *African American men in college* (pp. 95–111). San Francisco, CA: Jossey-Bass.

Tucker, I. B. (1992). The impact of big-time athletics on graduation rates. *Atlantic Economic Journal, 20*(4), 65–72.

Tucker, I. B. (2004). A reexamination of the effects of big-time football and basketball success on graduation rates and alumni giving rates. *Economics of Education Review, 23,* 655–661.

Weatherspoon, F. D. (2007). Black male student-athletes owe themselves, forefathers more. *Diverse Issues in Higher Education, 23*(25), 31.

12

ACADEMICALLY GIFTED BLACK MALE UNDERGRADUATES IN ENGINEERING

Perceptions of Factors Contributing to their Success in an Historically Black College and University

Alonzo M. Flowers

Overview

Extensive literature on academic achievement by Black college students primarily focuses on their academic failure rather than their success. Black students have historically faced underrepresentation in both gifted and talented programs and science, technology, engineering, and mathematics (STEM) areas of study (Bonner, 2010a; Ford, 2003; Fries-Britt, 1998; Grantham, 2004a; Harper, 2004). Jackson (2003) suggested that an increase in research focusing on the academic experiences of gifted Black males in STEM is warranted. To date, research that focuses on the academic and social experiences of academically gifted Black male college students has been limited. Recent findings on college persistence stress the role of institutions of higher education in providing educational opportunities; however, the minimal literature which exists suggests that academically gifted Black males have had limited access to these opportunities. Academically gifted Black males in higher education encounter social and institutional factors that guide the direction of their educational experience, particularly in engineering disciplines.

This chapter explores the perceptions of academically gifted Black male undergraduate students majoring in engineering disciplines at an historically Black college/university (HBCU) to identify factors that contribute to academic and social development. To provide information about academically gifted Black males in engineering, this chapter discusses retention and persistence of Black males in this field, provides a context for academically gifted Black male achievement and identity formation, and presents practical recommendations aimed to assist Black males in their navigation of engineering programs.

Black Males' Persistence in Engineering

Recent studies have highlighted the importance of examining persistence among college students of color (Moore, 2006). Moore's study of Black male students majoring in engineering focused on the impact of the students' academic experiences as a factor in persistence. In many cases, insufficient academic preparation in science and mathematics at the early levels of education has influenced Black male students' scholastic trajectory (Moore, 2006). The economic and social issues that academically gifted Black males encounter during college may also affect their persistence (Davis, 1994). In contemporary studies on persistence and STEM, there has been an increased emphasis on the importance of fostering persistence during the critical sophomore year (Gahagan & Hunter, 2006; Graunke & Woosley, 2005; Schreiner & Pattengale, 2000). The struggles that students tend to encounter during the sophomore year have been associated with a high level of attrition (Sanchez-Linguelinel, 2008). On one hand, Bowen, Chingos, and McPherson (2009) claimed that "nearly 44% of all college withdrawals occur after the second year" (p. 35). In contrast, Moore and Herndon (2003) contended that, despite the multitude of challenges faced by academically gifted Black males in engineering, they are inclined not to let negative experiences, attitudes, and perceptions hinder their academic development.

The academic and social experiences of Black male college students are often tainted by negative stereotypical social stigmas that operate on a deficit frame, consequently affecting their academic process (Palmer, Davis, & Hilton, 2009). For academically gifted Black males the collegiate experience becomes a continuous battle of redefining the nature of their identities (Bonner, 2001, 2010a; Lynn, 2002). Contemporary research on the issue of Black male persistence in engineering confirms that academic success is connected with the students' self-perception (Whiting, 2006a). In addition, issues of college persistence for academically gifted Black males have been linked to concerns with the level of student engagement with their disciplines and satisfaction with their instructional context (Allen, 1992; Bonner 2001; Davis, 1994). Given the problems and underrepresentation of Black males in engineering in general and academically gifted Black males specifically, this chapter will make a compelling contribution to the literature.

Academic Giftedness in Black Males

Academic giftedness has been defined in mainstream literature in terms of IQ or other cognitive ability assessments (Renzulli, 1986). However, the findings presented in this chapter offer a distinctively new perspective on giftedness. For the participants in the case study reported in this chapter, conceptualization of giftedness was not framed in the same manner as described in the literature. Academic giftedness from the perspective of the Black males in the study was based on factors associated with Whiting's (2006a, 2006b) *scholar identity model*. Whiting contended that the following characteristics contribute to a scholar identity: (a) self-efficacy, (b) future orientation, (c) willingness to make sacrifices, (d) internal locus of control, (e) self-awareness, (f) need for achievement greater than need for affiliation, (g) academic self-confidence, (h) racial identity, and (i) masculinity. Whiting's scholar identity model posits that Black males' identities are constructed by interactions between the school environment and several internal characteristics, such as self-efficacy and willingness to make sacrifices. *Self-efficacy* refers to one's belief about one's ability to perform a specific task. According to Bandura (1997), "Efficacy is a generative capability in which cognitive, social, emotional, and behavioral sub-skills must be organized and effectively orchestrated to serve innumerable purposes" (pp. 36–37). In other words, by organizing and executing a necessary course of action, people self-regulate their learning, in addition to setting proximal goals as a means to increase their beliefs not only about their ability to perform a task but also their persistence in the task.

Leading scholars when writing about gifted Black students have maintained that a "strong sense of self" is an essential characteristic of academically gifted Black males (Bonner, 2001, 2010b; Ford, 1996; Grantham, 2004b; Hilliard, 2003). Whiting (2006a, 2006b) asserted that, when self-efficacy is positive for Black males, they tend to share similar characteristics: (a) high resilience, (b) high self-confidence, (c) high self-control, (d) a strong sense of self-responsibility, and (e) a clear understanding of the tasks that they face and the belief that they can accomplish all of the subtasks associated with their goal. Bonner and Bailey (2006) claimed that "establishment of a positive identity for the [Black] male student is significant in that it serves as the foundation upon which the student can develop some sense of agency and in turn determine where he 'fits' within the academy" (p. 28).

Many of the experiences of academically gifted Black males are parallel to those of other gifted minority groups. They face issues concerning both academic and social integration in college environments. Interactions between internal (psychological) and external (social and institutional) factors may trigger responses that affect the academic and social development of academically gifted Black male college students. Moreover, because of their identification as gifted, Black males are likely to encounter race hostility and stereotyping both from within the Black community and from outside (Bonner & Bailey, 2006).

The chapter is based on a larger study, which employed case study methods to understand the experiences of academically gifted Black male engineering students at an HBCU. Consequently, the subsequent section will discuss the study's methodology.

Research Methods

Qualitative research uses a naturalistic approach to provide the researcher with an understanding of key phenomena in context-specific settings (Denzin & Lincoln, 1994; Lincoln & Guba, 1985; Patton, 2001). In a broad sense, qualitative research is defined as "any kind of research that produces findings not arrived at by means of statistical procedures or other means of quantification" (Strauss & Corbin, 1990, p. 17). Qualitative research emerged as a way to describe, interpret, and learn about people and how they construct their realities (Travers, 2001). Essentially, researchers using qualitative methodology do not seek to provide "the truth" through the data that they collect. Instead, qualitative researchers use elements of interaction such as words, gestures, and participants' actions to "form conclusions" about experiences of the participants and gather "detailed description of situations, events, people, interactions, and observed behaviors" (Patton, 2001, p. 22) to contextualize the participants' world. Qualitative research allows for an examination of various dimensions of truth. Ultimately, qualitative researchers are characterized as "intrigued with the complexity of social interactions as expressed in daily life and with the meanings the participants themselves attribute to these interactions" (Marshall & Rossman, 1999, p. 2). Consequently, the nature of qualitative research is to explore social phenomena through the participants' perspectives.

Research Design

This study followed a qualitative, single case study design. A case study is an empirical inquiry that investigates a contemporary phenomenon within its real-life context (Merriam, 1998; Yin, 2008). Yin (2008) indicated that case studies are essential to the investigation of one's perception. Specifically, case studies are based on a constructivist paradigm that allows the researcher to recognize the importance of the subjective human creation of meaning (Yin, 2008). Thus, case studies provide a context in which to understand a phenomenon from the participants' viewpoint. Yin (1994) presented four applications for a case study model: (a) to explain complex causal links in real-life interventions, (b) to describe the real-life context in which the intervention has occurred, (c) to describe the intervention itself, and (d) to explore situations in which the intervention being evaluated has no clear set of outcomes. In general, case studies allow for an exploration of a particular context. Yin categorized case studies as follows: explanatory, descriptive, and exploratory. In this study an exploratory single-method (two institutions) case study was employed. An exploratory single-method case study explores the *how* and *why* of a phenomenon, particularly in relation to how participants construct their perceptions about the phenomenon.

Participants and Site Selection

Participants were chosen based on criteria established by the researcher: Black, male, high achieving/academically gifted, seniors, and majoring in an engineering program. The target HBCU was the first state-supported college for Blacks and the second oldest public institution in the state. Initially, the curriculum of the university was designed to serve as preparation and training for teachers. After the Morrill Act of 1890 was implemented, the curriculum at the university was expanded to include subjects such as the arts, science, agriculture, nursing, and mechanics. The expansion of the curriculum created a strong tradition in agricultural research, community service, and educational excellence, a tradition that continues at the institution. Currently, the university is considered one of the top HBCUs in the state. Enrollment exceeds 8,500, including more than 2,000 graduate students.

Key Findings

This study was designed to investigate how academically gifted Black male engineering majors perceived their college experience within the HBCU context. Based on the participants' responses, it was concluded that institutions of higher education must understand the various factors (e.g., peer and faculty support, institutional congruence) that influence the academic and social integration of academically gifted Black male students. Specifically, these institutions must recognize the importance of family involvement and mentoring for Black male engineering students. Because Black males are far more likely to be underrepresented in engineering programs, it is vital that institutions of higher education provide proactive interventions. This section summarizes the responses given by participants, with quotations from the participants' responses to provide a context for the participants' reported experiences.

Participants' Perceptions of Their Abilities. Participants constructed their self-perception based on internal and external factors that they had experienced throughout their educational careers to date. Shavelson, Hubner, and Stanton (1976) broadly defined self-perception as "a person's self-perceptions formed through experience with and interpretations of his or her environment" (p. 411). They contended that self-perception is not an entity within the person but rather a hypothetical construct that is potentially useful in explaining, predicting, and understanding human behavior. Because self-perception influences self-determination, how students perceive themselves is vital to their academic outlook. For these participants, self-perception about their ability to be academically successful affected their perception of being high achievers. Participants' self-assurance about their academic capabilities often led to positive academic outcomes. Johnny, a senior majoring in electrical engineering with a

3.1 grade point average (GPA) described the importance of believing in one's abilities:

> You have to work hard to get somewhere in life but you have to believe in yourself and your abilities. So if you have the talent and you're gifted academically then you should believe you can do it and not let anyone or anything keep you from reaching your goals.

Thus, for Johnny, the belief in his academic abilities led to a positive self-perception. Throughout the interviewing process, these high-achieving Black males associated their ability to achieve academically with maintaining a positive self-perception. For instance, Isaiah, an electrical engineering major with a minor in physics said, "I'm great in math so I have always to strive for the best grades in all my classes." The participants discussed how their positive self-perceptions had been shaped. Each associated his strong academic identity to factors such as institutional influences and early interest in academics.

Many of the participants maintained that their academic self-perception was influenced by their institutional environments. For instance, the participants described how the supportive nature of the campus influenced their ability to achieve academically. Charles, a senior chemical engineering major with a 3.2 GPA said, "This college was built to support us Blacks; there is support in all aspects of campus life." Chase, a senior computer engineering major with a 3.3 GPA, claimed, "[This university] is like home; people want you to succeed here." The availability of academic support increased the participants' connection to the institution. In related literature it has been noted that institutional support is one of the fundamental factors for achievement by Black males (Moore, 2006). Success for Black male college students is fostered when the academic system is well organized and provides support services that promote academic achievement for all students (Hrabowski, 2003).

Defining Giftedness

The definition of *giftedness* varied among participants. For each of the participants, defining himself as gifted was not part of his self-constructed identity. While the notion of giftedness was seen as a positive attribute by all participants, they were not inclined to self-identify as gifted. Johnny jokingly emphasized that he does not walk around and talk about his abilities, telling people he is gifted in mathematics. Instead, he attributed giftedness to a divine power. "Giftedness is something that God has given you. It is something that you cannot go and get out on the streets. It is a gift!"

For the participants in this study, giftedness entailed not only the necessary academic skills to be successful but also the confidence in their ability to be successful. Some participants noted that giftedness is a combination of ability and effort. Chase stated, "Giftedness is not only one's natural intelligence.

Someone can be naturally smart but [if] they don't apply themselves, then their abilities mean nothing. But my ability to achieve comes from not only my brain but also my determination to succeed." Parenthetically, Johnny declared that his conceptualization of giftedness represented *something different*. From his perspective, the label of giftedness did little for his sense of identity, primarily because he did not realize the importance of being labeled as gifted. He commented, "Being labeled as 'gifted' just meant I was put in classes where teachers would give me more work." Johnny noted that, in retrospect, his enrollment in advanced classes in high school had kept him out of trouble.

For these participants, giftedness starts with the individual. Each of the participants discussed the importance of recognizing one's academic capabilities. It is important to note that the participants' framing of high achieving and their inability to connect this with the premise of giftedness compelled the researcher to use these terms interchangeably because these participants simply did not view themselves as gifted. Isaiah a senior electrical engineering major with a 3.2 GPA described his idea of giftedness:

> Ever since I can remember, learning and gaining new knowledge has always been important to me. I remember being young and watching television and seeing this commercial stating "Knowledge is Power" and I was like, "Wow,… I want power! So I must be willing and open to attaining knowledge." To this day, I still seek to gain all the power I can through my attainment of knowledge.

These data suggest that the cultivation of the participants' self-perception was a multifaceted process that was influenced by their educational experiences. Moreover, the participants' construction of their academic abilities (i.e., giftedness) was encouraged within educational settings that provided both academic and socioemotional support (i.e., support from teachers and positive reinforcement with regard to students' academic abilities). Specifically, the participants sought to define their educational experiences as the mechanism by which they conceptualized giftedness within themselves.

Majoring in Engineering

For each of the participants, majoring in engineering offered a sense of personal and academic self-fulfillment. Some participants commented on the importance of pursuing engineering degrees. The participants' ability to integrate academically and socially in their engineering programs was a critical factor in their success. A student's ability to integrate academically and socially in college is vital for academic success. Academic and social integration refers to the student's ability to connect with the essential elements within the institutional context. The participants in this study noted that to be a successful engineering major involves a feeling of connectedness with the department. This connectedness includes interactions with peers and faculty in the department.

Some participants noted that majoring in engineering had allowed them to integrate into a community of learners with similar academic aspirations. Charles stated, "In my program we are like a family; there are seven of us who have made it to senior year together." Johnny, an electrical engineering major, explained how he integrated academically and socially into his engineering department. He indicated that his transition to his engineering program was initially difficult but he realized that, if he wanted to be an engineer, he had to persist. Johnny acknowledged that his classmates, whom he viewed as friends, and his professors were "*all* in the same boat." His remark suggests that at HBCUs both peers and faculty play an integral role in the successful integration of Black students in engineering programs. Chase noted, "The professors made it easy for the students to academically and socially integrate with our peers; it was almost automatic." He explained that, during his first semester, the students worked in collaborative teams that were evaluated as a group, a method of instruction that forced students to work together. Faculty–student interaction can influence a range of educational outcomes, including attitudes toward college, personal development, and degree completion. Several participants indicated that faculty mentorships assisted in their success in college. Charles claimed, "We have a great chemical engineering department; if you need to talk to your advisor, a professor, or even the Dean of the College, their doors are always open." Johnny noted that faculty support occurs inside and outside of the classroom.

> The faculty at my college, no matter what department, wants you to do well in school. My junior year I took a fine arts course. I still remember how supportive the professor was. He was so interested and invested in my learning. When I first signed up for that course, I didn't think I was going to enjoy it. But after the second week that class ended up being one of my favorite courses.

Participants commented that they benefited intellectually and academically when they interacted with faculty. Seniors Isaiah and Chase shared similar positive experiences about their faculty mentors. Isaiah explained, "From the first day we met, my mentor and I got along very well. I guess it was due to our similar experiences growing up." Chase reported positive interaction with the faculty: "Faculty members in the College of Engineering definitely fight for us. When I couldn't find an internship, my mentor got on the phone and made some calls. Three days later I had an interview with a local engineering firm." Chase shared that faculty were eager to serve as mentors and to help students in the program. His experience highlights another role that faculty play for their students: networking. In this case, Chase's mentor used his networking skills to arrange an interview for an internship.

The participants noted that factors such as positive peer influence and faculty support were essential to their integration into the institution. However, they indicated a stronger sense of peer and faculty support inside and outside the classroom. As an HBCU, the school seeks to develop and educate the "whole" student. Kannerstein (1978) noted that HBCUs have two missions:

> The Black college, thus, has a dual mission. It is about human excellence, the superior education and training of tender minds, nourishment of the creative imagination, and reverence for learning; it is also the development of moral character and the production of better men and women for a more humane, decent, and open world.
>
> *(p. 55)*

Charles claimed that the campus climate was based on student support, especially within his engineering department. He noted that the engineering faculty and staff just wanted students to succeed; thus, they provided all necessary resources for success (e.g., mentoring, tutoring, and career advice). For Black males majoring in engineering, positive peer interaction and faculty support are vital for their success. The campus climate plays an integral role in successful integration of academically gifted, poor Black males. The establishment of a positive identity for the Black male student is significant in that it serves as the foundation upon which the student can develop some sense of agency and in turn determine where he "fits" within the academy (Bonner & Bailey, 2006, p. 28). Clearly, the campus environment has the potential to encourage or discourage academic and social transition of students. Bonner (2010) and Jackson and Moore (2006) asserted that institutional context influences students' ability to achieve. As seen through the experiences of these participants, academic success began within the context of their learning environments. Based upon the findings in this study, practice recommendations are offered.

Recommendations for Practice

1. *Reevaluate traditional applications of academic giftedness.* Participants viewed giftedness as multifaceted and multidimensional; that is, they viewed giftedness as applicable in a range of contexts, such as practical and creative abilities. They stated that giftedness was not limited to one specific definition. For these participants, giftedness was not a fixed trait; it was seen as the use of one's abilities. They agreed that gifted persons need a strong sense of their ability. Their conceptualization of giftedness is compounded by factors such as self-perception, need for achievement, future orientation, and willingness to make sacrifices. The findings suggest that a high sense of confidence is a critical factor in success in engineering. Participants were not intimidated by academic challenges in their programs; their increased sense of confidence supported their identity as high achieving.

To this end, faculty, staff, and student affairs practitioners should consider expanding their conceptualizations of *academic gifted* beyond the traditional definition. Additionally, there needs to be more focus on research and practices that include new methods of understanding multiple perspectives of students' academic abilities.

2. *Reexamine notions of Black male identity development.* When examining the perceptions of academically gifted Black male engineering students, it is essential to understand how their experiences are influenced by the intersection of multiple theories. Three distinctive theories comprised the conceptual framework employed in this study: (a) Sternberg's (2003) triarchic theory of intelligence, (b) Tinto's (1993) student integration model, and (c) Whiting's (2006a, 2006b) scholar identity model. Each of these theories served as a frame to understanding the participants' conceptualization of their experiences. The components of the conceptual framework led to a holistic understanding of achievement identity. Specifically, the models enabled an understanding of giftedness, college academic and social integration, and the participants' self-perceptions of being gifted. Based on the participants' conceptualization of their experiences, the conceptual framework illustrates the interconnectedness between participants' experiences and each of these three theories. Participants' perceived notions of their ability, willingness to integrate socially and academically, and framing of their giftedness all occurred simultaneously to create an "achievement identity."

All of the study participants stressed that they believed in their ability to achieve. As a result, they were able to perform successfully in their respective majors. However, each participant asserted that academic success was dependent on the willingness to make sacrifices. For instance, Isaiah said that his need to achieve was greater than the need to participate in unimportant social experiences such as parties. He claimed that other students considered him an outsider but that their perceptions were irrelevant to him because his academic goals took precedence over nonacademic events. Thus, Black male engineering students who have an achievement identity understand the necessity for *self-sacrifice* to reach academic goals. The participants stressed that the time commitment to homework, study, and in-class assignments seemed to be more daunting in their major than in other college majors but they declared that they were willing to sacrifice now to realize gains in the future. Given this finding, perhaps faculty and student affairs practitioners should increase their knowledge of the various developmental issues academically gifted Black males encounter. Further, it is imperative that faculty and student affairs practitioners are provided with the information necessary to create realistic programs and agendas to benefit students, while fitting within the scope of their other professional obligations.

3. *Create a mandatory mentoring program that focuses on Black male engineering majors.* Mentoring can have a significant impact on the experiences of Black engineering majors. Otto (1994) defined mentoring as a relationship based on mutual respect and made by choice. Mentors are identified as persons with recognized success who help others to interpret and learn to navigate unfamiliar environments (Daloz, 1986). According to Sutton (2006), mentoring has the potential to decrease students' feelings of marginality, increase their sense of personal significance (that they "matter"), and provide important validation of belonging to the campus environment. The availability of mentors is extremely valuable for Black males majoring in engineering disciplines. A mandatory mentoring program could enhance development of self-concept, self-esteem, and self-confidence in first-year Black engineering students. Administrators, faculty, senior engineering students, and graduate engineering students, regardless of race, could serve as mentors for incoming majors. Their goal would be to work with their mentees to help them to acclimate to the institution and the department. Mentors would aid in mentees' achievement of academic excellence and social integration on campus, as well as increase retention in engineering

Implications for Future Research

The findings of this study provide insight into experiences of academically gifted Black male students majoring in engineering disciplines. While this case study provides insight into the academic and social perceptions of the participants, research that extends to various other aspects of their experiences is necessary. First, researchers should reframe traditional notions of giftedness to reflect inclusiveness of multiple perspectives (e.g., analytical, creative, and practical intelligences). Second, research should focus on multiple statuses (e.g., race, masculinity, socioeconomic status, workforce transition) that academically gifted Black males encounter as they navigate engineering undergraduate degrees. A holistic understanding of this demographic is warranted if researchers and universities intend to meet the needs of academically gifted Black males in engineering disciplines. Third, future studies should explore issues of academics and masculinity, the influences of mentoring, and effects of long-term goal setting by Black male students in engineering disciplines. Fourth, researchers should examine the factors that motivate Black males to study engineering disciplines. Fifth, there is a need for more research publications that contribute to the dialogue about Black male engineers and their transition into the engineering workplace. Because there is minimal research that examines the experiences of this demographic group, further research could examine the nuances of this student population.

This chapter provides a glimpse into the experiences of academically gifted Black male students in engineering disciplines at an HBCU. Their stories chronicle their ability to achieve their academic goals despite adversity. The findings in the study can serve as a basis for future inquiry into areas of student and academic development of academically gifted Black males pursuing undergraduate engineering degrees. More important, this chapter demonstrates the need to study the varied nature of the Black collegiate experience and creates a frame for understanding achievement identity within this student population.

References

Allen, W. R. (1992). The color of success: African American college student outcomes at predominantly White and historically Black public colleges and universities. *Harvard Educational Review, 62,* 26–44.

Bandura, A. (1997). *Self-efficacy: The exercise of control.* New York: W. H. Freeman.

Bonner, F. A. (2001). Making room for the study of gifted African American males. *Black Issues in Higher Education, 18*(6), 80.

Bonner, F. A., (2010a). *Gifted African American male college students.* Santa Barbara, CA: Praeger.

Bonner, F. A. (2010b). *Academically gifted African American males in college.* Santa Barbara, CA: ABC-Clio.

Bonner, F. A., & Bailey, K. W. (2006). Enhancing the academic climate for African American college men. In M. J. Cuyjet & Associates (Eds.), *African American men in college* (pp. 24–46). San Francisco, CA: Jossey-Bass.

Bowen, W. G., Chingos, M. M., & McPherson, M. S. (2009). *Crossing the finish line: Completing college at America's public universities.* Princeton, NJ: Princeton University Press.

Daloz, L. (1986). *Effective teaching and mentoring: Realizing the transformational power of adult learning experiences.* San Francisco, CA: Jossey-Bass.

Davis, J. E. (1994). College in Black and White: Campus environment and academic achievement of African American males. *Journal of Negro Education, 63,* 620–633.

Denzin, N. K., & Lincoln, Y. S. (1994). *Handbook of qualitative research.* Thousand Oaks, CA: Sage.

Ford, D. Y. (1996). *Reversing underachievement among gifted Black students: Promising practices and programs.* New York: Teachers College Press.

Ford, D. Y. (2003). Beyond self-concept and self-esteem for African American students: Improving racial identity improves achievement. *The High School Journal, 87*(1), 18–29.

Fries-Britt, S. L. (1998). Moving beyond Black achiever isolation: Experiences of gifted black collegians. *Journal of Higher Education, 69,* 556–576.

Gahagan, J., & Hunter, M. S. (2006). The second-year experience: Turning attention to the academy's middle children. *About Campus, 11*(3), 17–22.

Grantham, T. C. (2004a). Rocky Jones: Case study of a high-achieving Black male's motivation to participate in gifted classes. *Roeper Review, 26,* 208–215.

Grantham, T. C. (2004b). Multicultural mentoring to increase Black male representation in gifted programs. *Gifted Child Quarterly, 48,* 232–245.

Graunke, S. S., & Woosley, S. A. (2005). An exploration of the factors that affect the academic success of college sophomores. *College Student Journal, 39,* 367–377.

Harper, S. R. (2004). The measure of a man: Conceptualizations of masculinity among high-achieving African American male college students. *Berkeley Journal of Sociology, 48*(1), 89–107.

Hilliard, A. G. (2003). *Young, gifted, and Black: Promoting high achievement among African American students.* Boston, MA: Beacon Press.

Hrabowski, F. (2003). Raising minority achievement in science and math. *Educational Leadership, 60*(4), 44–48.

Jackson, J. F. L., & Moore, J. L. (2006). African American males in education: Endangered or ignored? *Teachers College Record, 108,* 201–205.

Jackson, S. A. (2003). *Envisioning a 21st-century science and engineering workforce for the United States: Tasks for university, industry, and government.* Washington, DC: National Academy Press.

Kannerstein, G. (1978). Black colleges: Self-concept. In C. V. Willie & R. R. Edmonds (Eds.), *Black colleges in America: Challenge, development and survival* (pp. 29–50). New York: Teachers College Press.

Lincoln, Y., & Guba, E. (1985). *Naturalistic inquiry.* New York: Sage.

Lynn, M. (2002) Critical race theory and the perspectives of black men teachers in the Los Angeles public schools, *Equity & Excellence in Education, 35*(2), 119–130.

Marshall, C., & Rossman, G. (1999). *Designing qualitative research* (3rd ed.). Thousand Oaks, CA: Sage.

Merriam, S. B. (1998). *Qualitative research and case study applications in education: Revised and expanded from case study in research and education* (2nd ed.). San Francisco, CA: Jossey-Bass.

Moore, J. L. (2006). A qualitative investigation of African American males' career trajectory in engineering: Implications for teachers, school counselors, and parents. *Teachers College Record, 108,* 246–266.

Moore. J. L., & Herndon, M. K. (2003). Editorial. *Journal of Men's Study, 12,* 1–2.

Otto, M. L. (1994). Mentoring: An adult developmental perspective. *New Directions for Teaching and Learning, 57,* 15–24.

Palmer, R. T., Davis, R. J., & Hilton, A. A. (2009). Exploring challenges that threaten to impede the academic success of academically underprepared African American male collegians at an HBCU. *Journal of College Student Development, 50,* 429–445.

Patton, M. Q. (2001). *Qualitative evaluation and research methods* (2nd ed.). Thousand Oaks, CA: Sage.

Renzulli, J. S. (1986). The three-ring conception of giftedness: A developmental model for creative productivity. In R. J. Sternberg & J. E. Davidson (Eds.), *Conceptions of giftedness* (pp. 53–92). New York: Cambridge University Press

Sanchez-Linguelinel, C. (2008). Supporting "slumping" sophomores: Programmatic peer initiatives designed to enhance retention in the crucial second year of college. *College Student Journal, 42,* 637–646.

Schreiner, L. A., & Pattengale, J. (Eds.). (2000). *Visible solutions for invisible students: Helping sophomores succeed* (Monograph No. 31). Columbia, SC: National Resource Center for the First-Year Experience and Students in Transition, University of South Carolina.

Shavelson, R. J., Hubner, J. J., & Stanton, G. C. (1976). Self-concept: Validation of construct interpretations. *Review of Educational Research, 46,* 407–441.

Sternberg, R. J. (2003). Giftedness according to the theory of successful intelligence. In N. Colangelo & G. Davis (Eds.), *Handbook of gifted education* (pp. 88–99). Boston, MA: Allyn & Bacon.

Strauss, A., & Corbin, J. (1990). *Basics of qualitative research: Grounded theory procedures and techniques.* Newbury Park, CA: Sage.

Sutton, E. (2006). Developmental mentoring of African American college men. In M. Cuyjet & Associates (Eds.), *African American men in college* (pp. 95–111). San Francisco, CA: Jossey-Bass.

Tinto, V. (1993). *Leaving college: Rethinking the causes and cures of student attrition* (2nd ed.). Chicago, IL: University of Chicago Press.

Travers, M. (2001). *Qualitative research through case studies.* London: Sage

Whiting, G. W. (2006a). From at risk to at promise: Developing scholar identities among Black males. *Journal of Secondary Gifted Education, 17,* 222–229.

Whiting, G. W. (2006b). Promoting a scholar identity among African American males: Implications for gifted education. *Gifted Education Press Quarterly, 20*(3), 2–6.

Yin, R. (1994). *Case study research: Design and methods* (2nd ed.). Thousand Oaks, CA: Sage.

Yin, K. (2008). *Case study research: Design and methods* (3rd ed.). Newbury Park, CA: Sage.

13

INNOVATIVE INITIATIVES AND RECOMMENDATIONS FOR PRACTICE AND FUTURE RESEARCH

Enhancing the Status of Black Men at Historically Black Colleges and Universities and Beyond

J. Luke Wood and Robert T. Palmer

As discussed throughout this volume, Black males encounter challenges in college that can impede their success (Geiger, 2006; Lundy-Wagner & Gasman, 2011; Provasnik, Shafer, & Snyder, 2004). These challenges are directly and indirectly impacted by both student factors (e.g., help seeking behaviors, selection of major; Palmer, Davis & Hilton, 2009; Palmer & Strayhorn, 2008) and institutional factors (e.g., dilapidated infrastructure, inequitable distribution of funding, campus conservatism, and reduction of remedial programming; e.g., Davis & Palmer, 2010; Harper & Gasman, 2008; Hawkins, 2004; Kimbrough & Harper, 2006; McClure, 2007; Palmer & Davis, in press; Palmer, Davis, & Gasman, in press; Palmer & Griffin, 2010). Together, these factors create a complex array of considerations needed to address the barriers facing Black males in both historically Black colleges and universities (HBCUs) and other types of institutions of higher learning.

While challenges persist, some institutions have turned potential barriers into opportunities through programming that is both preventative and interventional in nature. Many of these programs fall under the broad umbrella of minority male initiatives (MMIs). Nevarez and Wood (2010) describe MMIs as "a wide variety of entities (e.g., private organizations, individual campuses, districts, nonprofit organizations), which provide a platform for dialogue, research, and direct action (e.g., conferences, workshops, speaker series, retention programs) to increase the persistence and graduation rates" among male students of color (p. 88). Thus, MMIs are inclusive of programming designed to enhance the success of minority males in education. Under this spectrum of initiatives are programs developed specifically for Black males, often referred to as Black male initiatives (BMIs).

Essentially, BMIs are MMIs that focus specifically on addressing the unique experiences, barriers, and supports for Black males in educational institutions (Bobb, 2006a). Consistent with MMIs, their activities can range from small programs (e.g., mentor and tutor programs) to university-level task forces. As Bobb (2006b) discussed, there are core functions of BMIs, two of which include: (a) data gathering to define, identify, and understand the barriers facing Black male admission and retention in postsecondary institutions; and (b) using the data obtained to design programmatic features which mitigate the barriers and provide multiple sources of support for Black males. One focus of this chapter is on the latter, to discuss innovative programs designed to enhance the enrollment, persistence, achievement, and graduation rates of Black males in HBCUs.

Throughout this chapter, the editors present innovative programs designed to serve Black males. Highlighted in this chapter are four BMIs that are reflective of diverse programming taking place across the nation. These programs are provided as a point of information for researchers and practitioners interested in understanding efforts already underway for Black males in HBCUs. After the presentation of these programs, the authors discuss metalevel recommendations derived from the implications for practice sections from chapters in this text. All recommendations presented herein are proffered as practical strategies that researchers, faculty, staff, administrators, community members, and students can use to enhance the status of Black males in HBCUs and predominantly White institutions (PWIs). The editors conclude this chapter with several recommendations for future research.

Innovative Programs Aiding Black Males

The section provides an overview of several programs that are aiding the success of Black men at HBCUs. The programs discussed include: (a) the Black Male Initiative Program at Philander Smith College; (b) The Male Initiative on Leadership and Excellence (MILE) at Morgan State University; (c) The Man Up program at Howard University; and (d) the Student African American Brotherhood (SAAB) at several HBCUs. A description of the purpose, functions, structure, and impact of each program is discussed.

Black Male Initiative Program at Philander Smith

The Black Male Initiative (BMI) program at Philander Smith College (PSC) began in 2007 in response to disappointing success rates among Black males at the institution. In 2006, PSC had a 6-year Black male graduation rate of only 11%, 10% lower than the female rate at the institution. In response, President Walter Kimbrough launched a presidential initiative with diverse programming designed to impact at least 50% of the Black men at PSC each semester (Philander Smith, 2009). Given funding challenges, the initiative sought to maximize on a meager budget by utilizing a research-based foundation for understanding the Black male experience in higher education. For instance, the BMI targeted noncognitive factors relevant to student success; in particular, focus was given to facilitating students' academic and social integration into the campus setting by creating an affirmative campus environment (Redden, 2009).

An inextricable part of this focus is the mission of the BMI at PSC to "provide relevant experiences for males that will ensure success academically, professionally, and socially through developing a male student's success factors" (Philander Smith, 2011, para. 8). In particular, the BMI focuses its programming in five core areas: education, leadership, social justice, community engagement, and cultural and spiritual development. Initially, the program had more stringent operations, with a key coordinating body and monthly meetings with students. However, the program now operates on a more "organic" model, where faculty, staff, and students interested in working on different events and activities do so under the direction of the program coordinator. In this revised model, there are no formal monthly meetings.

Overall, the BMI at PSC operates on an event model, where multiple events are held each year that allow for widespread participation in the initiative. These events are planned and implemented by faculty, students, academic affairs staff, and alumni. There is a wide range in the type of events that take place. For example, BMI hosts mentor luncheon events to encourage informal mentorship between faculty and students. Faculty–student mentor dyads are not formally composed; rather, faculty and students are encouraged to establish their own mentor bonds. BMI also hosts special study sessions where male students gather at specified locations for large-group study. In 2008, one event hosted by BMI was a dinner with filmmaker Byron Hurt, producer of *Beyond Beats and Rhymes*. The dinner featured a video that addressed the role of some hip-hop music in distorting Black masculinity and portraying sexist and misogynistic images of women, Black women in particular (Kimbrough, 2008). Another BMI event sought to provide insight into the experiences of the blind. During this event, BMI participants ate a meal where they were blindfolded. To amplify the effect, the lights in the room were turned off.

BMI also focuses on providing students with skills needed for success in their professional lives. For example, given the importance of golfing in business and political areas, BMI teaches participants to play golf (e.g., the rules of the game, holding, swinging, and selecting clubs). Furthermore, the program has an etiquette course and a professional closet. The etiquette course teaches students a range of skills needed to present themselves to employers, ranging from learning how to tie a necktie to pleasantries essential for business meetings (e.g., proper introductions). The closet is used to collect professional clothing (e.g., ties, suit jackets). Students can borrow clothing from the closet for campus career days, formal events, and interviews. Another example of BMI's focus on etiquette training is an activity where BMI staff provided female students with gentleman cards. For the period of a week, men who illustrated courteous actions (e.g., opening doors for others) were given gentleman cards by campus women. Unbeknownst to the males, the cards were part of a contest where prizes were awarded to BMI participants. Assessment and evaluation is integrated with BMI events and activities. Events are primarily assessed using a postevent questionnaire where participants remark on the success of the event and provide ideas for future events.

Also as part of the initiative, PSC's retention office has developed an early alert system. Early alert systems (also referred to as early warning systems) are structurally integrated protocols where college officials (e.g., faculty, staff, and administration) report concerns about student success (Wood, 2011). Students with low class attendance or academic performance are reported through the early alert system. After being reported, the college provides additional support mechanisms (e.g., mandatory tutoring, meetings with counselors) to support students' success. To date, 43 male students have been identified through this system.

As discussed earlier, the BMI sought to "impact" 50% of the males on campus. BMI operationalized impact to make sure that a student participated in at least one of the many BMI events. In 2011, BMI has surpassed the initial goal, already reaching nearly 75% of the Black male students on campus. In tandem with other PSC efforts (e.g., revised orientation, admissions standards), BMI has led to a significant increase (12%) in the 6-year Black male graduation rate at the institution, from 11% in 2006 to 23% in 2009. In addition, the campus has also enjoyed higher grade point averages among BMI participants. In the 2009 academic year, the average GPA among non–BMI students was 2.26, while the average GPA for BMI students was 2.38, a grade point difference of .12. In the following year, the overall GPA rose for BMI students and non–BMI participants to 2.56 and 2.43, respectively. These data indicate that over the 2009 and 2010 academic years, BMI participants enjoyed *slightly* higher GPAs than nonparticipants. BMI participants also benefit from high retention rates. During the 2009–2010 academic year, the one-year retention rate from program participants was 98% (M. Hutchinson, personal communication, May 20, 2011).

Because of the program's focus and apparent success, the Winthrop Rockefeller Foundation has provided BMI with grant funding. The grant funding is in stark contrast to the program's origins where the operating budget was so meager that BMI staff would obtain donations from faculty and staff to purchase pizza. Winthrop Rockefeller monies support the BMI peer educators program where students work as peer tutors in the PSC Student Success Center. Peer tutors provide supplemental classroom support through one-on-one tutoring, specifically in mathematics and English. The activities of BMI peer educators are not solely limited to tutoring. They are also responsible for:

(a) recruitment of students for participation in the BMI; (b) developing and implementing advertising campaigns for BMI events; (c) using a text-messaging system to encourage participation in BMI events; and (d) maintaining a BMI Facebook page which serves as a platform for participants to build community and to learn about upcoming events and campus support service offerings. The peer educators program is assessed by the number of students served by peer tutors in the center, including both tutor requests (requests for aid) and tutor responses (aid provided). The program has a high degree of participation, receiving support requests from 70% of males in the Integrated Campus Center (M. Hutchinson, personal communication, May 20, 2011).

The Morgan MILE at Morgan State University

The Male Initiative on Leadership and Excellence (MILE) at Morgan State University, referred to as the Morgan MILE, was founded in 2003 as an initiative to improve success rates among male students of color at the institution. Prior to the initiation of the program, Black male retention and graduation rates at Morgan were declining sharply (Freeman & Addison, 2008). The program was begun to curb the declines and to begin increasing success rates. The program was founded by Dr. Jason DeSousa, then Assistant Vice President of Academic Affairs, and was started as a campus–based initiative, though it is now housed in the Office of Residence, Life, and Housing.

The mission of the Morgan MILE is to "enhance the quality of student life and engagement for male students at Morgan State University" (Morgan MILE, 2009a, para. 1). This mission is pursued through the program's purpose, which is to: (a) aid Black male students toward graduation; (b) instill a sense of purpose in Black males; and (c) inspire participants to be academically and personally confident (Morgan MILE, 2009b). MILE is funded through Title III monies, which support program operations centered on leadership activities, developing academic skill sets, and values building (Palmer, Maramba, & Dancy, in press). In particular, the program is organized around the Afrocentric virtue of collectivity, where successes and challenges are shared. This orientation is evidenced by the program's motto of "learn together, lead together, graduate together" (Morgan MILE, 2009a, para. 5).

Unlike programs designed for a small subset of participants, the Morgan MILE is unique in that it is open to all male students. In this structure, membership is defined as having attended three program events and completed an application (Morgan MILE, 2009d). Additionally, no fee is required for participation in MILE. Students are recruited through direct communication with program staff and MILE participants.

The program model is based on monthly themes. Each month the group has a general body meeting where the monthly theme is introduced. This theme is reinforced by guest lecturers, videos, and through group and panel discussions.

Meetings are designed to build a supportive community where intergroup communication and support are fostered. At the end of each month, an excursion (field trip) is organized where Morgan MILE participants engage in off-site learning, community building, and leadership development activities. Excursions are based around five themes and applicable activities, including: (a) educational excursions, where participants engage in academic-oriented activities; (b) exploratory excursions, where "fun" and social interaction are the primary focus; (c) executive excursions, where MILE participants visit state and federal policy-making engagements to represent the university and the program; (d) exclusive excursions, activities designed for Morgan MILE members only; and (e) expressive excursions, activities where participants engage in community service related projects (Morgan MILE, 2009c).

One example of an expressive excursion was a 2007 excursion to New Orleans to participate in Hurricane Katrina community service activities. Participants have also engaged in community service oriented activities in the states of South Carolina and Georgia during which they fed the homeless and supported the efforts of homeless shelters. Excursion activities are followed up with critical reflections where students are required to consider the meaningfulness of each event in light of their personal experiences and perceptions. Follow-ups are conducted through group dialogues and individual journaling (Palmer et al., in press).

As with the other initiatives discussed in this chapter, the Morgan MILE is a research-based endeavor. Program interventions emphasize the importance of academic and social engagement. In particular, the program strives to promote two concepts, *integrated identity* and *mature relationships*. The integrated identity concept refers to the development of students' understanding of self, which thereby facilitates their ability to engage in decision making about what is and is not best for them. The mature relationships concept deals with the notion that students must operate in a diverse society. Therefore, the ability to develop and sustain healthy relationships that cross cultural, racial, and gender lines is of importance (Chickering, Peters, & Palmer, 2006).

MILE has documented positive participant perceptions as well as successful achievement and graduation results. Palmer et al. (in press) indicated that qualitative findings from MILE point to the importance of strong programmatic leadership, where students felt that the director was passionate, encouraging, and dedicated to their academic and personal success. Of the original class of 20 participants, 18 graduated in 4 years with an average GPA of 3.2 (Freeman & Addison, 2008). MILE participants have also shown progressive GPA gains each semester. For instance, in 2004 the average GPA of a MILE participant was 2.1. This increased to 2.4 and then to 2.8 by the end of the fall and spring semesters, respectively. In like manner, 2005 illustrated similar gains where MILE participants began the year with a 2.3 GPA, rising to 2.7 and 3.1 by the end of each semester (Chickering et. al., 2006).

Man Up Program at Howard University

The Man Up program was founded in 2004 and began operations in spring 2005 at Howard University. Man Up is housed in the John H. Johnson School of Communications. Like other programs described in this chapter, Man Up was implemented in response to poor success rates among Black males at the institution. Several faculty and staff members were concerned about factors that contributed to high attrition among male students, particularly Black males (e.g., family obligations, financial issues, academic challenges). Organizers were also concerned with the low representation of male students at Howard, where less than a third of students are men (Brown, 2010).

In response, male faculty and staff at the school, led by Bernadette Williams (a senior academic advisor), met together and formed the structure of the group. Man Up is an unfunded initiative whose operations are supported by male faculty and staff. Its success led to the development of a similar program for women at Howard called Sister Stars (Alexander, 2006). Both programs are guided by the following core values: "integrity, empowerment, education, wholeness, positive self-esteem, compassion, partnership, perseverance, [and] opportunity/access" (Williams & Brown, 2010, para. 12).

As indicated by Lincoln Brown, the director of the program, "Man Up is a program that helps to reach beyond the social and classroom problems to help students as they matriculate through the university and through life" (L. Brown, personal communication, May 27, 2011). Man Up follows the unofficial theme "being there for them," which indicates the program's focus on providing support, encouragement, and resources for male students at Howard. This is accomplished through monthly meetings that are organized around a group counseling model. Essentially, Man Up is a confidential "male support group aimed at tackling issues and concerns faced by young men" (J. Brown, 2008).

Monthly meetings consist of group discussions, where males sit in a large circle and talk about issues they are confronting in their lives. Meetings begin with "check-ins" where participants are encouraged to air the challenges and triumphs they face in their personal, professional, and academic lives (Brown, 2010). The importance of discussion that is honest and free from judgment is emphasized by the program leadership (Harris, 2010). As part of this initiative, Man Up organizers provide college success and academic oriented workshops where all students in the communications college can learn about time management, study skills, and how to enhance their writing ability. Aside from these meetings, Man Up staff work with students during discussion sessions to identify their needs. Once identified, the staff refers students to the workshops and offices that are most applicable. In addition, Man Up has also aided students in their professional endeavors through resume critiques and interview etiquette sessions (Valbrun, 2010).

Additionally, conversations focus on attaining multiple perspectives on select topics. Man Up conversations are guided around topical conversations. Each year, an annual word is selected which serves as a platform for multiple conversations on topics of interest associated with that word. For example, during the 2010-2011 academic year, each monthly topic was based upon the word *choices*. Program staff and participants used this yearly word to guide monthly conversations, with discussions ranging from how participants make choices in life to what determines whether a choice is right or wrong. However, conversations are not solely limited to the monthly topic and also include discussions on "depression, money, sexual orientation, balancing school with an active social life or just showing affection…and students' relationship or lack of relationship with their fathers" (Harris, 2008, para. 18).

Monthly meetings occur on the first Monday of each month, unless that date is a holiday. While housed in the School of Communications, Man Up participation is open to all male students at Howard. Initially, participants were concentrated at the freshman and sophomore levels. However, the program is not solely limited to students, and it now includes faculty, alumni, and community members. While Man Up participation is optional for most students, male students in the School of Communications whose GPAs fall below 2.0 are required to join the program (Farmer, 2009). Man Up activities are often supported by the Mankind Project, a nonprofit organization which conducts trainings and seminars on men's issues. While Man Up participants are predominantly Black, given that Howard University is an HBCU, program participants are multicultural. Participants are reflective of varying racial/ethnic backgrounds (e.g., Black, Hispanic, White, biracial), cultural groups, class standings, and orientations. The program notes that many Man Up alumni still participate in meetings, remain engaged in the program, and serve as a network of support for Howard males.

While program operations center on the monthly meeting structure, some supplemental programming also occurs outside of these meetings. Black male leaders in various capacities are invited to speak with students about various topics. For instance, a recent special guest lecture included Arthur Burnett, Sr., a senior judge in the DC Superior Court and National Executive Director of the National African American Drug Policy Coalition. Judge Burnett spoke with students about the importance of having high goals and striving beyond mediocrity.

Each year, during the university's mandatory freshman orientation in August, all male students in the School of Communications are required to participate in Man Up. This annual activity hosts conversations with 80 or more new students and serves as a recruitment mechanism for ongoing participation in the program. Regular monthly meetings are more limited in number, with an average meeting hosting conversation circles with 20 to 30 participants. Meetings feature a core set of participants with a number of students who periodically attend Man Up meetings. While not structured to facilitate formal mentorship, Man Up staff encourage informal mentoring, often connecting students with individuals who they believe will serve as good mentors and role models.

Although Man Up does not engage in formal research assessment and evaluation, anecdotal information is used as part of Howard's major outcomes assessment (Howard University, 2009). These data suggest that the program has a profound impact on the lives of the men it serves. The program director reports that the School of Communications has enjoyed an increase in the retention of male students, which he attributes to Man Up (Harris, 2008). Students who are facing issues associated with their sexual orientation have found the Man Up network to provide a safe space for open dialogue, encouraging words, and a network of supportive men. Students with financial issues air their concerns at Man Up meetings and are directed to resources and opportunities that can lead to their stability. During Man Up meetings, some participants have broached their intentions to leave Howard and have been deterred from doing so, using the Man Up network to find actual and verbal support and uplift. Male students without fathers are reported to find male role models, particularly from faculty, staff, and alumni, who aid students in developing a positive perception of Black masculine identity (L. Brown, personal communication, May 27, 2011). Man Up has also resulted in dropouts returning to Howard to finish their academic pursuits (L. Brown, 2010).

Student African American Brotherhood (SAAB) at Several HBCUs

The Student African American Brother (SAAB) is an organizational initiative designed to increase success rates among Black and Latino males in college. SAAB was founded by Tyrone Bledsoe in 1990. Bledsoe was formerly Vice President of Student Life at the University of Toledo but now serves as Executive Director for SAAB (SAAB, 2009a). Founded in 1990, the organization has grown to over 200 chapters on college campuses across the country that are representative of multiple institutional types (e.g., 2-year, 4-year, HBCUs, PWIs, and both public and private). SAAB has chapters at multiple HBCUs with North Carolina Central University being the first HBCU to start a SAAB chapter (Bledsoe & Rome, 2006).

Like other initiatives discussed in this chapter, SAAB began as a response to alarming challenges facing Black males in education and the wider society. The mission of SAAB is to assist members to "excel academically, socially, culturally, professionally, and in the community" (SAAB, 2009b, para 1). SAAB is an open-access organization. Unlike fraternities and some collegiate clubs, SAAB does not have an intake process, GPA requirement, or membership fee. SAAB chapters are student operated, and these chapters function under the approval of the national SAAB headquarters. Chapters vary in size, but usually range from 20 to 40 members. While the vast majority of SAAB members are Black and Latino, chapter members are also inclusive of other racial/ethnic groups (e.g., White, Asian, Native American). SAAB chapters are sometimes referred to as Brother to Brother (B2B) chapters, especially when chapter membership is representative of multiple racial/ethnic groups (SAAB, 2009c).

All SAAB chapters are required to conceptualize, develop, and implement a strategic plan that accounts for the needs faced by males of color at their respective institutions. In general, SAAB chapters meet twice a week, including an Executive Board meeting with chapter leaders and advisors and a general meeting with the full SAAB membership. Strategic plans are implemented by a chapter's members who are urged to develop relationships with stakeholder partners both within and outside their institutions. In general, stakeholders work with SAAB members to determine the viability of a SAAB chapter, the establishment of a taskforce to begin the SAAB strategic plan, and the identification of community issues. SAAB program operations adhere to the Afrocentric notion of collectivity, which is exemplified by the program principles "I am my brother's keeper, and together we will rise" (SAAB, 2009d, para 1). These principles are seen in program operations, such as the program's requirement that all members serve as role models, mentors, and tutors. For instance, all members participate as tutors and mentors in local high schools.

Each SAAB chapter is composed of six standing committees. These committees are responsible for developing programming related to academics, personal development, service-learning, spiritual and social enrichment, financial affairs, and public relations. The academics committee is responsible for connecting SAAB members with campus support services and facilitating academic achievement among members. Further, this committee organizes weekly study sessions. The personal development committee is accountable for ensuring that members have resumes and current personal development plans (PDPs). PDPs are 5-year plans for personal and professional goals. The "service" learning committee is designed to provide opportunities for SAAB members to participate in community service initiatives, particularly with Habitat for Humanity, Boy Scouts of American, and Big Brothers Big Sisters. The financial affairs committee is responsible for hosting financial seminars to create awareness of money management, consumer credit, investments, entrepreneurship, the development and implementation of business plans, and financial literacy. The membership/public relations committee oversees the membership database and works to create a sense of community among SAAB members.

Mentoring is a primary component of SAAB, which "emphasizes mentoring from a developmental approach by enhancing participants' understanding of their responsibilities as mentors, role models, future fathers, husbands, and productive citizens" (Bledsoe, n.d.). SAAB operates on a three-tier mentoring model: SAAB members receive mentorship from their chapter advisors; peer-to-peer mentoring where SAAB members co-mentor one another; and student-to-young-student mentoring, where members mentor youth in middle and high schools. SAAB's mentorship model adheres to four core principles: developing proactive leadership, accountability, self-discipline, and intellectual maturity.

SAAB has enjoyed noticeable success. This has resulted in an array of funding organizations that support SAAB efforts, such as AT&T, the Lumina Foundation, and the Rising Oak Foundation (SAAB, 2009e). In order to evaluate the organization's success, SAAB has developed a data collection and analysis system. Findings from SAAB's data collection indicate that 86% of SAAB members have graduated from college; this is 44 percentage points greater than the national graduation average of Black males (SAAB, 2009f). SAAB also boasts an 80% first-year persistence rate among collegians. Eighty-seven percent of participants reported that they are happy with their experiences in SAAB while 82% remarked that SAAB made their collegiate experience better. Qualitative findings suggest that SAAB serves to create community among participants. Other emergent themes indicate that participants were pleased with the organization's focus on developing professional skills, opportunities for leadership, networking, and an environment that is conducive to academic success.

Program Themes

This chapter has described several programs that are working to improve outcomes for Black males at HBCUs. These programs are suggested as potential models for practitioners to consider as they: (a) design programming for their respective campuses; or (b) identify existing programs in their institutions that could be expanded. In particular, the editors suggest that practitioners consider several emergent themes evident from the programs examined. First, the BMIs examined were research-based in that program development and implementation were informed by extant research and theory. In particular, these programs were developed with research on academic and social integration, student engagement, and the creation of a welcoming and affirmative campus environment. Second, most programs had a focus on collectivity, as exemplified through program slogans, mottos, and themes. Collectivity suggests that successes and failures are mutually shared. Under this value, collaboration, community, otherness, and equity are important virtues. Third, the majority of programs held mentoring in high esteem. Through formal and informal mentor models, these programs facilitated faculty-to-student, student-to-student, and student-to-youth mentoring. Fourth, program assessment and evaluation were integrated into most programs examined. This allowed for program officials to better understand the impact their programs had on the students served and led to enhanced partnerships. Fifth, many of the BMIs examined had programming designed to facilitate students' critical reflection of their personal, academic, and professional goals and philosophical outlook on life.

These reflections were facilitated by journaling as well as small and large group discussions. Finally, the editors' investigation of each program illustrated that social networking technologies (e.g., Facebook) were used to facilitate recruitment, networking, and communication among participants. This section has described innovative programs, and the next section will present metalevel recommendations for practice generated from chapter contributors.

Metalevel Recommendations from Chapter Contributors

This volume has examined the experiences of Black males of varying backgrounds (e.g., high performing, low-income, fathers, immigrants). These experiences underscore the diverse lives of members of Black subgroups who face unique barriers and supports in college. While this volume has heralded a new conception of Black men, one that negates their monolithic treatment by researchers and practitioners alike, the editors of this volume also recognize the existence of metalevel themes for practice. These themes are elicited from recommendations proffered by chapter authors in this volume and are presented below. The highlighting of metalevel themes should not minimize the importance of specific recommendations outlined by chapter authors which addressed the unique needs of subgroups. Rather, the recommendations presented recognize and reaffirm the importance of student diversity, while acknowledging that *certain* uniform practices can serve to enhance institutions' support of diverse Black male collegians.

Avoid Homogenous Treatment

Authors in this volume have repeatedly called for the avoidance of programming and policies that homogenize Black males into one sociocultural group. This call reaffirms the spirit of this volume in acknowledging the differential identities, experiences, and backgrounds of Black males in colleges. As Baber indicated, approaching Black males as a lumped category can serve to detract from efforts to increase parity in enrollment, retention, and graduation. This can result in the use of theories and models which are not dynamic enough to account for the diversity that is to be found within groups of Black males. For instance, as noted by Dancy and Johnson, Black fathers encounter unique challenges associated with maintaining a work-life-school balance. Certainly, programming that does not recognize that Black fathers can encounter larger persistence issues in certain areas than nonfathers may be ineffective. Moreover, Flowers noted that programming for engineering students should address the challenges faced by these students but also take into account their professional obligations. He stated that such programming required that faculty and student affairs practitioners better understand the unique developmental issues experienced by academically gifted Black males. To this end, the editors believe that *continuing to treat Black males as a monolithic group* will result in wasted resources that could have been better maximized through other uses which address the primary and direct challenges facing subgroup persistence and success.

Learning Communities

The need for learning communities was discussed in chapters written by Bonner and Scott. Learning communities are collections of students that are coordinated via coursework; they are similar to cohorts. However, a unique attribute of learning communities is that students are grouped around specific background factors (e.g., values, identities, academic plan). In some cases, learning communities also have residential components, where students live together in dormitories and participate in ongoing social programming to facilitate the notion of community (Weiss, Visher, Teres, & Schneider, 2010). Scott suggested the use of a residence model that was supported by ongoing activities designed to enhance student engagement. Bonner noted that learning communities could foster intellectual and psychosocial development through discourse among groups of like-minded collegians around important academic matters and challenges. Further, he noted that these enclaves of students serve as communication networks where information on college life is passed from one student to another. He suggested that practitioners use these communication networks to infuse information needed to ease academic concerns.

Countering Stereotypes

Several chapter authors called for campus officials (e.g., faculty, staff, administration) to counter pervasive stereotyping of Black men. In particular, emphasis was placed on discourse, actions, and values which validate racialized and hypermasculine stereotypes about Black men. As noted by Baber, it is difficult to counter such stereotypes given that they are so prevalent in society and continually reinforced through popular culture and the media (e.g., Internet, radio, television, newspapers). However, he suggested that institutions can share the sociocultural climates of their own campuses to avoid reifying stereotypical practices, behaviors, and messages. Similarly, Dancy and Johnson noted that colleges can shape students' outlook on racial and gender messages by raising consciousness around the detrimental effect of such images. They caution that, in some cases, institutional officials buttress male-dominance and hypersexual messages. As such, critical dialogues between multiple institutional stakeholders (e.g., faculty, students, staff, and community members) are needed to discuss and delineate truths about what it means to be both Black and male. These conversations can serve as a platform to deconstruct ill-informed and misguided perceptions of Black masculinity. In addition, Black male students themselves also have a responsibility to counter stereotypes. As noted by Horton, Black male athletes may not be perceived by faculty as being serious about their academic performance. Thus, they must strive at all times to counter these notions by presenting themselves in a studious manner during class and in interactions with their faculty.

Mentoring

By far the most recurrent theme elicited from chapter recommendations was the importance of mentoring. Both faculty–student and peer–peer mentor dyads were discussed as being integral to student success. Gasman and Spencer focused on faculty–student mentor pairs. They recommended that mentor relationships expand beyond informational bounds, to become systemic pairing—by systemic they mean that every student, upon entering college, should be assigned a mentor (e.g., alumnus, faculty, administrator). Similarly, Flowers noted that mentoring programs for engineering students should be mandatory, drawing support from mentors in all capacities regardless of race (e.g., administration, faculty, and senior engineering students). Furthermore, Bonner noted that colleges must avoid a philosophy that assumes students will seek out mentorship on their own. Rather, he suggested that colleges should be proactive in linking students to mentors. In contrast to Gasman and Spencer, Baber emphasized the importance of peer-to-peer mentoring. He suggested that mentor relationships be constructed with considerations beyond race and gender, but taking into account other forms of identity (e.g., immigrant status). Scott discussed the importance of mentor programs, suggesting that they can serve to create a welcoming and affirming campus climate. He recommended that mentors be responsible for: (a) acclimating students to the campus environment; (b) informing students about campus involvement (e.g., clubs, organizations, activities) and professional opportunities (e.g., internships); and (c) serving as guides as students continue through college. Scott also indicated that noninstitutional mentor relationships can be established, which allow students to engage with leaders in the local business community or in service-related activities.

Early Warning System

As noted in this chapter as well as by Gasman and Spencer, there is a need for early warning/alert systems. These systems track students' progress and have mechanisms (e.g., policies, processes, procedures) in place to report impending issues. Thus, when students are facing academic troubles, as exemplified by low performance and attendance rates, they can receive additional support from the campus. As noted by Gasman and Spencer, at Philander Smith, when a student falls behind, the campus engages in intrusive support efforts, often including direct interventions and conversations with the campus president, Walter

Kimbrough. While not all university executives can commit to this level of intervention, there is a need for early warning system development, implementation, and refinement which is championed by college executives. Given the focus of this text, the editors encourage campus officials to consider the need for diverse intervention strategies that are indicative of the diverse Black male populations served by HBCUs and beyond.

Supportive Campus Environments

As noted by several contributors, there is a need to develop and sustain supportive campus environments which allow all students, regardless of identity (e.g., immigrant, fathers, low-income, gay) to feel welcome and affirmed. There is a need to seek broader levels of inclusion in campus activities, organizations, and events which celebrate differences. Further, there is also a need to challenge and deconstruct negative messages about student groups in all campus spaces (e.g., classrooms, common areas, dormitories). In this vein, Strayhorn and Scott noted the important responsibility shared by both faculty and students to counter homophobic messages, whether intentional or unintentional. As stated by Dancy and Johnson, HBCUs must strive to maintain environments indicative of "equity, tolerance, and inclusion." When these virtues are not achieved, students can lack a sense of belonging to the campus, which fuels division and thereby, negatively affects their social and academic engagement. In addition to challenging identity stereotypes, there is also a need to affirm students in academic matters. Scott suggested that administrators and faculty can facilitate supportive academic environments by using encouraging language with students which illustrates their concern for students' academic and personal well-being, development, and success.

Cultural Awareness Workshops

Some authors pointed to the importance of establishing cultural awareness workshops. These workshops would be platforms for dialogue relevant to students' cultural identities. As noted by Dancy and Johnson, these workshops could focus on generating discussions around issues of spirituality, skin color, gender, and other important topics. They suggested that these workshops take place on a routine basis and that their occurrence should be codified in institutional policy. Similarly, Strayhorn and Scott noted the importance of similar workshops and seminars relevant to addressing issues of homohatred and harassment. In particular, they posited that these workshops take place in residence halls. Dancy and Johnson believe that these workshops serve a purpose beyond discussions of cultural awareness. Rather, they see cultural awareness workshops as necessary groundwork for needed institutional conversations relevant to enhancing Black male enrollment, retention, and graduation in college. Specifically, they suggest connecting these workshops to campus climate issues, noting that they can serve to create a welcoming environment where differing perspectives and *difficult* conversations around marginality are accepted.

College Success Workshops

Several chapter contributors noted the importance of creating college success workshops that provide students with critical information needed for collegiate success. Gasman and Spencer recommended that these workshops be part of both orientation and as an ongoing series throughout students' first year in college. Workshops could range in size, duration, and locale. Workshops could cover a variety of topics including (but not limited to): time management, goal setting, awareness of campus resources and services, academic productivity, promotion of student involvement in extracurricular activities as well as campus clubs and organizations, financial planning and financial aid. The importance of financial aid workshops was advanced by Scott, who noted that low-income students may lack critical information to successfully engage the financial aid process. He cites research which suggests that low income students and their families typically have little information on the process of obtaining education funding. Given the range of topics needed to both demystify and engage the policies, processes, and procedures of college, college professionals of all positions (e.g., faculty, staff, and administrators) could serve as workshop facilitators. Some institutions may even consider making certain workshops mandatory in order to ensure that students have received accurate and up-to-date information.

Facilitate Social Integration

The need to facilitate students' social integration was a recurrent theme through many recommendations offered. In particular, authors suggested that college officials (e.g., faculty, staff) make concerted efforts to connect students with campus clubs, intramural activities, student government, and other organizations. Scott noted that campus officials, while not responsible for ensuring involvement, are responsible for informing students about opportunities as well as the benefits derived from involvement. He also broached that campus officials partner with Black Greek Letter Organizations (e.g., Alpha Phi Alpha, Kappa Alpha Psi, Omega Psi Phi, Phi Beta Sigma) to foster campus involvement. In like manner, Strayhorn and Scott suggested that off-campus organizations (e.g., LGBT alliances) be recruited to bring their services to campus as a way of promoting enhanced inclusion and involvement for gay students. They noted that some students may be more inclined toward participating in off-campus organizations; thus, by partnering with the institution, the goal of enhanced involvement can still be achieved.

Understanding Learning Modalities

Chapter contributors discussed the need to understand how students learn and advocated the use of alternative teaching strategies which capitalize on differing learning styles. Scott noted the importance of group exercises, activities, and assignments, which allow for greater levels of student involvement in class. He cites research which denotes the vital need to integrate students into the learning process in a manner that empowers them as authentic contributors to classroom learning and discourse. Scott believes that this approach allows for students to develop a positive academic self-concept, thereby leading to enhanced academic performance. Bonner posited that campus officials (e.g., faculty, staff) should be trained in up-to-date theory and research in student development to explicate learning styles as well as cognitive and affective development. He believes that this will provide campus officials, specifically faculty, with tools needed to understand students' learning and motivation. Armed with this information, he suggested that this enhanced understanding will lead to enhanced institutional functioning, which will improve outcomes for students.

Important recommendations were proffered by chapter authors. The editors suggest that practitioners consider using these research-based recommendations to further the success of Black males at their respective institutions. The next section will turn its attention to researchers of the Black male experience, particularly at HBCUs, by providing suggestions for future research on this population.

Implications for Future Research

We conclude this chapter and this volume with several recommendations for future research. First and foremost, as made evident throughout this text, the editors strongly urge that future research avoid homogenous depictions of Black males in postsecondary education. Intersectionalities must be addressed with respect to student characteristics (e.g., class, age, sexual orientation, immigrant status), parental and family attributes (e.g., parents' highest level of education, dependency status), religion (e.g., religious affiliation, religiosity, spirituality), regional differences (e.g., Southern, Western, Eastern, Midwestern), environmental characteristics (e.g., employment status, peer influences), campus involvement (e.g., Greeks, student leaders), institutional type (e.g., 2-year, 4-year), and control (e.g., public, private not-for-profit, private for-profit). We argue that no lens is too fine; rather, that fine levels of analysis allow for greater levels of insight. In particular, this book has emphasized the experience of Black males in Black colleges, and we emphasize the importance of additional investigations of Black males in other institutional types. For instance, too little is still known about their experiences, challenges, and successes in community colleges, liberal arts colleges, and even in for-profit institutions. The sheer number of Black males represented in these postsecondary education locations demands extensive research, revised models and theories, and unique insights which account for the heterogeneity of the Black male experience.

Enhanced insight can in turn lead to better practices which can serve to improve outcomes for diverse Black males. However, this will only occur when researchers present practical suggestions for policy and practice. As is evident from the discussions in this volume, research on the Black male experience is more meaningful when concrete recommendations are provided. Thus, we urge scholars to continue making connections between research, theory, and practice. We suggest the need to understand the reciprocal relationship between these three concepts in that each informs, relies upon, and advances the others. This occurs in a cyclical and dynamic relationship that advances the work of researchers and practitioners alike.

Quigley (2011) stated that "a great deal of time and energy is invested [by educators] into efforts to modify maladaptive behavior and remediate academic deficits." A noticeable trend in caricatures of Black boys and men in society takes a deficit approach. A cultural deficit approach assumes that the challenges and problems facing Black males are a product of the students themselves as well as their families, communities, and culture. For instance, a deficit approach would suggest that Black male underachievement in HBCUs is a byproduct of Black males themselves: *their* lack of adequate preparation for collegiate course-work; *their* lack of motivation or interest in college; and *their* families' lack of involvement in their educational development. This approach minimizes and disregards the role of institutions, their affiliates (e.g., faculty, staff, administration), and societal forces (e.g., racism, genderisms, classisms) in manifesting destructive processes and structures. Altogether, these factors systematically can negate, marginalize, and alienate Black males and other students of color. HBCUs are well-known for fostering climates where students are affirmed (Allen, 1992; Berger & Milem, 2000; Bonous-Hammarth & Boatsman, 1996; Fries-Britt & Turner, 2002; Outcalt & Skewes-Cox, 2002; Palmer & Gasman, 2008), but academicians must guard against applying deficit perspectives to select subpopulations of Black males (e.g., low income, academically under-prepared). With this in mind, researchers must be attuned to instances where deficit perspectives are evident and address them in their scholarship.

Several initiatives and programs were examined in this chapter that are designed to advance the status of Black men at HBCUs. The strength among these programs is their understanding of the diverse backgrounds and needs of the Black males they serve. While some of these programs have embedded assessment and evaluation into their operations, others have relied upon anecdotal data. The editors suggest that scholars can aid these programs in better understanding what elements of their programming are successful in producing positive outcomes for Black males. Further, and more important, research on these programs will allow program officials to determine what aspects of their programming are ineffective. Thus, we urge scholars to work collaboratively with these programs to aid them in assessing and evaluating their practices. In doing so, when programming is found to be "effective" in shaping positive outcomes, these data can be used by program officials to advocate for additional funding from institutional, foundation, and private donors. Additionally, such investigations will better situate the programs for expansion on their respective campuses as well as to other institutions of higher education.

References

Alexander, A. (2006). So much to do, so little time … Sister Stars shining beyond the school of communications. *The Hilltop online: The student voice of Howard University.* Retrieved from http://www.thehilltoponline.com/news/so-much-to-do-so-little-time-1.463699

Allen, W. R. (1992). The color of success: African American college student outcomes at predominantly White and historically Black public colleges and universities. *Harvard Educational Review, 62,* 26–44.

Berger, J. B., & Milem, J. F. (2000). Exploring the impact of historically Black colleges in promoting the development of undergraduates' self-concept. *Journal of College Student Development, 41*(4), 381–394.

Bledsoe, T. (n.d.). *Student African American brotherhood: Key components and core elements.* Toledo, OH: University of Toledo.

Bledsoe, T., & Rome, K. D. (2006). Student African American brotherhood. In M. J. Cuyjet & Associates (Eds.), *African American men in college* (pp. 257–264). San Francisco, CA: Jossey-Bass.

Bobb, K. (2006a, October 11). Perspectives: Disentangling the paradox of Black male initiatives. Retrieved from http://diverseeducation.com/article/6498/

Bobb, K. (2006b, March 23). The paradox of Black male initiatives. *Diverse Online, 10,* 43. Retrieved from http://diverseeducation.com/article/5641/

Bonous-Hammarth, M., & Boatsman, K. (1996). *Satisfaction guaranteed? Predicting academic and social outcomes for African Americans college students.* Paper presented at the Annual Conference of the American Educational Research Association, New York.

Brown, J. (June 2, 2008). Man Up events calendar. Retrieved from http://www.howard.edu/calendar/main.php?calendarid=default&view=event&eventid=1183990883404-0011&timebegin=2008-06-02+00%3A00%3A00

Brown, L. Jr. (2010). Man Up. Retrieved from http://communications.howard.edu/prospective/undergrad/special-programs/man-up.htm

Chickering, A. W., Peters. K., & Palmer, R. T. (March, 2006). *Assessing the impact of the Morgan male initiative on leadership and excellence (MILE).* Baltimore, MD: Morgan State University.

Davis, R. J., & Palmer, R. T. (2011). The role and relevancy of postsecondary remediation for African American students: A review of research. *Journal of Negro Education, 79*(4), 503–520.

Farmer, E. (2009). Colleges fight to get and keep Black males. *New American Media.* Retrieved from http://news.newamericamedia.org/news/view_article.html?article_id=c91a1a8470fc42d78d0d522717ed3a61

Freeman, R. T., & Addison, E. (2008). Building successful Black men: MILE and warrior institute programs boost retention of male students. *Morgan Magazine, 2,* 4–7.

Fries-Britt, S., & Turner, B. (2002). Uneven stories: Successful Black collegians at a Black and a White campus. *Review of Higher Education, 25*(3), 315–330.

Geiger, S. M. (2006). *Understanding gender at public historically Black colleges and universities: A special report of the Thurgood Marshall Scholarship Fund, Inc.* New York: Thurgood Marshall Scholarship Fund.

Harper, S. R., & Gasman, M. (2008). Consequences of conservatism: Black male undergraduates and the politics of historically Black colleges and universities. *Journal of Negro Education, 77*(4), 336–351.

Harris, R. (2010). Faculty and staff take truth and service to heart. *Howard University Capstone.* Retrieved from http://www.howard.edu/capstone/dec2010/feature1.html

Hawkins, D. B. (2004). Doing more with less. Black Issues in Higher Education. Retrieved from http://diverseeducation.com/article/3759/

Howard University. (2009). *2009 self-study supporting documents: Assessment measures utilized in the university's academic program.* Washington, DC: Author. Retrieved from http://www.gs.howard.edu/middle_states/mse/supportingdocs/Chapter%2017%20%20Assessment%20of%20Student%20Learning/17.8%20Assessment%20Measures%20Utilized%20in%20the%20University's%20Academic%20Programs.pdf

Kimbrough, W. (2008, August 23). Black male initiative [Web log message]. Retrieved from http://www.philander.edu/blog/2008/08/24/BlackMaleInitiative.aspx

Kimbrough, W., & Harper, S. R. (2006). African American men at historically Black colleges and universities: Different environments, similar challenges. In M. J. Cuyjet & Associates (Eds.), *African American men in college* (pp. 189–209), San Francisco, CA: Jossey-Bass.

Lundy-Wagner, V., & Gasman, M. (2011). When gender issues are not just about women: Reconsidering male students at historically Black colleges and universities. *Teachers College Record, 113*(5). Retrieved from http://www.tcrecord.org/content.asp?contentid=15936

McClure, M. L. (2007). Collegiate desegregation: Can historically Black colleges and universities maintain their mission and identity in the midst of desegregating? In O. G. Brown, K. G. Hinton, & M. Howard-Hamilton (Eds.). *Unleashing suppressed voices on college campuses: Diversity issues in higher education* (pp. 35–42). New York: Lang.

Morgan MILE (2009a). Morgan MILE core values. Retrieved from http://www.morgan.edu/Administration/Student_Affairs/Office_of_Residence_Life/Morgan_MILE/Core_Values.html

Morgan MILE (2009b). Morgan male initiative on leadership and excellence. Retrieved from http://www.morgan.edu/Administration/Student_Affairs/Office_of_Residence_Life/Morgan_MILE.html

Morgan MILE (2009c). Meeting structure. Retrieved from http://www.morgan.edu/Administration/Student_Affairs/Office_of_Residence_Life/Morgan_MILE.html

Morgan MILE (2009d).Membership and participation. Retrieved from http://www.morgan.edu/Administration/Student_Affairs/Office_of_Residence_Life/Morgan_MILE/Membership.html

Nevarez, C., & Wood, J. L. (2010). *Community college leadership and administration: Theory, practice, and change.* New York: Lang.

Outcalt, C. L., & Skewes-Cox, T. E., (2002). Involvement, interaction, and satisfaction: The human environment at HBCUs. *Review of Higher Education, 25*(3), 331–347.

Palmer, R, T., & Davis, R. J. (in press). "Diamond in the rough": The impact of a remedial program on college access and opportunity for Black males at an historically Black institution. *Journal of College Student Retention.*

Palmer, R. T., Davis, R. J., & Gasman, M. (in press). A matter of diversity, equity and necessity: The tension between Maryland's higher education system and its historically Black institutions over the OCR agreement. *Journal of Negro Education.*

Palmer, R. T., Davis, R. J., & Hilton, A. A. (2009). Exploring challenges that threaten to impede the academic success of academically underprepared Black males at an HBCU. *Journal of College Student Development, 50*(4), 429–445.

Palmer, R. T., & Gasman, M. (2008). "It takes a village to raise a child": The role of social capital in promoting academic success for African American men at a Black college. *Journal of College Student Development 49,* 52–70.

Palmer, R. T., & Griffin, K. (2009). Desegregation policy and disparities in faculty salary and workload: Maryland's historically Black and predominantly White institutions. *Negro Educational Review, 60*(1–4), 7–21.

Palmer, R. T., Maramba, D. C., & Dancy, T. E. (in press). The magnificent "MILE": Impacting Black male retention and persistence at an HBCU. *Journal of College Student Retention.*

Palmer, R. T., & Strayhorn, T. L. (2008). Mastering one's own fate: Non-cognitive factors associated with the success of African American males at an HBCU. *National Association of Student Affairs Professionals Journal*, *11*(1), 126–143.

Philander Smith College. (2009). Black male initiative program. Retrieved from http://www.philander.edu/current-students/blackmaleinitiative.aspx

Philander Smith College. (2011). Black male initiative program. Retrieved from http://www.philander.edu/current-students/blackmaleinitiative.aspx

Provasnik, S., Shafer, L. L., & Snyder, T. D. (2004). *Historically Black colleges and universities, 1976 to 2001*(NCES 2004-062). Washington, DC: National Center for Education Statistics.

Quigley, M. (2011). *Multicultural/Multiethnic education acceptance speech*. Speech presented at the Annual Meeting of the American Educational Research Association, New Orleans, LA.

Redden, E. (2009, July 14). Reaching Black men. *Inside Higher Ed*. Retrieved from http://www.insidehighered.com/news/2009/07/14/blackmale

SAAB (2009a). The SAAB founder. Retrieved from http://saabnational.org/founder.htm

SAAB (2009b). The SAAB mission. Retrieved from http://saabnational.org/mission.htm

SAAB (2009c). About the SAAB organization. Retrieved from http://saabnational.org/about.htm

SAAB (2009d). The SAAB profile. Retrieved from http://saabnational.org/profile.htm

SAAB (2009e). SAAB friends and partners. Retrieved from http://saabnational.org/chapters.htm

SAAB (2009f). SAAB successes. In the Student African American Brotherhood website. Retrieved from http://saabnational.org/successes.htm http://saabnational.org/successes.htm

Valbrun M. (2010). Black males missing from college campuses. *America's Wire*. Retrieved from http://www.chicagodefender.com/article-9288-black-males-missing-from-college-campuses.html

Weiss, J. M., Visher, M. G., Teres, J., & Schneider, E. (2010, August). Learning communities for students in developmental reading: An impact study at Hillsborough community college. *National Center for Postsecondary Research: NCPR Brief,* 1–4.

Williams, B., & Brown, L. Jr. (2010). Howard University HU School of Communications Retention Program. Retrieved from http://communications.howard.edu/prospective/undergrad/special-programs/remedial-services.htm

Wood, J. L. (2011, September). Black males in the community college—"Falling through the cracks": The need for early warning policies. *Diverse issues in Higher Education*.

ABOUT THE CONTRIBUTORS

Lorenzo DuBois Baber is Assistant Professor in the Department of Educational Organization and Leadership at the University of Illinois, Urbana-Campaign. He received his PhD in higher education from Pennsylvania State University. His scholarship focuses on experiences of traditionally underrepresented students in postsecondary education and the role of higher education in reducing social, political, and economic stratification among racial/ethnic minorities and individuals from low-income backgrounds.

Fred A. Bonner, II is Professor of Higher Education Administration and Educational Psychology and Associate Dean of Faculties at Texas A&M University, College Station. He received an EdD in higher education administration and college teaching from the University of Arkansas, Fayetteville. Dr. Bonner has published articles and book chapters on academically gifted African American male college students, teaching in the multicultural college classroom, diversity issues in student affairs, and success factors that influence the retention of students of color in higher education.

Brian A. Burt is a doctoral student and research assistant in the Center for the Study of Higher and Postsecondary Education (CSHPE) at the University of Michigan. His scholarly interests include graduate student retention and persistence, STEM education, and the Black student experience. Brian is a member of the Association for the Study of Higher Education, (ASHE), the National Association of Student Personnel Administrators (NASPA), and the American Education Research Association (AERA). He earned a bachelor's in secondary English education from Indiana University, Bloomington, and a master's in higher education administration from the University of Maryland, College Park.

Joelle Carter, PhD serves as the Director of Undergraduate Programs in the School of Business at George Washington University. In this capacity, she is primarily responsible for developing and coordinating efforts for the School's first-year development program for more than 300 undergraduate students and coordinating the School's Research Experiences for Undergraduates (REU) program. Dr. Carter's research interests are centered on the status of minority-serving institutions in the United States, increasing diversity on historically Black college and university (HBCU) campuses, and specifically the engagement of non-Black students attending HBCUs. Prior to completing her doctoral studies, she received a grant from the National Association for Student Personnel Administration (NASPA) Foundation and the Connie Cox Scholarship from the University of Maryland, College Park's College of Education that supported her qualitative data collection. Since the completion of her doctorate in 2010, Carter has been invited to serve on academic panels focused on HBCU research and strategies to increase student engagement.

T. Elon Dancy, II is Assistant Professor of Adult and Higher Education at the University of Oklahoma in Norman. His research agenda investigates the experiences and sociocognitive outcomes of college students, particularly related to the intersection(s) of race, gender, and culture. Dr. Dancy is editor of *Managing Diversity: (Re)Visioning Equity on College Campuses* (Peter Lang, 2010). His papers have been published in *American Behavioral Scientist, Journal of Negro Education*, and *Review of Higher Education*, among other publications. Dr. Dancy has participated in more than 30 peer-reviewed or invited talks and symposia. He has received awards and recognition for his work from the Association for the Study of Higher Education, the American Educational Research Association, as well as the American Enterprise and Thomas B. Fordham Institutes, and he is Senior Editor of the *College Student Affairs Journal*.

Alonzo M. Flowers has a doctorate in higher education administration from Texas A&M University. Dr. Flowers specializes in educational issues including academic giftedness, teaching and learning, and student development theory. He holds a master's in adult and higher education administration from the University of Texas at San Antonio and a bachelor's degree in political science with a minor in multicultural studies from Texas State University. Dr. Flowers's dissertation research topic focuses on academically gifted poor African American males in engineering disciplines. He has just recently completed a book chapter in a volume titled *Diverse Millennial College Students* (Stylus, 2011). He is also on the editorial board of the landmark *Journal of African American Males in Education* (JAAME). Noteworthy too is his recent article in *Tempo*, a leading peer reviewed journal for the Texas Association for the Gifted and Talented (TAGT), titled "Becoming Advocates for the Gifted Poor."

Tiffany P. Fountaine is Assistant Director of the Center for Academic Success and Achievement at Morgan State University. In this role, she coordinates and assesses a broad range of support services for a diverse set of student populations including first-year, academically underprepared, and first-generation minority learners. Fountaine is also an adjunct faculty member for graduate programs in Higher Education Administration and Community College Leadership in the Department of Advanced Studies, Leadership, and Policy at Morgan State University. Her research interests have focused on issues of access, participation, and outcomes for students of color, the impact of strengths-based educational approaches on student success and program efficacy, and Black doctoral education, particularly the role of HBCUs. Fountaine's work has been published in a national refereed journal and she has authored a book chapter and several papers for regional and national conferences. In 2011, she was recognized by the American Education Research Association for her efforts in producing scholarship which advances multicultural and multiethnic education and commitment to underserved communities with its Carlos J. Vallejo Award for Emerging Scholarship. Fountaine earned a bachelor's degree in communication from the University of Maryland, College Park, a master's of science in communications management from Towson University, and a doctorate in higher education administration from Morgan State University. Fountaine serves on the editorial board for the *Journal of Student Affairs Research and Practice*, and as a reviewer for the *Journal of College Student Retention: Research, Theory and Practice* and the *Journal of Negro Education*.

Khadish Franklin is completing a doctorate in higher education policy at the University of Maryland, College Park where his research focuses on high achieving African American collegians matriculating at predominately White institutions; policy implications for equal access and affirmative admissions policies outcomes of undergraduate education; retention of underrepresented students; and campus diversity initiatives that impact student success. Franklin also serves as the Associate Director for Higher Education Policy, Research, and Student Success at *CommunciationWorks*, LLC, a policy strategy firm in Washington, DC. Franklin has previously served as a graduate fellow at the Institute for Higher Education Policy, doctoral intern at the Pell Institute for the Study of Opportunity in Higher Education, and the National Association for Student Personnel Administrators. He has presented scholarly papers and led symposia at the annual meetings of the Association for the Study of Higher Education, the American Education Research Association, the National Association of Student Personnel Administrators, and the Institute on College Males. Franklin earned a master's of science degree in higher education from the Florida State University and a bachelor's degree in communication from the University of Arkansas.

Sharon Fries-Britt is Associate Professor in the College of Education at the University of Maryland, College Park. Her research focuses on the experiences of high-achieving Black collegians and issues of race, equity, and diversity in higher education. Prior to her academic appointment, she served for 12 years as an administrator in higher education. She has developed and implemented innovative programs in multicultural and racial relations for professional organizations in and outside of higher education.

Marybeth Gasman is Professor of Higher Education at the University of Pennsylvania. She is an historian and her work focuses on African American higher education, including historically Black colleges and universities, African American leadership, Black philanthropy, and the postwar period in higher education. She is the author of 13 books, including *Envisioning Black Colleges: A History of the United Negro College Fund* (Johns Hopkins University Press, 2007). She has authored numerous articles related to African American philanthropy as well as Black colleges. In 2006, Dr. Gasman received the Association for the Study of Higher Education's Early Career Award. She is also the recipient of a University of Pennsylvania Excellence in Teaching Award. Dr. Gasman was named a Penn Fellow by the president and provost of the University of Pennsylvania. Just recently, Dr. Gasman was awarded the Ozell Sutton Medallion of Justice by Philander Smith College for her research on historically black colleges and universities. Her research on Black colleges and African American philanthropy has been cited by *The Washington Post*, the *Wall Street Journal*, the *Chronicle of Higher Education*, *Diverse Issues in Higher Education*, National Public Radio, *U.S. News and World Report*, and CNN.

David Horton, Jr., is Assistant Professor in the Higher Education and Student Affairs program, Patton College of Education and Human Services at Ohio University. Horton earned a bachelor's of science and a master's of liberal arts in history from Dallas Baptist University, and a doctorate in higher education administration from the University of Florida. In 2009, he was awarded the 2009 Outstanding Dissertation Award from the Southeastern Association for Community College Research (SACCR) for his dissertation titled, *A Comparative Study of the Persistence and Academic Success of Florida Community College Student-Athletes and Non-Athlete Students*. Recently, Horton was named 2011 Outstanding Young Alumnus by the College of Education at the University of Florida. At Ohio University, Horton's teaching and research areas include the organization, governance, and funding of higher education; multicultural student development; diversity in higher education; the persistence of community college students; and the academic success of student-athletes. Horton has presented and published several manuscripts and book chapters on the experiences of student-athletes at community colleges. In 2009, he coedited a New Directions for Community Colleges volume with Linda S. Hagedorn that was devoted exclusively to the topic of athletics and student athletes.

Gralon A. Johnson recently received a master's degree from the University of Arkansas, Clinton School of Public Service. Johnson holds a bachelor's of science degree in human development and family studies from the University of Arkansas at Pine Bluff. He is interested in issues of disadvantaged families, environmental socialization, and minority male persistence.

Dorian L. McCoy is Assistant Professor in the Higher Education and Student Affairs program at the University of Vermont. His research focuses on experiences of people of color in higher education. More specifically, his research explores the socialization experiences of faculty, administrators, and graduate students from historically underrepresented groups and issues of access to higher education. Current research projects include examining how historically underrepresented students develop a scholarly identity and acquire the cultural capital necessary to navigate the transition to graduate education and a phenomenological study of first-generation students of color at an *"extreme"* predominantly White institution.

McCoy has published in the *Journal of the Professoriate* and *Enrollment Management Journal* and written chapters in several higher education texts. He has presented numerous peer-reviewed papers at national and international higher education and student affairs conferences and is a 2008 American College Personnel Association *Annuit Coeptis* honoree for emerging scholars/professionals. He serves on the editorial board of the *Journal of Student Affairs Research and Practice* and *The Journal of College and University Student Housing*. McCoy earned his PhD from Louisiana State University, a master's in education from the University of Arkansas, and completed his undergraduate studies in business administration-management at Henderson State University.

Robert T. Palmer is Assistant Professor of Student Affairs at the State University of New York, Binghamton. His research examines issues of access, equity, retention, persistence, and the college experience of racial and ethnic minorities, particularly Black men at historically Black colleges and universities. Since completing his doctorate in 2007, Palmer's work has been published in national refereed journals, and he has authored more than 60 peer-reviewed journal articles, book chapters, conference papers, and other academic publications in 4 years. In addition, he serves as a major author for a monograph for the ASHE-Higher Education Report that provides context for racial and ethnic minority students in the STEM educational pipeline. In 2009, the American College Personnel Association's (ACPA) Standing Committee for Men recognized his excellent research on Black men with its Outstanding Research Award. In 2011, Palmer was named an ACPA Emerging Scholar. Palmer is on the editorial boards of the *Journal of College Student Development, Journal of Negro of Education, and Journal of Student Affairs Research*. Palmer is working on two books: *Black Students in Graduate/Professional Education at HBCUs* (with Adriel A. Hilton and Tiffany Fountaine) and *Minority Serving Institutions and STEM* (with Dina Maramba and Marybeth Gasman). More recently, Palmer was commissioned by the College Board to author a policy brief on supporting and retaining Black male collegians.

Jameel A. Scott is a doctoral student at the University of Maryland, College Park, where his interests are philanthropy and higher education finance, particularly at HBCUs, and minority student retention and persistence at minority serving institutions. In 2010 he was a consultant for the Counsel of Opportunity in Education and a doctoral intern at the Pell Institute for the Study of Opportunity in Higher Education, where he researched trends affecting low-income and first-generation students, and developed *Black College Dollars*, a scholarship guide for African-American Students. Jameel earned his bachelor's degree in African American studies at Morehouse College, Atlanta GA, a master's in theology from Drew University, Madison NJ, and a master's in science in higher education, where he primarily focused on historically Black colleges and universities (HBCUs) from the University of Pennsylvania.

Dorsey Spencer Jr. is the Director of Student Activities and Involvement at the American University of Nigeria, Yola, Nigeria. He previously served as Assistant Director of Campus Activities and Programs at Bucknell University in Pennsylvania and was Graduate Assistant for Events and Programs at the University of Massachusetts, Amherst. His research interests include leadership development among minority students, historically Black colleges and universities, and the experiences of administrators of color in higher education. He is also interested in international education, specifically in Africa. He earned a bachelor's degree in sport and recreation management from Temple University and a master's degree in higher education administration from the University of Massachusetts, Amherst.

Terrell L. Strayhorn is Associate Professor and Senior Research Associate in the Kirwan Institute for the Study of Race and Ethnicity in the School of Educational Policy and Leadership at the Ohio State University. His research program centers on issues of access and equity, diversity and student learning as well as retention and post-bachelor's degree outcomes. Author or editor of five books and over 70 refereed journal articles, book chapters, and reports, Strayhorn is PI of a 5-year National Science Foundation grant. In 2010, he coedited *The Evolving Challenges of Black College Students: New Insights for Practice* *and Research* with Melvin Cleveland Terrell of Northeastern Illinois University. He serves on six journal editorial boards, is associate editor of the *NASAP Journal*, and governing board member of the American College Personnel Association and Association for the Study of Higher Education, both prestigious organizations in his field. Strayhorn has received numerous awards and accolades including being recipient of the 2009 ASHE Promising Scholar/Early Career Award, 2007 ACPA Emerging Scholar Award, and was recognized as Emerging Scholar by *Diverse Issues in Higher Education* in 2011.

J. Luke Wood is Assistant Professor of Administration, Rehabilitation and Post-Secondary Education (ARPE) at San Diego State University. Wood is Coeditor of the *Journal of African American Males in Education* (JAAME) and Chair of the Multicultural and Multiethnic Education (MME) special interest group of the American Educational Research Association (AERA). He received his doctorate in educational leadership and policy studies with an emphasis in higher education from Arizona State University (ASU). His research focuses on ethical leadership and decision making in community colleges as well as Black male achievement in the community college. Wood is coauthor of the textbook, *Community College Leadership and Administration: Theory, Practice, and Change* (2010). Dr. Wood is a recipient of the Sally Casanova Pre-Doctoral Fellowship from which he served as research fellow at the Stanford Institute for Higher Education Research (SIHER), Stanford University. His scholarship and professional practice have been lauded through awards/honors, including: the Mildred Garcia Award for Exemplary Scholarship (ASHE-CEP); Outstanding Graduate Award (ASU-Alumni Association); Dean's Excellence Award for Graduate Research (ASU Fulton College); Top 30 under 30 Award (Sacramento Observer); Robert H. Fenske Fellowship for Higher and Postsecondary Education (ASU Fulton College); and the Distinguished Fellows Presentation Co-Awardee (ISETL).

INDEX